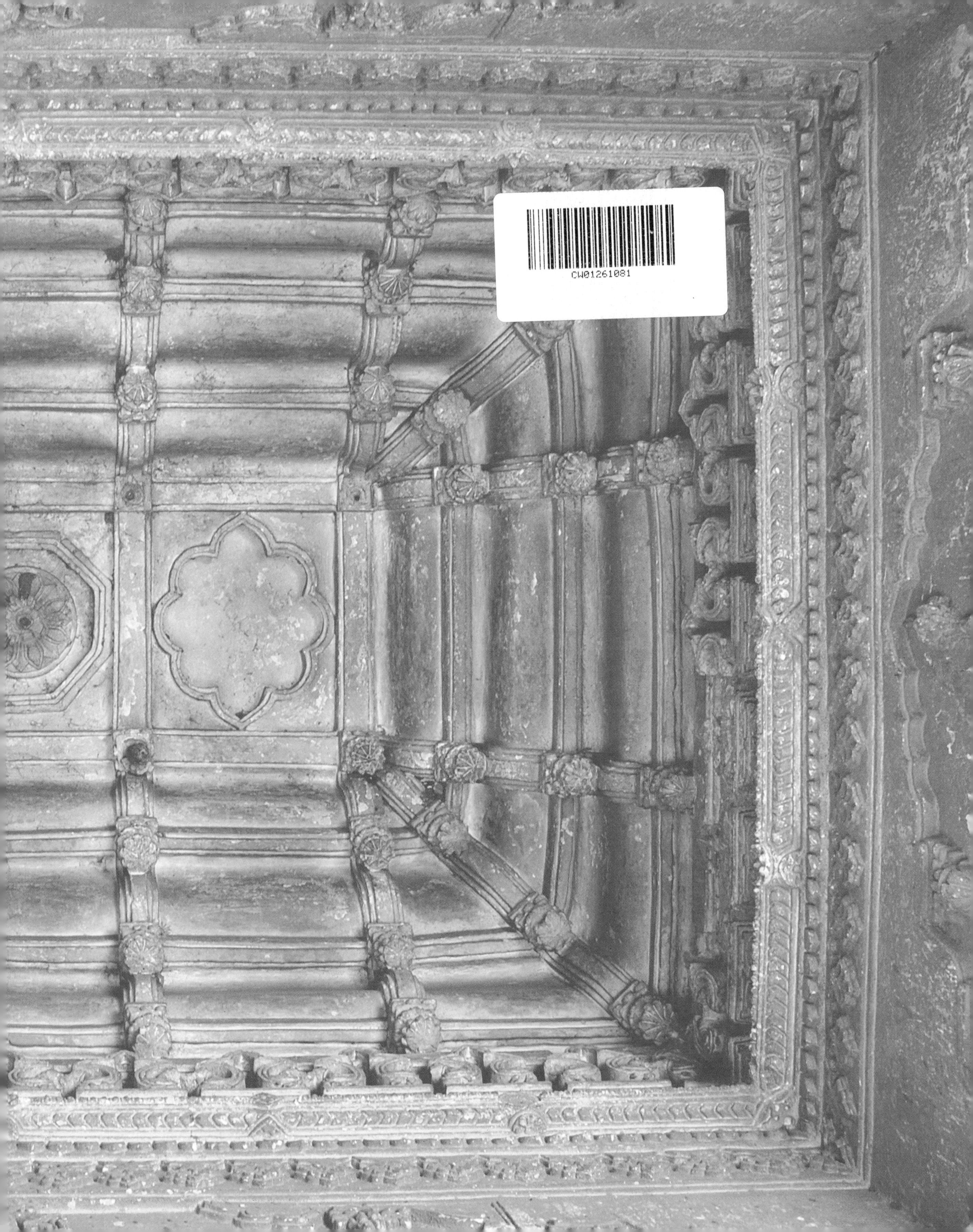

June 21, 2010

My Dearest Simon,

Congratulations on having finished your exams! Thank you so much for everything you have done for me these past three years. I am so lucky to have had you as my college father and indeed am so lucky to have you as a friend. I wish you the best of luck next year and in the years to come. I will miss you very much.

Love always,
Yours,

Zain.

Princess Shamina Talyarkhan is noted in the arts community for her many cultural interests and gracious patronage. A collector of Indian and Islamic art, traditional as well as modern, Princess Shamina has generously supported major institutions and projects devoted to Indian and Islamic art for more than a decade. Among her most notable achievements, she was the principal patron for the Brooklyn Museum of Art's groundbreaking exhibition on the historic 16th-century Imperial Mughal manuscript the Hamza Nameh. She is also a longtime supporter of the Islamic Art Department of the Metropolitan Museum of Art through the Friends of Islamic Art program and of the Museum of Modern Art in New York, as well as of the Victoria and Albert Museum in London, among others. Formerly married to a member of the royal family of Johor, Malaysia, Princess Shamina has a son, Zain, and divides her time between India, Europe, and America, where her work and various projects take her.

Layla S. Diba, PhD
Former Hagop Kevorkian Curator of Islamic Art
Brooklyn Museum of Art

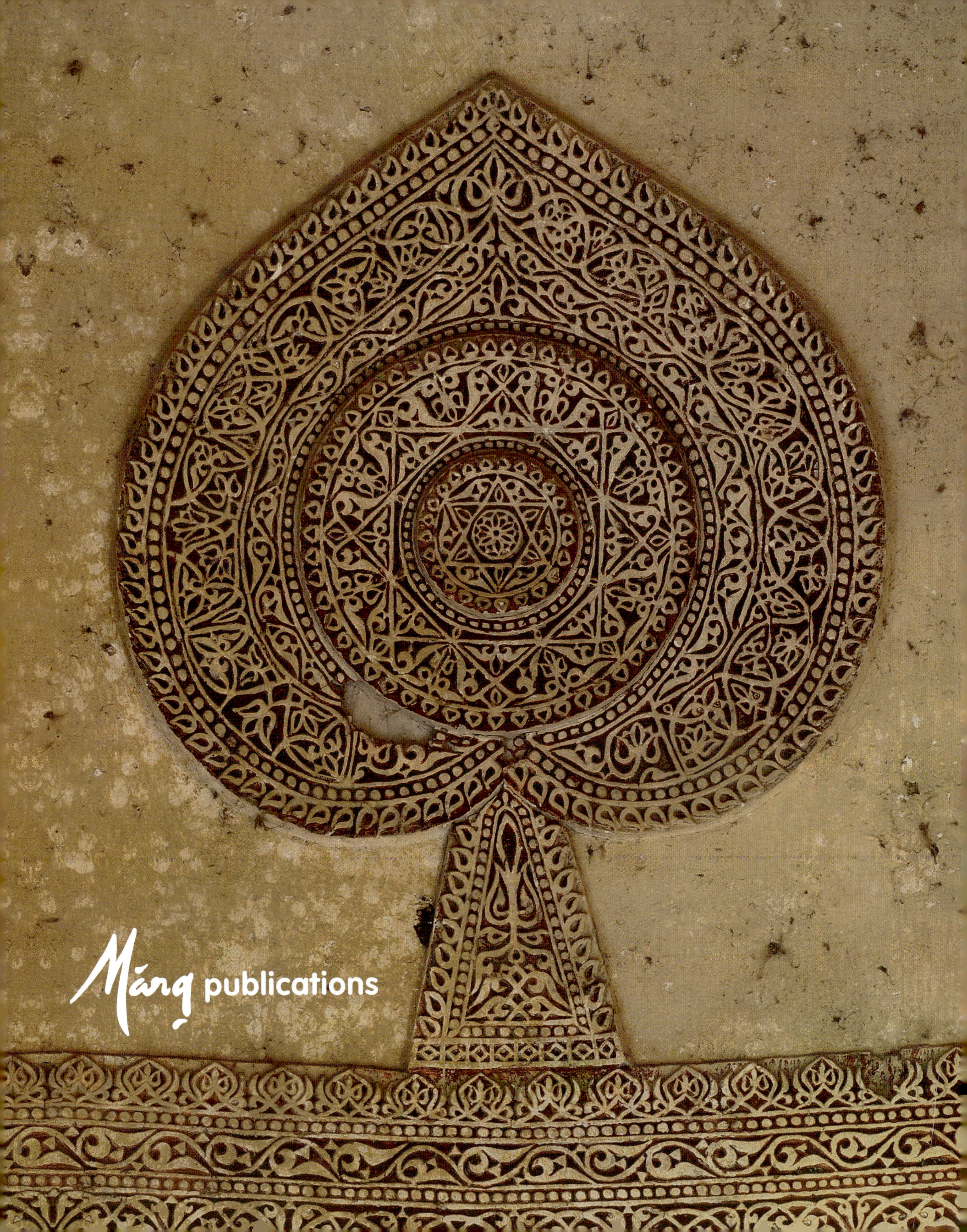
Marg publications

Silent Splendour
Palaces of the Deccan
14th–19th centuries

edited by **Helen Philon**
photographs by **Clare Arni**
with a foreword by **Pratapaditya Pal**

General Editor *Pratapaditya Pal*
Associate Editor *Rashmi Poddar*

Senior Executive Editor *Savita Chandiramani*
Executive Editor *Gayatri W. Ugra*
Senior Editorial Executive *Arnavaz K. Bhansali*

Text Editor *Rivka Israel*

Designer *Naju Hirani*
Senior Production Executive *Gautam V. Jadhav*
Production Executive *Vidyadhar R. Sawant*

Vol. 61 No 3
March 2010
Price: Rs 2500.00 / US$ 68.00
ISBN: 978-81-85026-96-1
Library of Congress Catalog Card Number:
2010-319015

Marg is a registered trademark of Marg Publications
© Marg Publications, 2010
All rights reserved

No part of this publication may be reproduced, stored, adapted, or transmitted, in any form or by any means, electronic, mechanical, photocopying, recording, or otherwise, or translated in any language or performed or communicated to the public in any manner whatsoever, or any cinematographic film or sound recording made therefrom without the prior written permission of the copyright holders.
This edition may be exported from India only by the publishers, Marg Publications, and by their authorized distributors and this constitutes a condition of its initial sale and its subsequent sales.

Published by Radhika Sabavala for Marg Publications on behalf of the National Centre for the Performing Arts at NCPA Marg, Nariman Point, Mumbai 400 021.
Processed at Marg, Mumbai 400 001.
Printed at Thomson Press (India) Ltd., Navi Mumbai 400 708.

Captions to preliminary pages:
Page 1: Bijapur. Pani Mahal, cypress trees carved on stone, 1656–72.
Page 2: Gulbarga. Chor Gumbad, painted plaster decoration on dome, c. 1430.
Page 3: Sagar. Shah Darwaza, open flower motif, 1407.
Page 4: Bidar. Solah Khamba, domes, c. 1460.
Page 5: Bidar. Ashtur, baoli, 15th century.
Pages 6–7: Bidar. Solah Khamba, hypostyle hall, leaf motifs on columns, c. 1460.
Page 8: Gulbarga Fort, Great Mosque/Hazar Sutun, c. 1407.

Marg's quarterly publications receive support from the Sir Dorabji Tata Trust – Endowment Fund

CONTENTS

- 8 **Foreword**
  Pratapaditya Pal

- 10 **Background Note**
  George Michell

- 11 **Acknowledgements**

- 12 **Maps**
  Klaus Rötzer

- 14 **Introduction**
  Helen Philon

- 26 **Fortifications**
  Klaus Rötzer

- 34 **Daulatabad, Gulbarga, Firuzabad, and Sagar under the Early Bahmanis (1347–1422)**
  Helen Philon

- 44 **Bidar under the Later Bahmanis and Baridis (1432–1619)**
  Helen Philon

- 56 **Ahmadnagar under the Nizam Shahis (1496–1636)**
  Pushkar Sohoni

- 66 **Bijapur under the Adil Shahis (1490–1686)**
  Mark Brand

- 78 **Golconda and Hyderabad under the Qutb Shahis (1495–1687)**
  Marika Sardar

- 88 **Daulatabad and Aurangabad under the Mughals (1660–1707)**
  George Michell

- 98 **Hyderabad under the Asaf Jahis (1724–1950)**
  Alison Mackenzie Shah

- 106 **Hydraulic Works and Gardens**
  Klaus Rötzer

- 114 **Architectural Decoration**
  Helen Philon

- 122 **Plans**
  Klaus Rötzer

- 140 Glossary
- 142 Bibliography
- 146 Index
- 148 Contributors

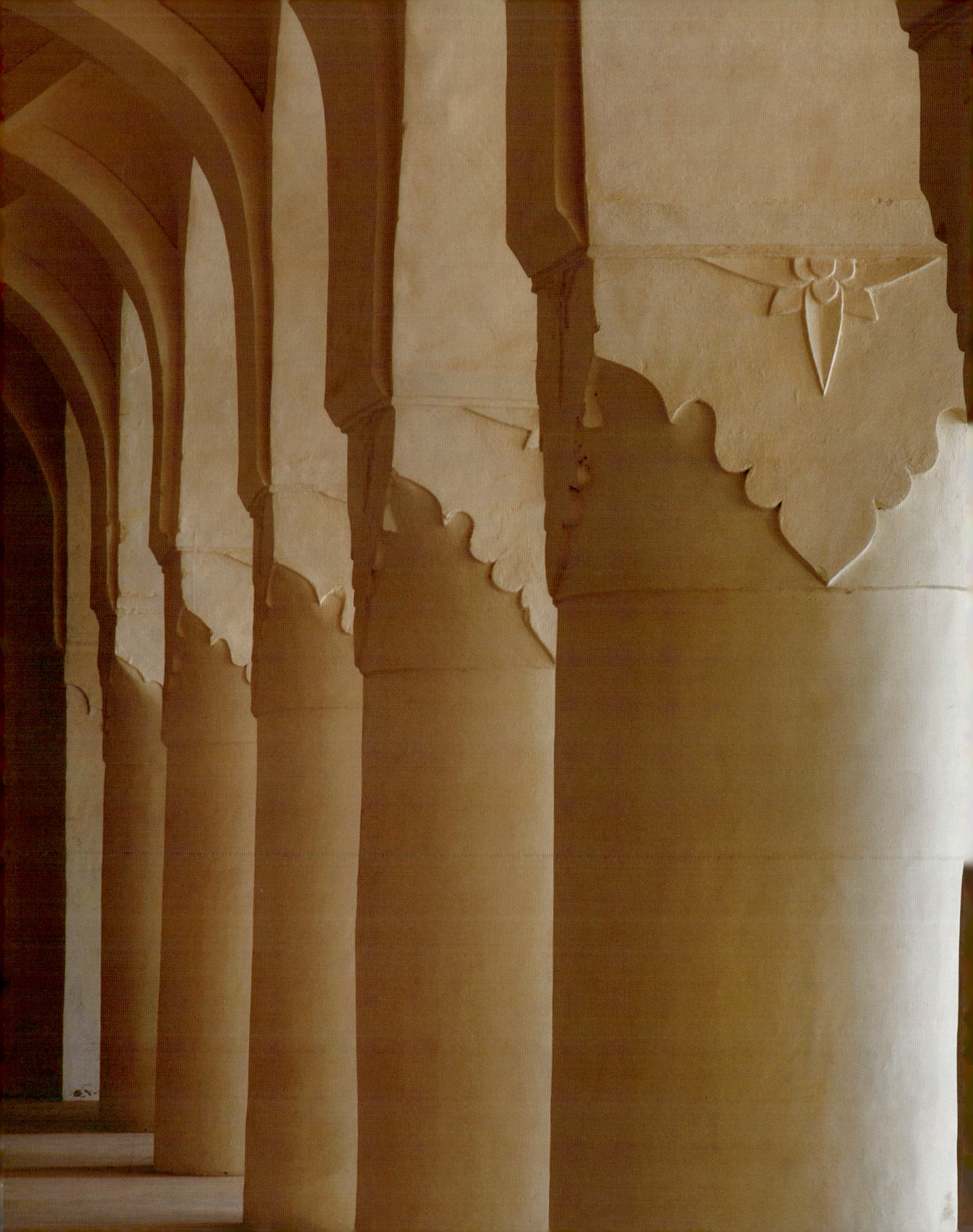

The publication of this book has been made possible with a donation from Shamina Talyarkhan

FOREWORD

Pratapaditya Pal

It is a great pleasure to contribute a foreword to this handsomely illustrated volume – the first in many decades – on the great architectural achievements of the Deccani Sultans, for at least two reasons. First, the expression "Deccan" has always had a romantic resonance for me even before I came to know that it is an Anglicization (hopefully it will survive) of *dakkhan*, the colloquial form of the Sanskrit *dakshina* meaning south. Secondly, the book brings together two individuals I have long admired.

Although the expression generally means south, Deccan really denotes only the elevated plateau south of the Vindhya mountain range, that girdles the hip of the subcontinent, and separates the Sanskritic north from the deep south, the bastion of Dravidian culture. The region has always been the crucible where the two cultures have commingled from ancient times, creating some of the most fascinating architectural monuments of the country.

I first encountered the expression during my early childhood when, like most boys, I was fascinated by trains. The "Deccan Queen" along with "Toofan Mail", I thought, were the most magical and romantic trains in the world. Later I had the pleasure of riding the latter, but the Deccan Queen has remained elusive. By the age of 15, in 1950, when the last kingdom of the Deccan, Hyderabad, was integrated into the new Indian nation, the Deccan was securely entrenched in my imagination as the land of magic and fabulous wealth – of the Nizam (at the time the richest man in the world), of the diamonds of Golconda, especially the Kohinoor, the luxuriant muslins and fabrics, and of course the famous Hyderabadi biryani. By the time I was 20, the Charminar of Hyderabad, though not as beautiful, was as familiar as the Taj Mahal, not for its architecture but because of an inexpensive, eponymous cigarette, the favourite of the proletariat and the intellectuals at the time. It was only as a graduate student of fine arts that I became aware of the artistic heritage of the Deccan – the great Hindu, Buddhist, and Jain rock-cut monuments, the awesome murals of the Ajanta caves, the elegant temples and sculptures of Badami and Aihole, and, of course, the picturesque ruins at Hampi, mute witness of the glorious kingdom of Vijayanagar, which was destroyed in the 16th century by the combined efforts of the Sultans to lay the foundations of their own architectural ambitions in turn.

My familiarity with the material remains of the Islamic sultanates and culture of the subcontinent had to wait for almost another decade, until I joined the Museum of Fine Arts, Boston in 1966 as the keeper of the Indian and Islamic collections. I began reading about the history and culture of the Deccan though from my study of Mughal history as an undergraduate I did know that it was for his obsession with the conquest of the Deccan that Aurangzeb (r. 1658–1707) sacrificed the Mughal empire. Once again my romantic notion of the Deccan was only augmented by the rich beauty of the paintings of the Deccani school whose appreciation was further encouraged by the writings of and numerous discussions with Karl Khandalavala, Edwin Binney, 3rd, and, of course, Mark Zebrowski. This interest and knowledge was further enhanced by several visits to the Deccani sites over many a summer (which is quite pleasant on the plateau) in the late '70s and '80s. I was of course familiar with the distinctive architecture of the Deccan through paintings and photographs but seeing them in the flesh, even as magnificent ruins, was no less viscerally and visually exciting than the first visit to Ajanta. These excursions also confirmed my firm belief in the innate genius of the Indian architects and craftsmen, who never hesitated to imbibe and adapt diverse ideas and techniques with equal facility and open minds from the days of the Satavahanas to those of the Nizams.

Part of that remarkable narrative covering the Sultanates of the Deccan and the distinctive eclectic and diverse architectural traditions is recounted here by some of the most eminent specialists and historians in the field today. But as one reads the chapters, as I did, one cannot fail to notice the discrete vision behind the book which is that of its editor, Dr Helen Philon. Her Greek background afforded an innate advantage to study the architecture of India, and especially of the Deccan. This passion as well as her vast knowledge of the subject have contributed to this remarkable book of fresh historical insights as well as visual richness.

This is where my second friend Shamina Talyarkhan comes in. As everyone knows, publishing such lavish art books is expensive and Marg being non-profit, cannot depend on bank loans but must rely on the generosity of donors. It is a double pleasure therefore that Shamina, a common friend of both Helen and mine, has proved to be an angel for this volume. This is appropriate in another sense, she herself is a coastal Deccani and both in her personality and munificence – for she is a generous patron of the arts in New York as well – she continues to reveal the grace and nobility that one imagines were characteristics of the men and women who built the monuments that have inspired this book.

The efforts of the Greek Helen (and her fellow contributors) and the Deccani Shamina, along with Marg's dedicated staff, will be rewarded when the neglected architectural treasures of the Deccani Sultanates become as well known as those of the Delhi Sultans and the Mughals. Hopefully, names such as Bijapur and Golconda will resonate as much as Delhi and Agra in the imaginations of Indian and foreign visitors. As they wander around the magnificent ruins of the region they may recall that poignant quatrain of the Persian poet-philosopher Omar Khayyam (d. 1123):

> Since All is unsubstantial as the air
> And naught save loss and ruin; whatsoe'er
> Exists in this world, thinks doth not exist,
> And what on earth is not, *imagine* there.[1]

Note

1 Eben Francis Thompson, *The Wisdom of Omar Khayyam*. New York, Citadel Press, 1967, #54.

BACKGROUND NOTE

George Michell

It is now more than 20 years since I edited a volume for Marg entitled *Islamic Heritage of the Deccan*. At that time there were very few scholars specializing in Deccan architecture and art. Among them were Elizabeth Schotten Merklinger and Mark Zebrowski, who had made particular studies of the architecture and painting traditions of this region respectively. Nonetheless, the volume was brought out and seems to have had a certain impact. There is now a new generation of scholars, both in India and abroad, who have decided to concentrate on the Deccan. One consequence of this renewed interest has been a series of academic conferences on Deccan architecture and art traditions in Hyderabad, Oxford, and New York in 2007 and 2008. Another is the present volume, which showcases research by a new and dedicated band of art historians. It is heartening to read through the articles that have been assembled here under the expert editorship of Helen Philon. They cover the historical and religious background to the Deccan from the 14th to 19th centuries, the urban context of royal architecture, the formal typologies of palaces, and the significant interaction with indigenous building traditions.

The articles should be of interest to scholars, general readers, and travellers alike. While palaces at Deccan sultanate sites have already been published to a limited extent, the present authors offer much new data as well as fresh interpretations. To begin with, Klaus Rötzer offers insights into the fortified settings of palaces, commenting on layouts and building construction methods. In her discussion of both phases of Bahmani palace architecture Helen Philon challenges long-held opinions by arguing that the Great Mosque in Gulbarga and Solah Khamba Mosque in Bidar were originally conceived as sites of royal audience rather than public places of prayer. Her discovery of Sultanpur, a royal suburb on the outskirts of Gulbarga, is a significant contribution; so, too, her interpretation of the palaces within Bidar Fort. Pushkar Sohoni's description of the courtly structures of the Nizam Shahis in and around Ahmadnagar covers buildings that have hardly ever been published before. He draws particular attention to Farah Bakhsh Bagh, one of the most imposing palaces to have been erected anywhere in India in the second half of the 16th century. Mark Brand charts the changes in the religious cults promoted by the Adil Shahi sultans and their effect on the courtly architecture of Bijapur and its surroundings. Marika Sardar analyses the layout of the Qutb Shahi palace at Golconda, demonstrating an overall progression from private to public zones. I offer a few remarks on palaces erected at Deccan sites by Shah Jahan and Aurangzeb, both of whom were based in the Deccan for some years, while Alison Mackenzie Shah locates the Asaf Jahi palaces within the cosmopolitan aristocratic culture that was so enthusiastically promoted by the Nizams of Hyderabad in later times. To complete the volume, Klaus Rötzer examines the waterworks and gardens of palaces and associated buildings of the Deccan, and Helen Philon analyses the decorative themes of palaces, as realized in a dazzling array of materials and techniques.

Readers will be grateful to Klaus Rötzer, who has willingly undertaken the laborious task of preparing new maps and architectural drawings especially for this volume. Clare Arni's marvellous photographs offer a fresh look at both familiar and unfamiliar buildings, perfectly capturing the architectural inventiveness and sumptuous details of these now silent, but splendid palaces.

ACKNOWLEDGEMENTS

This publication was made possible thanks to the warm hearted support of Dr Pratapaditya Pal and Dr Rashmi Poddar who embraced the project with great enthusiasm. Their comments on the first draft of the manuscript prompted us to clarify certain thoughts.

Without the help of the previous Director General of the Archaeological Survey of India, Mrs Anshu Vaish, this work would not have been possible and I would like to thank her and the local representatives of the ASI for their help and assistance.

I am grateful to the Greek Ambassador to India, H.E. Mr Stavros Lykidis for assisting me in all possible ways during the preparation of this volume. Nor can I forget Mrs Meera Sikand, Greek Embassy Delhi, who for the last 20 years has helped me with all my scholarly pursuits. I am really thankful for her friendship and resolute support.

The group of scholars who are participating in this volume must be thanked for sharing their recent research and knowledge of the royal foundations and courtly edifices of the Deccan, much of which appears here for the first time.

I would like to single out Klaus Rötzer whose detailed knowledge of the terrain, building techniques, and hydraulic systems distinguishing the geology of the Deccani plateau has been invaluable. Visiting the various capitals of the Deccani kingdoms with him has been one of the most rewarding learning experiences. The drawings of the monuments he has so generously provided are amongst the most important contributions in furthering our understanding of Deccani architecture and culture in general. In Bidar he was assisted by Kushal Kamble and Digambar Thakur and I would like to thank them for their hard work. Without the help of Ameen Hullur we would not have been able to visit and photograph many of the buildings of Bijapur that are in this volume.

It is George Michell who introduced me to the Deccan almost 20 years ago. His profound knowledge of Deccani culture has been my shining light and I can not thank him enough for his invaluable help in organizing this volume.

I greatly appreciated Pushkar Sohoni's advice and help on many issues. Alison Shah deserves a special thank you for so graciously accepting to contribute a chapter on the palaces of the Asaf Jahis at the very last minute. In this context I would like to thank Anita Jacob, Archivist at the Alkazi Collection of Photography and Uma Jain of Fotocraft for their willingness to expedite the search for the illustrations to Alison Shah's text, and Rajesh Vora for allowing me to use his luminous photograph of the Chowmahallah.

It is however the seductive and revealing images of Clare Arni that highlight the new ideas and suggestions presented in this volume for the first time. Her photographs communicate the grandeur of Deccani architecture and palaces.

I would also like to thank Mr Ranga Reddy, who has with great commitment and efficiency organized my trips to India in the last ten years. Special thanks to Ian McDonald for his advice and help on a number of issues relating to the texts. Nor should I forget my husband Alexander for his constant encouragement and support in reaching new intellectual frontiers and developing new interests.

Finally I would like to thank the staff at Marg for their valuable help in putting this volume together.

To all I express my gratitude and thanks.

Helen Philon

MAPS

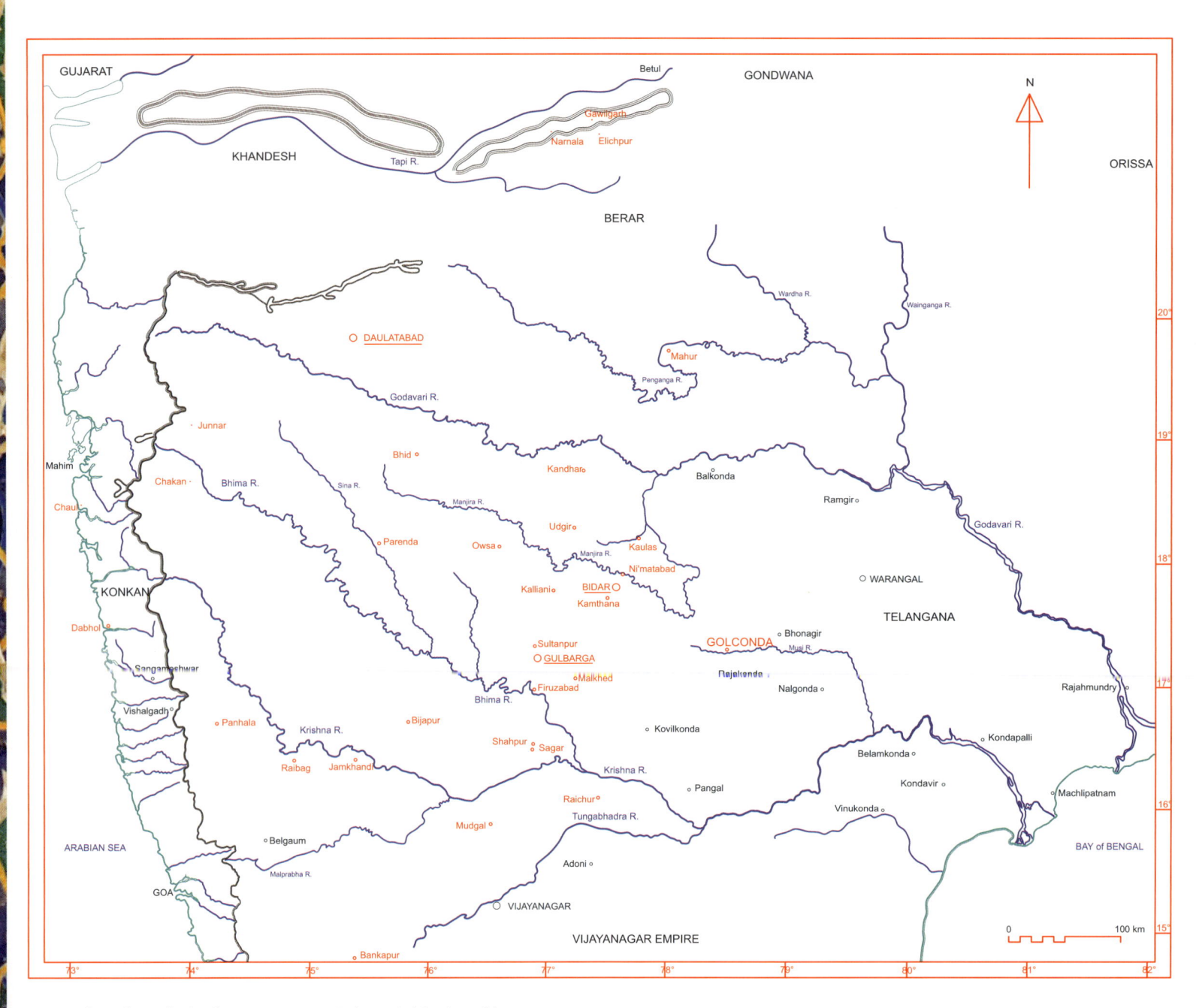

Map 1 The Bahmani Kingdom, 1347–1527. Bahmani cities in red letters.

Map 2 The Successor States:
The Baridis, 1487–1619. Forts and cities in blue.
The Qutb Shahis, 1495–1687. Forts and cities in magenta.
The Adil Shahis, 1490–1686. Forts and cities in green.
The Nizam Shahis, 1496–1636. Forts and cities in red.

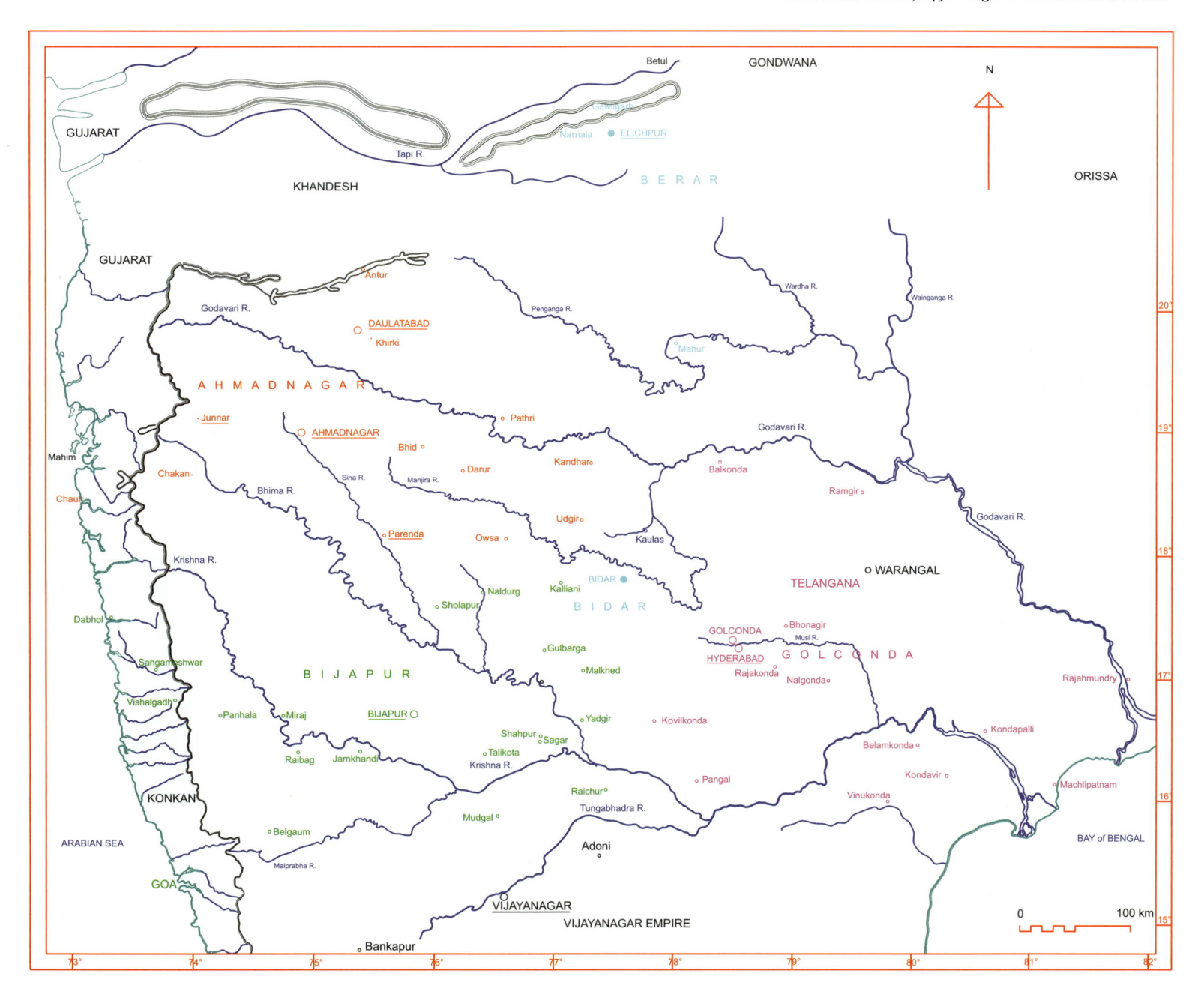

INTRODUCTION

Helen Philon

Political and Religious Background

The elevated plateau which forms the Deccan region of southern India lies at the heart of peninsular India, crisscrossed by the west-flowing Narmada and Tapti rivers, and by the east-flowing Godavari, Bhima, Krishna, and Tungabhadra. Fertile and rich in agricultural resources and mineral ore, the Deccan became a "Promised Land" for medieval adventurers, itinerant Sufis, and upstart Islamic dynasties. From 1296 onwards, a series of invasions by the Delhi Sultanate brought an end to the Hindu Yadava, Kakatiya, Hoysala, and Pandya dynasties of the Deccan. In 1327, the Sultan of Delhi, Muhammad Tughluq, established a permanent Islamic presence in the northern Deccan, when he brought leading military elite, merchants, and Sufis to the city of Devagiri. Renamed Daulatabad, the city became the secondary Tughluq capital. The power vacuum that ensued in the Deccan following Muhammad Tughluq's return to Delhi in 1334 offered an opportunity for the region's Tughluq governors to proclaim their independence. This resulted in the birth of two great Deccani powers: the Hindu kingdom of Vijayanagar at present-day Hampi (1336), and ten years later the Bahmani Sultanate – named after its founder Alauddin Hasan Bahman Shah – in the central Deccan, encompassing parts of present-day Maharashtra, northern Karnataka, and western Andhra Pradesh. The capital of this first Deccani sultanate was initially located in Daulatabad/Fatehabad (1347–50), then Gulbarga/Ahsanabad (1350–c. 1430), and finally Bidar/Ahmadabad (c. 1430–1527) (map 1).

The constant Vijayanagar–Bahmani wars over the much-coveted Raichur Doab, rich in minerals and agricultural land, did not, however, discourage trade activities. There was also a constant exchange of artistic traditions and building techniques between the two kingdoms, contributing to the genesis of a unique Deccani architectural vocabulary. This was augmented by Islamic traditions from Western and Central Asia, transmitted via an influx of immigrant Arabs, Persians, and Turks. In addition to these, the Deccan attracted East African slaves, known as Habshis, who later came to occupy leading positions in the political life of the Deccan and who also had an impact on the region's architecture. This multi-

1 Gulbarga Fort. Bazaar street, c. 1400. Pyramidal and lobed vaults cover each shop, and a stone chhajja runs along the facades.

2 Gulbarga. By Colin Mackenzie, 1797. Gulbarga Fort with its two townships. Gulbarga I is shown on the right side of the elliptical fort and Gulbarga II is below the fort. Inside the fort, the Hazar Sutun and the Bala Hisar are schematically drawn as squares. Courtesy The British Library, c0141-01.

ethnic environment enriched the culture of the Deccan, but was also responsible for socio-political and religious tensions between local Muslim communities, known as Dakhinis, and incomers from other Islamic lands, known as Afaqis. The power struggle between these two groups for control of the Bahmani court and state led to the fall of the dynasty during the first quarter of the 16th century, and the consequent rise of five successor states with Berar, four of which concern us here. These tensions continued up until the arrival of the Mughals, who began to intrude into the Deccan from the middle of the 16th century onwards.

By the end of the 1520s, the Bahmani kingdom had fragmented into a number of smaller states, each founded by a former provincial governor. The most important figures were Yusuf Adil Khan (r. 1490–1510), who founded the Adil Shahi dynasty with its capital in Bijapur, Karnataka (1490–1686); Ahmad Nizam Shah (r. 1496–1510), who established the Nizam Shahi kingdom in northwestern Maharashtra (1496–1636); and Quli Qutb al-Mulk (r. 1495–1543), with his capital at Golconda in Andhra Pradesh (1512–1687). Qasim Baridi retained his capital at Bidar, which was annexed in 1619 by the Adil Shahis (map 2). The history of these successor states is one of shifting alliances and intrigues, in which the hostile relations between the Dakhinis and the Afaqis played a primary role. For a while, these problems were avoided as the five kingdoms prepared to vanquish Vijayanagar. Following the battle of Talikota in 1565, and the removal of Vijayanagar as a political and economic force, two sultanate kingdoms emerged as the most powerful and prosperous: the Adil Shahis of Bijapur and the Qutb Shahis of Golconda. Both dynasties controlled territory with substantial mineral and agricultural resources, and their rulers became major players in international trade and vigorous patrons of architecture and the arts. The Mughals finally brought an end to local power struggles with their conquest of the Deccan, absorbing Bijapur and Golconda into their expanding empire during the second half of the 17th century. Over the next century, the eastern Deccan province of the Mughal empire became an independent state under the Asaf Jahis, who ruled from Hyderabad until modern times (1724–1950).

The Bahmani kingdom established itself at a time when the power of the Caliphate, the legitimator of political authority in the Islamic world, had eroded. In the Deccan, this authority was replaced by that of the Sufi saints and their dargahs or "courts". Under the early Bahmanis, the power of these figures overshadowed that of the ulema – the custodians, canonists, and theologians of orthodox Islam. Sufis acted as spiritual guides, serving as legitimators of political authority in the Deccan. Moreover, the popularity of Sufi dargahs extended well beyond their Muslim base, attracting support from the more numerous local Hindu communities. The dependence of the Sufis on sultans for patronage and civil authority led to the development of a relationship that blurred the boundaries between the domains of saint and sultan.

Architectural Symbolism

Architecture is the concrete embodiment of ideas and beliefs. It is one of the most enduring expressions of any dynasty's aspirations – and the Deccan is no exception. Summarizing the complex evolution of royal architectural forms

3 Gulbarga. By Colin Mackenzie, 1797. View of Firuz Shah's lake from the dargah of Sheikh Mujarrad. On the shores of the lake are the dargah of Gesu Daraz, with its Adil Shahi gate giving onto the lake (right); and the royal necropolis of Haft Gumbad, including the tomb of Firuz Shah with its two rows of arched openings (left). Courtesy The British Library, c0356-7.

in this region, we may argue that the iwan-like group of Bahmani palaces from c. 1400 – such as those partly preserved at Gulbarga, Firuzabad, and Sagar – continue the emblems of power introduced into the Deccan by the Tughluqs. Thanks to this architectural borrowing, a semblance of continuity was preserved when the Tughluqs were overthrown and the Bahmanis emerged as the new dynasts of the Deccan. With their power consolidated by the turn of the 15th century, the Bahmanis adopted architectural power-emblems from the universal pool of Islamic dynasties, harking back to the epic *Shahnama* of Iran and the Caliphal age of the Abbasids. By employing such forms, the Bahmani rulers attempted to claim their position in the universal world of Islamic kingship. One monument inspired by the descriptions of multi-columned palace halls in epic Persian literature is the Hazar Sutun or Chihil Sutun in the fort of Gulbarga – now known as the Great Mosque, even though this was not its original or prime function. A similar mix of political and spiritual references may also be seen in the small, elegant cross-in-square-plan edifice now known as the Dargah of Khalifat al-Rahman outside Firuzabad. Firuz Shah Bahmani (r. 1397–1422) was the first Deccani ruler to exploit the two aforementioned plan forms. We would argue that by using such building forms, he was able to resolve the ambiguous relationship between royal and religious centres of power (sultan and saint) that recurs throughout Deccani history and its architecture. Firuz Shah's brother and successor, Ahmad Shah (r. 1422–36), carried this idea of universal symbolism even further; his tomb at Ashtur outside Bidar is a meeting place of both Muslims and Hindus – and to this day this ruler remains a saint or a wali, revered by both communities.

The royal structures that Ahmad Shah and his successors patronized in Bidar broke away from the universal vocabulary of Islamic royal forms. They introduced a new architectural language of power that combined different local forms with adaptations of imported ones. We could argue that only with Ahmad Shah's move to Bidar did the Deccan become the setting for a genuinely unique style of royal architecture. The association of monumental, tripartite palace structures with water – first seen in Bidar and then imitated in later capitals – clearly evinces the influence of local traditions. By moving his capital to Bidar, Ahmad Shah tried to distance his rule from the different Muslim factions that seem to have prevailed in Gulbarga. This distancing from the past, and his intention to create a new identity for his kingdom, was further expressed in his choice of new architectural power-symbols, reflecting the political pragmatism of the Deccani sultans, being as they were a Muslim elite ruling a Hindu majority.

The Adil Shahis inherited this tradition; their courtly structures metaphorically express the position of the sultan as divine mediator and chief celebrant of the Nauras cult (see page 69), which combined popular Muslim and Hindu devotional traditions. The Bahmanis appear to have followed Sunni Islam, although their allegiances were more with the Sufi dargahs. The Baridis were Sunnis, the Qutb Shahis embraced Shia Islam, while the Adil Shahis vacillated between these two branches of the faith.

Capitals, Citadels, and Suburbs

Bahmani palaces are located within the forts of their capitals, and sometimes in the surrounding suburbs. Different ceremonial activities were probably practised in these domains, as implied by the existence of various courtly structures. The close juxtaposition of capital, secondary capital, and royal suburb was introduced to the Deccan at the time of Firuz Shah Bahmani. The concept of a royal suburb, and of combining two cities at a short distance from each other, is evident in Gulbarga, Firuzabad, and Sultanpur. It would appear that Bidar had no secondary capital, but rather boasted two royal suburbs – at Nimatabad and Kamthana – where the later Bahmanis built palaces (map 1). The "capital-and-secondary-capital-plus-suburb" scheme evolved under the Adil Shahis at Bijapur, Shahpur and Nauraspur (map 2), with a royal suburb and resort at Ainapur and Kumatgi respectively. Similarly, the Qutb Shahis built Hyderabad as a secondary ceremonial capital to Golconda, and surrounded both with palaces, mosques, caravansarais, and gardens. By contrast, the Nizam Shahis do not seem to have fostered any of these schemes. Their royal domain was confined to Ahmadnagar Fort and the adjacent, rectangular city, its surrounding royal edifices suggesting a more informal relationship between sultan and elite guests. This seems to have also been the pattern adopted by the Asaf Jahis, whose palaces, villas, and out-of-town residences in hybrid architectural styles bound together the nizams, the nobles, and the international world of princes.

Royal residences in the Deccani capitals of Gulbarga, Bidar, Daulatabad, Bijapur, Ahmadnagar, and Golconda were located in forts that were generally circular in layout, next to which were urban settlements enclosed by fortifications in concentric or elliptical configurations (plan 1). Cities with circular fortifications have a long history in India: they include Devagiri, capital of the Yadavas (850–1334) prior to the Delhi conquest; and Warangal, headquarters of the Kakatiyas (1083–1323) in Andhra Pradesh. During the Sultanate period, the one exception to this city plan is Firuzabad (plan 2), which

4 Firuzabad. Two-storeyed iwan-like audience hall, c. 1400.

5 Firuzabad. Dargah of Khalifat al-Rahman, audience hall, c. 1400.

18 HELEN PHILON

6 Firuzabad. East gate, c. 1400.

is quadrangular in layout. Hyderabad and Gulbarga have circular fortified royal enclosures, but neither has city fortifications.

Gulbarga comprised a fort and two unfortified satellite townships Gulbarga I and II (figure 2) that grew organically over a period of some 80 years. On the northwestern side of the city's elliptical fort is the oldest township (Gulbarga I) wherein was located the Shah Bazaar Mosque, which served as the Jami Mosque of Gulbarga. This quarter was linked through a northerly road to the unfortified royal suburb of Sultanpur, and to the fort of Gulbarga by a wide commercial avenue that continued into the citadel (figure 1). A later urban nucleus (Gulbarga II), possibly around 1400, originates at the northeastern gate of the fort (figure 2), where a street that opens on to a circular piazza continues to the royal necropolis of Haft Gumbad and the dargahs of Sheikh Mujarrad and Gesu Daraz – all of which face onto a great pre-Sultanate tank restored by Firuz Shah Bahmani. The tank no longer survives but was recorded on a watercolour by Colin Mackenzie (1754–1821), Surveyor General of India, at the end of the 18th century (figure 3). These tombs, dargahs, and associated water bodies probably served as conceptual "protective" concentric circles around the fort, enclosing both parts of the city.

Firuzabad – the secondary (or "twin") capital, which served as a royal residence as well as a pleasure retreat and military encampment – had a fortified enclosure. It differs from the other Bahmani capitals in that it takes the form of an irregular, square citadel which encloses both the royal domain and the city in which the ceremonial structures of the kingdom's governors were located. Its non-elite residential quarters and commercial zones, as indicated by the remains of a bazaar street (figure 1), lay outside this fortified compound. The audience hall of Firuz Shah Bahmani, the founder of Firuzabad, was located in a building now known as the Dargah of Khalifat al-Rahman (figure 5), which lay outside the walls and was connected to the city via a north–south axis.

Imposing gatehouses were the loci for welcoming visitors to the cities of the Bahmanis and later Deccani dynasties (figure 6). Here, taxes were

INTRODUCTION 19

levied and visitors conducted to the royal enclosures, which were endowed with additional ceremonial gates. A feature shared by many Deccani cities is a system of thoroughfares, linking these urban gates to streets within the fort, which generally cross at right angles. In Bidar, the junction of the two major urban thoroughfares is punctuated by a tower-like edifice known as the Chaubara; in Hyderabad the crossing is marked by the Charminar, a highly original ceremonial structure that combined a variety of functions. In all the capitals of the Deccan, the Jami Mosque, equipped with a minbar, lies inside the city. In military settlements and provincial headquarters, however, the Jami sits "astride" the urban and royal enclosures, as in Firuzabad, or on a route along which these two are axially aligned, as in Bijapur.

The irregular, circular fort of Bidar, within which the royal palaces are located, is attached on its southern side to the quadrangular city (plan 3). The city is furnished with religious, commercial, and public institutions, as well as elite residences. Bidar thus combines the circular layout of Daulatabad and Gulbarga with the quadrangular plan of Firuzabad. To the west of Bidar lay the military encampment of the Bahmanis, and beyond that the tombs of the Baridis; on its eastern flank was the enclosure of the powerful Habshi slave contingent. Situated at a greater distance from the city was the funerary complex of the later Bahmanis and their spiritual advisors, the Nimatullahi saints. Additionally, both Bijapur and Golconda revived the scheme of concentric circular zones, with the citadel located in the centre of the city. The secondary capital of Nauraspur (1599) contained a vast, nine-sided compound (plan 27) built by Ibrahim Adil Shah II (1580–1627). This was linked to Bijapur via a broad avenue lined with shops that entered the city through the Makka and Zorahpur gates. Hyderabad-Baghnagar, or "Garden City", built for official ceremonials, was laid out to the south of the Musi river, leaving Golconda for the more private activities of the court. Hyderabad was intended as a replica of heavenly paradise, and accordingly conformed to a grid plan centred on the Charminar. A short distance to the north of the Charminar was a great piazza with the Charkaman, or Four Arches, that seems to have imitated the great Safavid squares of Iranian cities. Palaces in Hyderabad were located along the river, while urban markets lined the avenues that converged on the Charminar.

Building Typologies

The more informal, private palaces in Daulatabad and Sultanpur share a tripartite plan and facade, and are built in both stone and timber. Timber, combined with stone bedded in mortar or earth and covered in stucco, was used for private edifices as well as for gates and iwan-like, vaulted audience halls. Such audience halls, which invariably had a north–south orientation, are first encountered in the Deccan in the buildings erected by the Delhi invaders. The earliest example of a north-facing, iwan-like structure in the region is the early-14th-century audience

7 Sultanpur. The royal country villa, c. 1400.

hall in Warangal known as the Khush Mahal. That iwan-like structures of this type were adopted by the Bahmanis is evident from the remains of such a hall in the middle of Gulbarga Fort (plan 8) – later engulfed by the masonry of the Bala Hisar – and a number of examples in Firuzabad (figures 4, 10). In Firuzabad, such halls are located at varying distances from the Jami Mosque and royal enclosure, suggesting that they may have been intended for provincial governors.

Yet another example of a vaulted audience hall is the Shah Darwaza at Sagar (pp. 36–37, figures 3–5), a gateway which is related in terms of vaulting techniques and decorative designs to the Firuzabad courtly structures. The Shah Darwaza, which combines ceremonial and private activities, is the first courtly edifice in the Deccan to stress verticality in its architecture. In the lapidary inscriptions embedded in its facades, it is compared to the Taq-i Kisra, the fabled, arched palace of the Sasanian kings in Ctesiphon, present-day Iraq. This comparison suggests that local, similarly shaped halls must have also evoked the fabled arch of Ctesiphon, thus establishing a link between Persian and Deccani concepts of kingship. The architectural apogee of universal kingship is, however the domed multi-columned hall, or Hazar Sutun, with its east–west alignment, inside Gulbarga Fort. Here, two concepts of power are combined – royal and spiritual. These dual Persianate architectural power-symbols adopted by the early Bahmanis – the iwan-like hall and Hazar Sutun – did not survive the move to Bidar, where architectural diversity was to be limited to essentially three building types.

The most widespread and long-lasting of these palace typologies is the tripartite scheme first used for the private palace structures of the Bahmanis in Sultanpur and Daulatabad. During the later Bahmani period the scale of this type of palace becomes monumental, as attested in the royal enclosure of Bidar. In the numerous audience halls of the Adil Shahis in Bijapur, the Qutb Shahis in Golconda, and the Nizam Shahis in Ahmadnagar, the tripartite scheme of their north-facing facades is expressed in different variations. Their size is expanded to contain additional rooms on three sides, including the most important ceremonial space to the rear (south) of the mandapa or hypostyle hall (marked C in all plans). The royal associations of these tripartite structures are indicated by domes, as well as by three novel features: water, change of level, and vertical progression. Another type of building found in Bidar, Bijapur, and Golconda is the suite of vaulted subterranean apartments in which to escape the heat of the summer months. To these basic palace layouts, each dynasty added its particular type of courtly structure.

In Bidar, tripartite palaces are associated with two cross-in-square-plan buildings, first encountered during the early Bahmani period, and with two domed square pavilions: the Gumbad Darwaza and the Solah Khamba Mosque, to which hypostyle halls were added later. The Gumbad Darwaza, Solah Khamba Mosque, and the edifice known here as Palace III (figure 9) lie along an east–west axis. The Takht Mahal (Palace II), in which the domed throne-room was located, combines a north–south "axis of movement" and an east–west "axis of gaze".

In Adil Shahi palaces, this tripartite scheme is expanded to a grander scale. Together with a loggia to accommodate a throne, these spaces are raised on

8 Nauraspur. Nauras Mahal, 1599.

9 Bidar Fort. Palace III, underground apartments, c. 1460.

a platform and preceded by a trio of monumental arches, which is reflected in a water body located in front. All these components follow a north–south alignment, as illustrated by the palaces of the Ark Kilah in Bijapur, though without any indication of how they relate to each other ceremonially. The Asar Mahal in Bijapur is an audience hall with an east–west alignment, which is located outside the royal enclosure. One type of structure particular to Bijapur is that of the water pavilion, which is found both in the royal enclosure and in the suburbs. In all these halls and pavilions, a vertical progression of receding spaces is evident.

This sequence of ceremonial spaces, moving from public to private zones with courtyards framed by palaces, is repeated in Golconda, where they ascend along a vertical axis reached by steps. In addition to these examples, underground courtly structures are also found, as are domed halls attached to residential apartments and octagonal spaces of uncertain function.

Courtly structures around Ahmadnagar, such as those in Kalawantinicha Mahal and the Manzarsumbah, repeat the tripartite scheme. Here, however, the scale is smaller and the vertical axis is not as obvious as it is in the Farah Bakhsh Bagh. This is a grandiose palace on the outskirts of Ahmadnagar, whose cross-axial layout recalls the audience hall in the Dargah of Khalifat al-Rahman at Firuzabad, while its octagonal plan and monumental portals imitate Persianate models. The same is true of the pleasure resort of Hasht Behesht Bagh a short distance to the north of Ahmadnagar. Significantly, both these edifices are situated in the middle of water bodies.

The palaces of the Asaf Jahis in Hyderabad and on its surrounding hilltops evince hybrid styles, in which occasionally – as in the case of the Chowmahallah – the tripartite facade of the Deccani palace is combined with styles that prevailed in Europe during the 18th and 19th centuries. Set on hilltops with commanding views of the surrounding areas, they recall the palace settings of the Nizam Shahis who chose similar locations in order to symbolically control and appropriate the land in question to their domains.

Interaction with Local Traditions

As has already been mentioned, the uneasy cohabitation of the Deccan sultans with the rajas of Vijayanagar by no means arrested cultural exchanges; there was considerable movement of craftsmen and artists between the Muslim and Hindu domains, which contributed to shared cultural and architectural traditions. Such interaction embraced the borrowing of building techniques, architectural forms, and decorative designs, as well as of ideas and beliefs.

Domed, square tombs and mosques at Vijayanagar testify to the presence of Muslims in the service of the rajas, as do multi-domed royal edifices that evoke the skylines of Deccani sultanate cities and palaces. Though the domes, arches, and decorative techniques of the Vijayanagar palaces relate to Bahmani and other sultanate examples, none are exact copies; in the process of borrowing there was evidently much re-invention. This seems also to be the case with the forms that the sultanates borrowed from Vijayanagar.

The ground plan and three-storeyed elevation of the Gagan Mahal at the later Vijayanagar palace in Penukonda stresses verticality and recalls the form of Deccani sultanate palaces, as do the overhanging balconies that frame its tripartite facade. It is possible that the Deccani palace plan originates in local vernacular traditions, in which temples and houses are preceded by mandapas (figure 11) and framed by side rooms. Whether realized in timber or stone, architectural elements such as mandapas, overhanging balconies

10 Firuzabad. Dargah of Khalifat al-Rahman, c. 1400. Interior. The iwan, with its ribbed vault, imitates timber structures.

on brackets, chhajjas, and square or octagonal columns are all of local origin. The vertical emphasis that distinguishes Deccani palaces seems, however, to be a purely sultanate innovation.

Pyramidal vaults – probably imitating the profiles of local, stepped temple towers – are often found here in conjunction with domes. Such a combination signals the symbiosis of the two Deccani cultures. Furthermore, so do rooms disposed in a cross-axial layout that precede spaces closely associated with the sultans, as is the case in Palace II and the Rangini Mahal in Bidar. Such a layout imitates mandala diagrams, which are held to regulate the divine and material realms that are presided over by (in this case) the sultans. To such formal and conceptual sharings must be added the emphasis on water – especially in relation to sultanate palaces, where water occurs in square, octagonal, or lotus-shaped pools, reflecting the audience hall or framing the throne-room. The association of these royal spaces with water symbolizes the divine

Introduction 23

power manifest in the sultan as world ruler. It is therefore, hardly surprising that the Persianate Hazar Sutun was eventually replaced by more indigenous symbols of divine power with wider local reverberations.

Contemporary Historians and Painters; Accounts of Foreign Travellers

The chronicles of Deccani history penned by Sayyid Ali Tabataba'i in 1592–96, by Muhammad Qasim Ferishta in 1606–11, Rafi ud-Din Ibrahim Shirazi (1608–35), Fuzuni Astarabadi in 1644 – and others – were written during the reigns of the successor states or later, well after the demise of the Bahmanis.

These chroniclers show greater interest in wars and political intrigues than in architecture. Their references to buildings are vague, and at best express a formal, somewhat predictable, appreciation of royal edifices. Nor do these writers shed much light on the tantalizing but often bewildering names of palaces in the Deccan. These names are later appellations, and afford few insights into the founders and functions of the buildings. While the dates cited in early modern sources prove doubtful at closer examination, inscriptions on the buildings themselves are a valuable source of information since they often mention patrons and builders. However, unless these records are an integral part of the edifice, as is the case on several Bijapuri monuments, they can prove problematic; in most cases, such records seem to belong to now-lost buildings and were attached to surviving ones at some unknown, later, date.

If the palaces of the Deccan did not in general attract the attention of contemporary chroniclers, the gardens closely associated with those palaces – together with their wells, water tanks, and reservoirs – certainly did. We are told that a poetic eye could even discern a qasida or verse in the lush vegetation, where mango, banana, coconut, tamarind, and other fruit trees were combined with scented flowers and vegetables. In Deccani miniatures, this association of water with fruit trees and scented plants is evident in the illustrations of luscious shaded and informal landscapes, in which playful and erotic activities take place and where poetry and music could be enjoyed.

There are no known surviving paintings from the Bahmani period, but there is an abundance of examples

11 Sagar. Mandapa in the village temple.

HELEN PHILON

from later centuries in which different activities are depicted, mostly in shaded, verdant garden settings. Rarer still are paintings portraying actual architectural environments. However, there are a number of relevant examples, some of which are cited below, and which can be found in Mark Zebrowski's book, *Deccani Painting* (1983).

The *Royal Picnic* in the India Office Library, London (Zebrowski, fig. 17), shows Sultan Burhan Nizam Shah II (r. 1591–95) seated on an architectural domed and canopied throne within a garden, and surrounded by courtiers and male musicians.

In a portrait of Sultan Ibrahim Adil Shah II (r. 1580–1627) in the British Museum, London (Zebrowski, plate VIII), the Bijapuri ruler is depicted at night in open countryside, with a distant palace occupying one corner of the background. This multi-storeyed structure, rising above a garden wall, boasts arched facades sheltered by chhajjas and guldastas of the typical Bijapuri type. Similarly, luminous white edifices crown the rugged hilltop in the famous early-17th-century painting, *Yogini* (Zebrowski, plate XII), in the Chester Beatty Library, Dublin. Their exaggerated, bulbous domes recall those of Bijapur, as well as the water-filled examples that crown the water pavilions at Kumatgi outside Bijapur. The pavilions at Kumatgi must also have been covered in gleaming white stucco, so as to shine like stars in the luscious, verdant landscape.

The poetic landscape in *A Lady Dozing in a Garden*, from the *Kulliyat* of Sultan Muhammad Quli Qutb Shah (r. 1580–1611) in the Salar Jung Museum in Hyderabad (Zebrowski, fig. 124), includes a courtyard with fountain and arcaded facades such as those that can still be discerned in the ruins of Golconda. In the *Darbar of Sultan Abdullah Qutb Shah* (p. 86, figure 9) the Golconda ruler (r. 1626–72) is shown enthroned in an audience hall with slender timber columns which carry canopied balconies. Such visual evidence offers invaluable clues as to the original appearance of Deccani palaces.

Unlike contemporary painters, chroniclers and foreign travellers to the Deccan refer to courtly buildings in a vague and eulogistic manner, while some describe the ceremonies that took place in these palaces (Zebrowski, p. 60, figs 71–72). However, Abdur Razzak, the envoy of the Timurid ruler Shah Rukh, visited the Deccan in 1442–46 and left us a vivid and often precise description of the flourishing rural life and crafts of the region. He was aware of the Bahmani kingdom, which he never visited – having stopped for a long time in Vijayanagar where he was impressed by the 100-pillared hall housing the revenue administration, which he refers to as a Chihil Sutun. Obviously, this type of building, even though located in a Hindu capital, evoked in him a reference to a mythical Iranian architectural model.

Of the European visitors, only the Russian, Athanasius Nikitin of Twer (1465–1505), visited the Arabian Sea Bahmani ports and the cities of Gulbarga and Bidar. He was impressed by the sultan's palace with its seven gates in Bidar: in "each gate are seated 100 guards and 100 scribes", but "foreigners are not admitted into the town". The number of gates mentioned by Nikitin is correct as is his observation that guards and scribes guarded the gates in order to protect and record the arrival and departure of visitors. He also noted: "The palace is very wonderful; everything in it is carved or gilded, and even the smallest stone is cut and ornamented with gold most wonderfully. Several courts of justice are within the building." It is now difficult to say exactly where the Bidari courts of justice were located, but the rich carving is still evident while gilding was noted at the time of the excavations undertaken by Ghulam Yazdani in Bidar in the 1940s. Nikitin also mentions the trading activities in the markets of Bidar, where he found silks and all sorts of merchandise as well as horses and "black people", or Habshis, but saw no goods deemed worthy to take back to Russia with him.

Ludovico di Varthema visited "beautiful and very fertile" Bijapur during the reign of Yusuf Adil Shah in 1505. Varthema noted that the city was "walled after the manner of the Christians" – an interesting comment, as at the time Bijapur had only earthen walls. He describes the palace of the king as beautiful and supplied with 44 rooms, an observation that is somewhat difficult to understand considering the size of the actual edifices. It could be, however, that he is referring to a whole complex of buildings, such as those that must have once surrounded the Gagan Mahal and the palace at Nauraspur (figure 8). Colin Mackenzie who spent some time in Gulbarga and other Deccani cities at the end of the 18th century has left us three drawings of Gulbarga. He was more interested however in recording products and revenues than in the description of the monuments of the past.

It is evident in the descriptions from these two European travellers, that they are recording impressions that were current in the market places of the Deccan, as they had no actual access to the forts where the palaces were located. Some visitors were, however, present at the royal ceremonies that unfolded in the cities of Bijapur and Golconda, and their accounts will be described in the relevant chapters.

FORTIFICATIONS

Klaus Rötzer

The fortifications built by the various sultans of the Deccan from the 14th to 16th centuries were intended to provide protection against enemies, as places of safety for state resources, and as potent symbols of power and prestige. In the minds of the population of the Deccan during this period, the enemies were not only the armies of neighbouring states, bandits, and uncontrollable tribes, but also hostile spirits responsible for drought, infertility, and disease. Consequently, fortifications had to be a prophylactic, guaranteeing protection for rulers and their subjects. From a more practical point of view, fortifications were places where taxes were paid by subjects in foodgrains (rice, jowar, dal), molasses, and oil, which were collected and stored in nearby granaries and warehouses (figure 1). This accumulated food stock demonstrated the real wealth of the sultan.

The fortifications of the Bahmanis and their successors can be classified according to their location into frontier, territorial, and metropolitan forts. Furthermore, forts must be distinguished from walled cities. Forts were more or less permanent military camps, while walled cities were intended for the protection and prestige of much larger social bodies. In this sense, the fort is related only to the ruler, while the fortified city is related to the elite inhabitants. The city walls reveal a desire for security and reputation on the part of the elite, which was composed not only of army commanders but also bureaucrats, merchants, religious figures, and craftsmen: that is, of people who needed peace to act efficiently.

The relation between fortifications and the conception people had of the duties of the sultan is difficult to apprehend because it changed continuously, depending on prevailing political, economic, and cultural conditions. To begin with, sultans like Alauddin Hasan Bahman Shah (r. 1347–58) and Yusuf Adil Khan (r. 1490–1510) were commanders of armed forces. They had to impose their authority, to cope with emergency situations and to demonstrate their ability to govern. On the other hand, sultans like Firuz Shah Bahmani (r. 1397–1422) or Ibrahim Adil Shah II (r. 1580–1627) succeeded to the throne as rightful heirs, born to rule, the heads of administrative bodies that, so to speak, were operational in themselves. For their reputation, they needed to

1 Shahpur. Granary in the royal enclosure, c. 1450.

2 Golconda Fort. View from the east, with the 14th-century fortifications on the Bala Hisar.

3 Bidar Fort. View from the northwest, including the lake in the lower garden. The promontory on which the palaces were built is buttressed by walls. The northern, arched facade of the western square tower of Palace II can be seen, and, in the distance, the dome of the Solah Khamba Mosque.

impress by means other than organizing and leading an army. Thus they came to erect impressive stone forts and palaces, and to promote ceremonials that could project them as agents of divine power in the imagination of their subjects.

Sites and Layouts

The choice of the site of a fort or town or capital city was determined essentially by the necessity of a good water supply, a general problem in the Deccan where sufficient water was not everywhere available. Daulatabad, for instance, was supplanted by Aurangabad at the end of the 17th century because of inadequate water supply. But forts needed also to be strategically located at a height, if possible, to command the surrounding terrain and for better defence, and to be visible far away and to impress outsiders. To benefit from both water and a commanding position, forts such as Daulatabad, Bidar, Mahur, Mudgal, Kaulas, and Golconda are all established on hill slopes (figures 2–4). Water was available at the lower level, while the structures associated with those in power were at the higher level. Bidar Fort provides a perfect illustration of such a situation: the lower western curtain wall is at the foot of a dam, while the palaces are at the top of a cliff.

The layout of a camp, fort, or urban area is determined by the natural terrain, but it can also be an imposed cultural concept. The figure of a mandala, round or square, can be discovered in most of the pre-Islamic capitals of the Deccan. The first layout of Devagiri, capital of the Yadavas in the 12th–13th centuries, copied a temple plan, with the principal gateway on the east leading westwards towards the royal palace and the huge basaltic mountain carved into the shape of a temple spire or shikhara, the abode of Shiva (plan 4). In this urban configuration, the ruler occupied the site of the god. Warangal, capital of the Kakatiyas in the 13th century, had three circular concentric walls, with a Shiva temple at the centre. The innermost wall, built of granite, was provided with principal gates facing the four points of the compass, with four secondary gates at the intermediate points. This mandala-like layout adapted the reality of the city to an ideal geometric image. Golconda is based on a similar plan, but here the fort and palaces are surrounded by city walls that create an irregular circle (plan 29). The locations of the gates, however, are determined by the actual needs of the flow of traffic and not by a symbolic model. The same is true of Bijapur (plans 25, 26).

The Bahmani fort of Firuzabad, established in about 1400 on a roughly rectangular plan, incorporates four gates facing the points of the compass, as in Devagiri (plans 2, 4) and Warangal. But here the eastern and western gates are more developed than the two others. It seems that a hierarchy or ranking existed between these gates, depending on the various activities they were supposed to shelter. Gulbarga Fort presents an ambiguous plan. The southern part is circular, probably in conformity with the configuration of an older earthen fort.

4 Daulatabad. Escarpment, baradari, 1636.

The northern part is rectangular. This was added when Gulbarga was chosen as the centre of Bahmani power towards the middle of the 14th century (plan 8).

These examples demonstrate that circular layouts are dominant, but not exclusive, before and after the Bahmani period. The Bahmanis had a clear preference for orthogonal figures, but most often adapted their planning to the local topology, as exemplified by the walls of Bidar Fort and Bidar city (plan 13). On the other hand, the circular layout is again dominant during the 16th century. Ahmadnagar Fort and the capital cities of Bijapur and Golconda, including their central citadels where the sultans resided, are clearly circular. Obviously the circle was at that time a strong symbol of power.

Gates and Towers

Gates in fortifications served as structures through which people had to pass in order to enter the fort or walled city. The main gates of Deccani fortifications are generally well defended with barbicans, towers, and brattices. They

28   KLAUS RÖTZER

5 Daulatabad. Kalakot: southern wall of the Rang Mahal with its pyramidal vaults (c. 1400) and, next to it, the ruined palace of the Nizam Shahis. Beyond, the long wide avenue that links Kalakot and Mahakot to Ambarkot. On either side of this avenue are the Charminar (1445) and the conquest mosque erected by Qutbuddin Mubarak Khalji, 1318.

were furnished with guards and clerks who exercised more or less control over the people who entered and exited. Here, goods could be checked and taxes collected. Lesser gates, such as posterns, are simple passages through curtain walls used by the people living within the defences, to fetch water at a well outside the walls or to answer calls of nature. The study of the gates of a fort or of a walled town offers many clues concerning its public and private life.

We have seen that at Warangal the four gates of the circular stone walls faced the cardinal points; they were all built on the same plan, and were evidently not positioned according to traffic needs. On the other hand, the first Bahmani forts at Gulbarga, Bidar, and Udgir display a large number of gates (plan 8). Some are elaborate structures; others are simple passages through curtain walls. A study of the main gatehouses of the forts of Daulatabad, Gulbarga, and Bidar offers the following results.

Daulatabad is an exceptional site with a long history. What is called Mahakot represents the city of the high castes during the Yadava period and the city of the elites during sultanate rule (plan 4). However, the site also had the functions of a fort. Mahakot has four main gates facing the four points of the compass. This indicates that they belong to the Yadava layout of Devagiri. They were renovated many times in later years. The north gate of Daulatabad leads to a water reservoir where people could wash and bathe. The east gate, which is today the only one still in use, was probably the most important for traffic; it is also located on a significant east–west axis. This axis continues through the city along an important road that leads westwards, directly towards the gate giving access to the palace area (figure 5). This latter gate was entirely rebuilt in the 16th century by the Nizam Shahis. Flanked by two massive sloping towers, it commands the whole city as an architectural manifestation of the power of the rulers. During the 14th and 15th centuries, the south gate of Daulatabad opened towards a maidan, a space used for public events; further south is situated the main idgah of Daulatabad dating from the Tughluq period. The gate has preserved two square towers of

FORTIFICATIONS 29

Yadava times, as well as a Bahmani-period barbican. On its eastern side, the curtain wall was reinforced at the end of the 15th century by two curved features with cannon ports and brattices. These features are built of well-dressed stone, and one cannon port is carved into the shape of an infuriated elephant (figure 6). The cannon placed here was probably not intended to fire stone or cast-iron or lead balls on the enemy; rather, it scattered tiny silver coins over a delighted populace during festivals.

Gulbarga Fort experienced many changes. It began as a circular mud fort located between the centres of the Yadava and Kakatiya kingdoms. By the middle of the 14th century it became the capital of the Bahmanis, a role it fulfilled until 1432 when it was replaced in that function by Bidar. Later, under Adil Shahi rule, Gulbarga again assumed the role of a frontier fort defended by powerful wrought-iron cannons. During the 17th century, it accommodated important ironworks where arms were produced. At the time of its greatest importance, Gulbarga Fort had three main gates. The northwest gate was the main entrance for traffic, connecting the fort to the city. In use without interruption since its foundation, it is a fine example to illustrate the development of gates in the Deccan. Starting with a well-built gatehouse situated between two towers and protected by a barbican, it expanded from the 16th century onwards to become a long, winding passage with five doors and three checkpoints. During this time the other gates of the fort were blocked up (plan 8). The northeast gate of Gulbarga was added at the beginning of the 15th century. It corresponds to the development of the city eastwards, which occurred during the same period (plan 1). The south gate opened towards a huge reservoir and a garden area that was developed during the Bahmani era. It has now been blocked up by a bastion, and being situated at the lowest level of the fort, it has been partly buried under sediment brought by the runoff. All that we can now see is its internal door, which had an arched frame. The structure flanking the passage of the gate is composed of pillars and lintels taken from a splendidly ornate Late Chalukya temple, with images of Hindu deities on the lintels (figure 7). Significantly, its inner arch faced north towards the audience hall, now obscured by the Bala Hisar. The size and elaboration of this gate, and its location on an axis with the Bala Hisar audience hall suggest that it was used for ceremonials. The fact that the images of Hindu deities on the columns inside the passageway were not chipped off suggests that the Bahmani rulers were anxious not to alienate their Hindu subjects.

Bidar Fort, inaugurated in 1432 by Ahmad Shah Bahmani (1422–36), has largely preserved its original shape. Its gates were many and it is quite possible to assign to each of them a particular use. The main gate, the Gumbad Darwaza (plan 17 and figure 8), is in the south wall of the fort that faces east; its octagonal inner space is covered by a huge dome; two rooms on the north–south axis look into this majestic inner space from behind a jali (lattice) window. Another window on the eastern facade could have been used by a ruler to appear to an audience assembled in the open square in front, which was an important meeting point connected by four secondary gates to roads. The first road ascended from the Manjira valley; the second road led to the adjacent city; the third road followed the outermost ditch until it reached the royal camp; the fourth road followed the innermost ditch and ended at the Karnatik Darwaza. This last road permitted service people in the western zone of Bidar Fort to arrive at the square in front of the Gumbad Darwaza without passing through the palace area. That the Gumbad Darwaza faced onto a ceremonial space is not surprising. As long as the sultans were essentially soldiers, touring their territories or leading military expeditions against their neighbours, their camps were often settings for courtly ceremonies. Such settings were generally of a temporary nature, made of wooden stakes and textiles. In the frontier forts of the early Bahmani sultans, at Sagar and Mahur for instance, a gatehouse was used for varied functions. At Sagar, the Shah Darwaza, built by Firuz Shah in 1407, is a structure with four levels, each level intended for a specific use: entrance, checkpost, audience hall, and residence (plan 10). At Mahur, the residential part of the Hathi Darwaza has preserved a pool and toilets; a meeting space was located at the top of the eastern flanking tower.

Curtain Walls and Ditches

Curtain walls and ditches are closely related to mud fortifications, since the earthen material to build such walls comes from the surrounding ditches. From a defensive point of view, mud walls are very efficient, as is illustrated by many examples in the Deccan. For instance, at the beginning of the 14th century, when the forces of the Delhi army twice besieged Warangal, they were held in check both times by the second ring of earthen walls. Subsequently, when gunpowder came into use, mud walls proved effective against cannons since they had the capacity to absorb the shot. Masonry walls, on the contrary, could more easily be broken down. In the Deccan, most of the curtain walls are actually of mud with a dressed stone facing. A wall showing courses of well-dressed stones of large size may be more imposing than a simple mud wall, but it was not necessarily more protective.

The stone facing of forts had essentially a symbolic purpose, contributing to the ceremonial show of the palaces that were inside. This

6 Daulatabad. Elephant bastion, end of 15th century. Polygonal tower with cannon port decorated with the head of an elephant.

7 Gulbarga Fort. South gate, 14th century. The platforms on both sides of the passage are built out of re-used Chalukyan material.

is particularly evident in the southern walls of Bidar Fort, completed by 1432 (figure 9). Here, the grey basalt wall is laid out in a straight line without flanking elements; in fact, it reuses pink granite blocks taken from older buildings, including Hindu temples and Muslim tombs! In front, a triple ditch was carved out of solid laterite. From a military point of view, this wall and the triple ditch provided a poor defence. If besiegers managed to reach the bottom of the first ditch, nobody on the parapet wall would be able to hit them, since they would be out of view. However, this wall with the triple ditch is visually impressive. The reused stones of the wall were emblems of a new power, while the triple ditch symbolized sovereignty.

The main task of frontier forts in the Deccan was to ensure the protection of the land, while territorial forts served as security posts and safe depositories for taxes collected in kind and cash. However, such forts were also conceived as architectural expressions of power, as were metropolitan forts. Mud walls would have been cheaper to build than stone ones, and as has already been pointed out more effective, but not as imposing. For this reason in the Vijayanagar empire only the imperial fort of the capital on the Tungabhadra river received a stone facing. The importance of the outward appearance of Vijayanagar Fort is evidenced by the shape given to the curtain walls that were built between about 1450 and 1550. The parapets here are burdened with brattices and merlons pierced by a line of loopholes. They ensured effective protection for the soldiers behind, and at the same time offered them opportunities of firing on

8 Bidar Fort. Gumbad Darwaza, 1432–36. Ensconced under the soaring arch is the darshan window. Beyond the round bastion is the facade of the Rang Mahal.

9 Bidar Fort. Southern wall, c. 1430. Grey basalt wall with pink granite blocks from Hindu temples and Muslim tombs.

besiegers. But their appearance was also meant to discourage assailants who were unable to determine from where the gunfire was coming. After the middle of the 16th century, with the introduction of heavy bombards, the appearance of forts in the Deccan changed. They were shielded by an earth embankment, which absorbed the balls fired by the bombards, thereby protecting the stone walls. The adoption of these new weapons led in fact to the reintroduction of mud fortifications, though in a different shape.

Conclusion

Fortifications in the Deccan had many purposes. Their appearance was as important as their actual defence value. To a certain extent, impressive gates flanked by towers, dressed stone facing, and elaborate masonry parapets were used for this purpose. Forts at capital cities served as crenellated settings for the royal camp as long as the ruler had to show his capability to rule by his grip on military power; once the leadership of the sultan was firmly established, this camp was gradually replaced by palaces, gardens, and administrative structures. Lesser forts were used as safe depositories, but had to present a potent image of royal power. As the sultan tended to visit frontier forts during military campaigns, a building had to be planned for his lodgings and ceremonials. That a gate could fulfil this purpose is evident at Sagar and Mahur.

DAULATABAD, GULBARGA, FIRUZABAD, AND SAGAR UNDER THE EARLY BAHMANIS (1347–1422)

Helen Philon

Gulbarga, capital of the early Bahmanis, is associated with a number of administrative, strategic, and royal establishments – all of them distinguished by different types of courtly structures. Firuzabad, the royal city of Firuz Shah Bahmani (r. 1398–1422), lay 20 kilometres southwest of Gulbarga, while some 6 kilometres to the northeast was the royal suburb of Sultanpur, and to the northwest lay Daulatabad, the short-lived capital of the Bahmanis and secondary capital of the Tughluqs. This last formidable citadel remained an important trading and administrative centre throughout the Bahmani period, and was the headquarters of one of the four tarafdars of the kingdom. Closer to the Krishna river and the kingdom of Vijayanagar lay Sagar, the most important Bahmani military outpost southwest of the capital Gulbarga (map 1).

Five types of courtly structures are recorded at these localities, suggesting a conscious gradation of importance in early Bahmani ceremonial practices. Private complexes of the ruler and his representatives are marked with edifices distinguished by tripartite plans and facades. These are found in the royal suburb of Sultanpur and in Daulatabad. The iwan-like, vaulted-hall structures at Gulbarga and Firuzabad recall the audience halls of the Tughluqs, predecessors of the Bahmanis in the Deccan. The same plan is found in gatehouses such as the one in Sagar. With the exception of the Bala Hisar inside Gulbarga Fort, all such structures, whether gateways or audience halls, are considerably smaller in scale, as if to acknowledge the pre-eminence of the original prototype (plan 10). The same is true of the cross-in-square Dargah, or "court", of the Sufi saint Khalifat al-Rahman, outside Firuzabad. A different architectural type is represented by the hypostyle interior of the Great Mosque (Hazar Sutun or Chihil Sutun) that stands in the middle of Gulbarga Fort (plan 8). The location of this building in the military centre of the capital and its bold, monumental style suggest its overriding importance for state ceremonials. The divide between courtly and religious domains is bridged by the Chor Gumbad, a commemorative structure with courtly ceremonial functions located a short distance northwest of Gulbarga Fort, on the periphery of the city (plan 12).

1 Sultanpur. Royal country villa, c. 1400. The spandrels of the transverse arches are decorated with stamped roundels in plaster, and on the apex of the arches are lotus motifs. The apex of the second transverse arch depicts regardant birds.

2 Daulatabad. Kalakot, Rang Mahal, c. 1400.

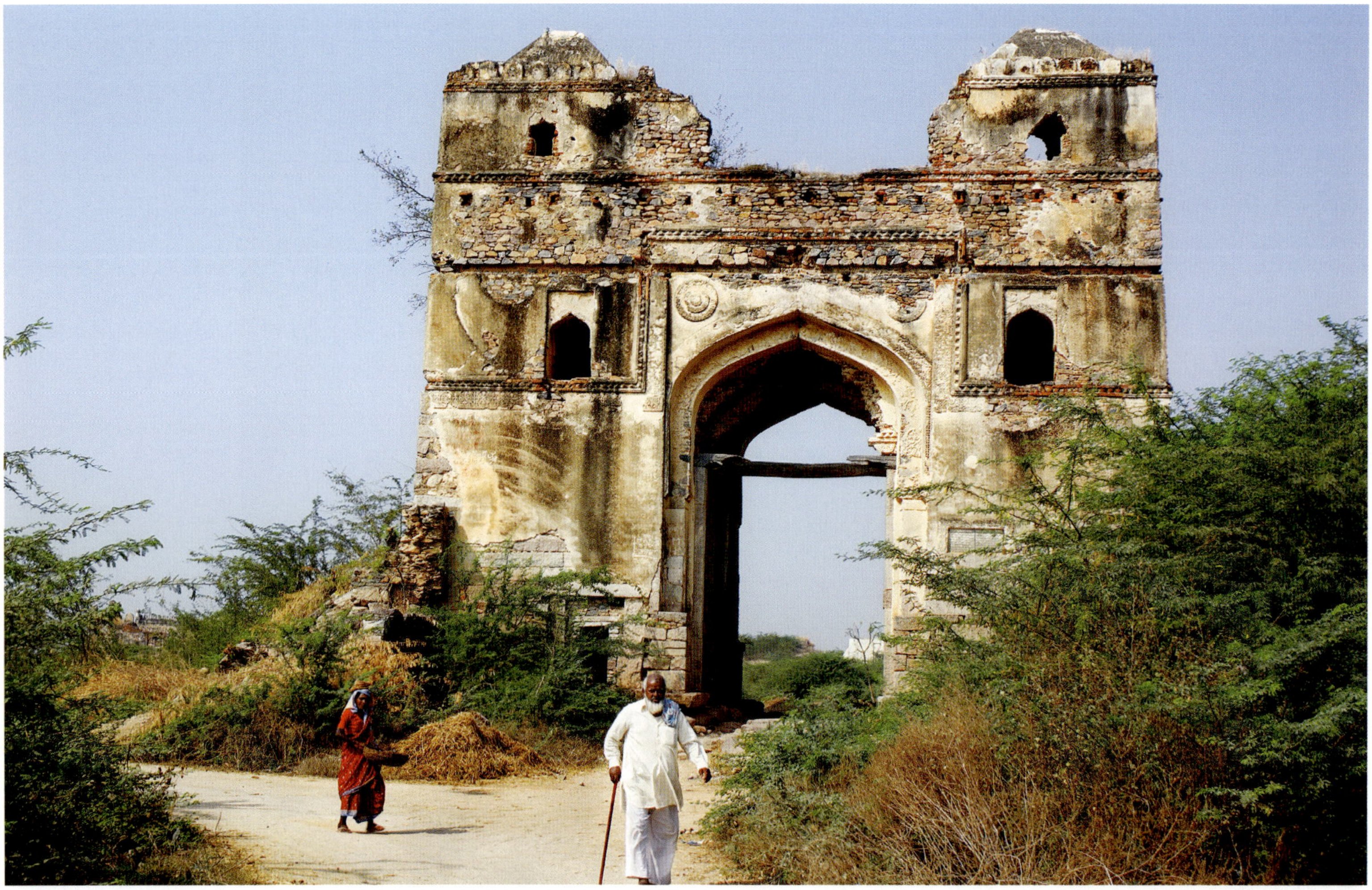

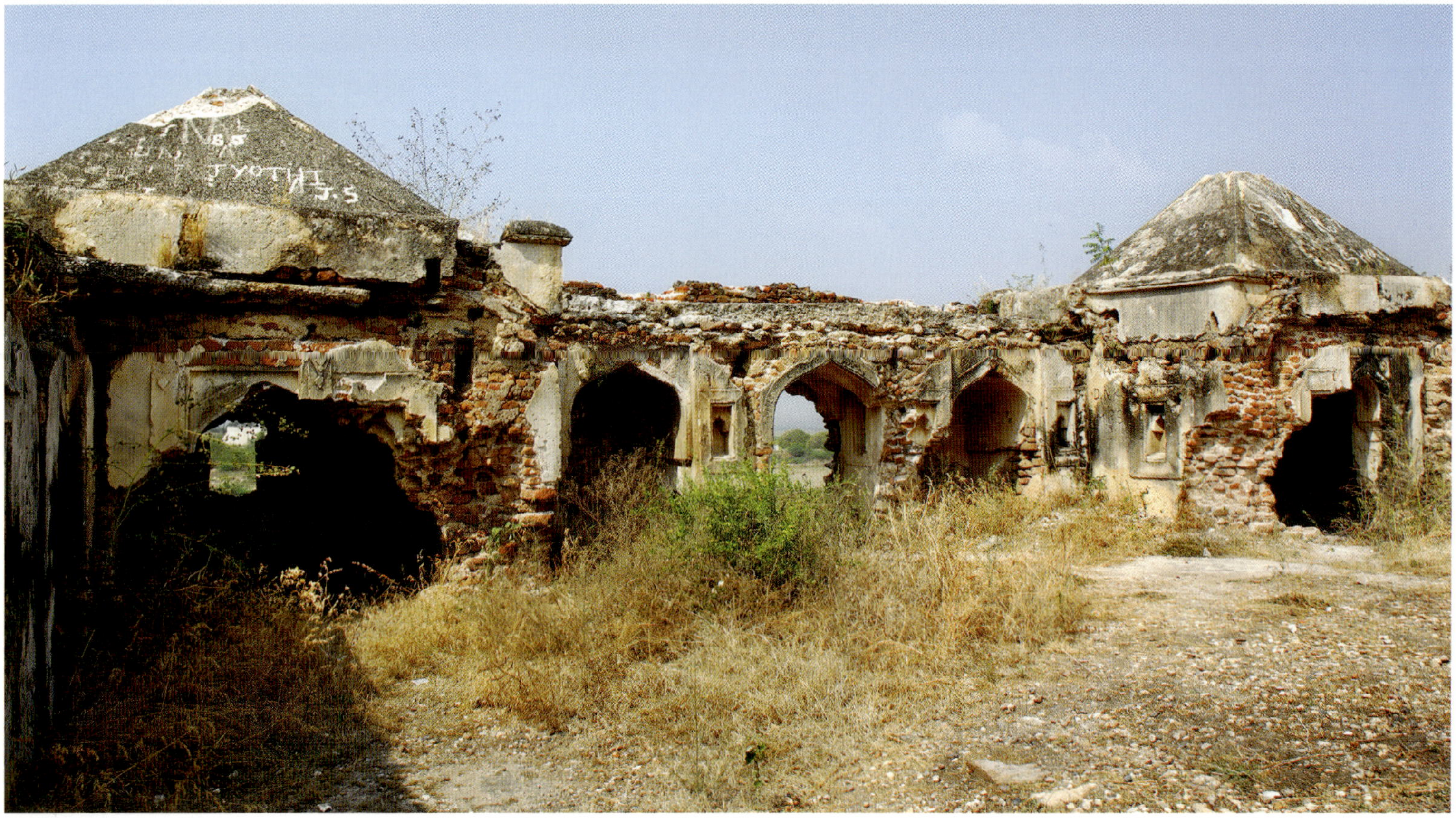

3 Sagar. Shah Darwaza, 1407. Side door for pedestrians.

4 Sagar. Shah Darwaza, 1407. Fourth level. The pyramidal vaulted rooms in the four corners were joined together by timber awnings.

5 Sagar. Shah Darwaza, 1407. Transverse arches of vaulted passage (see plan 10).

Tripartite Schemes: Palaces at Sultanpur and Daulatabad

One of the country estates of the Bahmani sultans and a gathering place of eastward-marching armies was Sultanpur (King's Village), where there is a villa dating most likely to the period of Firuz Shah. Northwest of this property is a re-used ornamental step-well. Numerous nearby canals, bridges, and wells testify to a sophisticated hydraulic system that serviced the surrounding farmlands. The Rang Mahal in Daulatabad is located within the Kalakot enclosure of the fort (plan 6 and figure 2). It is bounded by walls, and its southern side once probably abutted gardens with panoramic views of the city below. Both these Sultanpur and Daulatabad palaces exhibit a central arched section with side wings, with and without balconies, which create a characteristic tripartite facade. This architectural format was later to be repeated at a monumental scale in the courtly structures of the late Bahmanis in Bidar Fort (see following chapter).

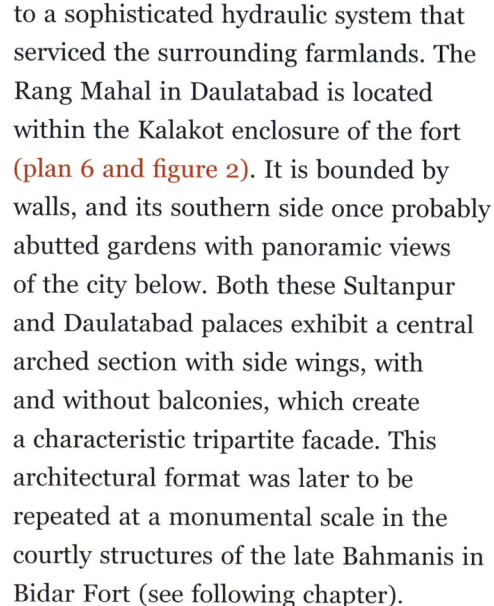

The central space of the Sultanpur villa comprises 3 by 3 stone-arched bays (figure 1). In the Daulatabad Rang Mahal this arrangement is present in the wings, where timber rather than stone columns frame the central rectangular space. A further departure from the Sultanpur example is the range of three rooms adjoining the smaller, central space, and the paired wings along their southern sides (plan 6). Steps attached to the exterior lead to the roof, and to two corner pavilions with pyramidal vaults, resembling those at the Shah Darwaza in Sagar. At Sultanpur, the flight of stairs leading to the roof is set within the northeastern wall that divides the central from the easternmost room. It is not clear, however, whether the rooftop arrangement here was similar to that of the Daulatabad Rang Mahal or the Shah Darwaza in Sagar, or whether a lighter construction in timber or even in fabric was employed. Unlike the Rang Mahal, the Sultanpur villa was endowed with timber balconies on its southeastern, as well as northwestern and northeastern, facades.

The absence of squinches or pendentives in both these buildings seems to indicate the use of flat timber roofs, like the ones surviving in the Rang Mahal, Daulatabad. Recesses in the walls

DAULATABAD, GULBARGA, FIRUZABAD, SAGAR

imply the use of timber, such as that in the Daulatabad mansion and the Rangini Mahal in Bidar Fort. The Sultanpur villa and Rang Mahal in Daulatabad share the same plaster foliate designs highlighting the shape and apexes of arches and niches and their spandrels. One feature unique to Sultanpur is the depiction of two affronted and regardant birds on the central arch of the northeastern room.

Iwan-like Audience Halls in Firuzabad and Gulbarga; Shah Darwaza at Sagar

Early Bahmani audience halls and gateways display commonalities with iwan-like audience halls. These rectangular structures are each distinguished by four transverse arches that originally supported vaults or flat timber roofs. Identified as audience halls, they are usually two-storeyed, with arched openings in their peripheral walls. They occur in the urban centre and royal enclosure of Firuzabad as well as in Gulbarga Fort (p. 18, figure 4 and plan 8).

Gates with platforms on both sides of their central passage, and an open-air rooftop verandah surrounded by merlons, are located along the earthen or stone walls of many fortified Bahmani enclosures. This type of gateway is typical of the early Bahmani period, the most significant example being the Shah Darwaza at Sagar (figures 3–5). However, the Shah Darwaza differs from other Bahmani gates in that it rises to four storeys (plan 10). The different layouts and decorative schemes on each floor suggest distinct usages, implying that ceremonial functions were not always separate from less formal activities. Such is certainly the case for the three, and

6 Gulbarga Fort. The Great Mosque, here identified as the Hazar Sutun, after 1407. View of the southwestern, or qibla, wall.

possibly four, two-storeyed audience halls with north–south alignments found in Firuzabad (p. 18, figure 4). These halls are located at different distances from the royal enclosure, where one additional such structure is recorded. The multiple occurrence of this type of hall argues against their being intended as royal audience halls, since such a structure should comprise a unique throne-room arrangement rather than a repeated type. Their disposition throughout Firuzabad suggests that they may have been intended for the different governors of the kingdom, reflecting the status of these figures within the Bahmani hierarchy. The only exception might be the ruined hall within the royal enclosure, which is associated with hammams and other courtly buildings, and which could indeed have functioned as a private ceremonial hall for Firuz Shah.

If these Firuzabad halls were intended to accommodate the official business of the different provinces and the military establishment of the Bahmani kingdom, a similar usage could be postulated for the Bala Hisar audience hall inside Gulbarga Fort (plan 8). This, however, is the sole example of such a structure within the fort. Indeed, it could well have been used as a royal audience hall by Firuz Shah's predecessors, perhaps changing function during the reign of Firuz Shah to serve as a ceremonial gateway to the Great Mosque. As we shall argue below, we believe that this mosque was in fact the Hazar or Chihil Sutun of Firuz Shah Bahmani.

By far the most imposing ceremonial entryway of the early Bahmani period is the Shah Darwaza at Sagar erected by Firuz Shah in 1407–08 (plan 10). This multi-purpose gateway was constructed in timber and stonework, the latter with decorative designs both impressed and carved into its plaster surface. It displays features that vary at each level, implying different functions for each storey. In plan, the Shah Darwaza seems a typical early Bahmani gateway. Its lofty arched entrance and vaulted hall with transverse arches recall the iwan-like spaces of the Bala Hisar in Gulbarga Fort and the halls of Firuzabad. This possibly explains the analogy with the fabled arch of Ctesiphon (in present-day Iraq), which is specifically

7 Gulbarga Fort. The Great Mosque, here identified as the Hazar Sutun, after 1407. Central dome.

8 Gulbarga. Chor Gumbad, c. 1430.

mentioned in the lapidary inscriptions embedded in the facades of the Sagar gateway. Only on its eastern entrance the passageway level was protected by teak doors set below a timber lintel. This lintel supported a balcony that could have been the setting for a royal darshan ceremony. High and wide enough for horses and elephants, this monumental entrance has a much smaller side door for pedestrians, which is the first occurrence of this feature in the Deccan.

The second level of the Shah Darwaza was probably meant for guards. It comprises two platforms, that to the north probably entered from two doors in its north wall (plan 10). Steps enclosed by doors permitted access to a southern platform, from which further steps ascended to a space, which follows a cross-shaped design, probably roofed by a shallow dome on its eastern side. This domed space could have been used as a throne-room for the visiting sultan. From this platform yet another stairway reached the third level, where we find vaulted halls linked by a passage located above the timber lintel of the monumental entrance. Only two windows on the eastern facade can be seen, as the other openings overlook the vaulted hall of the passage.

The fourth and most elaborately decorated level of the Shah Darwaza is reached by staircases from both southern and northern sides of the third storey. This topmost floor comprised an open court bounded on three sides by rooms that connected to four rectangular pavilions with pyramidal vaults, and which were joined by a timber awning that no longer survives. The vaults of these pavilions are decorated with open-flower motifs, geometric designs,

9 Firuzabad. Royal enclosure, hammam, c. 1400. Framing the central dome are pyramidal vaults and lobed domes, all perforated.

10 Firuzabad. Royal enclosure, hammam, c. 1400. Perforated dome supported on muqarnas.

and patterns imitating those of timber structures. This array of domes and pyramidal vaults decorated with varying patterns indicates a ceremonial rather than a defensive purpose for the gateway. Between the ribs of one of the vaults are "lotus-tree" motifs, a design with particular royal associations, which is also present in palaces in Firuzabad and a number of early Bahmani royal and elite tombs. The designs embellishing the domes and vaults of the Shah Darwaza can be compared with those from the cross-in-square building in the Dargah of Khalifat al-Rahman and other palace structures in Firuzabad, as well as with examples from the neighbouring kingdom of Vijayanagar.

The richness of the decorative repertoire found in the Shah Darwaza sets it apart from all other Bahmani structures. The likeliest explanation for such opulence is that the building was intended for the sultan's local representative in a crucial frontier province of the kingdom. This would explain the combined features of entryway, ceremonial hall, and private quarters. Architecturally, this multi-functional structure is the link between the city gates and the audience halls in Firuzabad and Gulbarga, all of which are distinguished by the use of transverse arches.

Great Mosque (Hazar Sutun) in Gulbarga and Dargah of Khalifat al-Rahman outside Firuzabad

The unique features of the Great Mosque in the middle of Gulbarga Fort suggest a new interpretation: rather than serving as the Jami Masjid of the city, this was the Hazar Sutun, or ceremonial audience hall (figure 6), of Firuz Shah, erected after his victorious and lucrative campaign against Vijayanagar in 1407. A number of architectural characteristics support this interpretation: the absence of the external wall projection that marks the presence of the mihrab on the qibla wall; the absence of a minbar, or pulpit, and other smaller mihrabs along the qibla wall; the overall plan of the hall, divided by piers into 90 domed-bay units, which imitates a hypostyle space; and the raised platform in the nine-bayed space immediately in front of the qibla wall, roofed by a soaring dome (plan 9 and figure 7). All these features indicate that the building may not have been intended primarily as a place of worship, though it could have been used as such since it faces towards Mecca.

DAULATABAD, GULBARGA, FIRUZABAD, SAGAR

Large, soaring domes emphasize the presence of the ruler within his palace, especially if, as here, there is no evidence of an original mihrab. The raised platform beneath the dome had a similar significance; it is recorded from examples of courtly architecture but is unknown in buildings with religious associations. If the combination of raised platform and dome is an indicator of royal presence and clearly relates to courtly architecture, then the same may be said of the multi-columned hypostyle hall. It is worth noting here that this hypostyle plan recalls Ibn Battuta's (1304–68/69) description of Muhammad Tughluq's palace in Delhi as a Hazar Sutun. In medieval Islamic lore, the great Apadana at Persepolis in Iran – described variously as a Chihil Sutun, Hazar Sutun, or Hazar Ustun – was the conceptual model for palaces belonging to dynasties eager to adopt Islamicate styles. This Iranian symbol of majesty was widely known throughout the Islamic world, as was the association of the dome with sovereignty. Significantly, both these architectural emblems are combined in the Great Mosque at Gulbarga.

Like the Great Mosque, the Dargah of Khalifat al-Rahman outside Firuzabad may be interpreted in a royal-ceremonial context. Its unique cross-in-square plan, lacking a fixed orientation, is without parallel in the funerary architecture of the Deccan (plan 11). The same is also true of the location of its graves. In Deccani tombs, burials are usually positioned beneath the dome. Here, however, they are located in the eastern iwan and in the southeast corner of the central domed space, suggesting that they were added later when the function of the building was changed. In fact, the burial place of the saint associated with this dargah adjoins the mosque, exactly as in other Islamic lands where funerary mosques are well attested. (The mosque and tomb have been replaced by a modern concrete mosque and only the domed square gate of the original survives, along with parts of its enclosure wall.) In the Deccan this is not usually the custom. This funerary mosque in this dargah is the only such Deccani example, implying the influence of imported traditions.

In Firuzabad, this funerary mosque and the cross-in-square layout seem to hark back to originals from western Islam, most likely Anatolia. In fact, the presence of Anatolian immigrants at Firuzabad, and indeed throughout the Bahmani domains, is well attested in lapidary inscriptions and contemporary records. Amongst these immigrants were master-masons who could have brought with them plans of buildings from their country of origin with which to impress the sultan. These documents may have included the cross-in-square-type layout and the hammam, both of which make their first appearance in the Deccan during Firuz Shah's reign. The symmetrical axial arrangement centred on a domed throne-room that distinguishes the Dargah of Khalifat al-Rahman in Firuzabad is not unique in Islamic courtly architecture. As in the case of the multi-columned hall wherein the concept of Persian kingship was embedded, so was universal majesty traditionally represented by the cross-in-square plan. This form focused on the central, square room beneath the dome, a space that was associated with concepts of kingship and caliphal power.

The quadripartite division of interiors has a long history in Islamic palace architecture. Two variants of it exist: one in which four iwans face into a square courtyard; another in which they meet under a square domed chamber. The Dargah of Khalifat al-Rahman belongs to the latter variant. The caliphal association of this cruciform plan is probably responsible for inspiring numerous later copies in India and indeed throughout the Islamic world.

The Chor Gumbad in Gulbarga

There is one more structure that should be added to the record of early Bahmani courtly architecture: the Chor Gumbad. This square, domed building stands west of Gulbarga Fort (plan 12 and figure 8).

11 Firuzabad. "Tiger" gate to royal enclosure, c. 1400–22.

It was probably built by Ahmad Shah Bahmani (r. 1422–36) to commemorate his gratitude towards his spiritual mentor, or pir, Gesu Daraz, and his victory over his brother Firuz Shah.

In plan, the Chor Gumbad recalls the cross-in-square courtly arrangement of the previously discussed dargah near Firuzabad (plan 11). Instead of four iwans, however, here there are only three. Furthermore, these have been reduced in depth to resemble wide recesses; the space where the fourth iwan would have been located is instead occupied by the mihrab. The size of the dome that roofs the central space has been increased to monumental proportions, comparable only to the dome of the throne room in the Great Mosque. Indeed the domes of the Chor Gumbad and Great Mosque share a number of other features, including the trefoil squinches that support the dome. The band of muqarnas at the base of the Chor Gumbad's dome is also found in the domes of the tombs of Firuz Shah and Gesu Daraz in Gulbarga, the two most prominent funerary monuments of the early Bahmani era, and at the hammam in Firuzabad. The absence of a burial in the Chor Gumbad provides further evidence that it was not a tomb. Thus, this building unites elements of domes belonging to the most important ceremonial and commemorative structures in Gulbarga.

A further feature differentiating the Chor Gumbad from other Bahmani funerary structures is the interior staircase leading to an upper-level corridor. This was screened by geometric openwork jalis, and probably accommodated the royal ladies. From there, they could follow the ceremonies that took place beneath the dome, where the throne of the sultan would have been located. The stairs continue to the rooftop, where a quartet of chhatri kiosks, an architectural form with courtly antecedents, could have been used as observation posts by the sultan's guards. In the Chor Gumbad, therefore, we have yet another hybrid structure, combining religious and royal activities.

Hammams

The earliest baths to be preserved at any sultanate site in India are those in the walled city and royal enclosure of Firuzabad. Royal hammams in both these locations exhibit a volumetric interplay between domes and pyramidal vaults set at different heights. However, the example in the royal complex is grander in scale and more elaborately decorated than those elsewhere in the city. The decorative schemes of the hammams are confined to the ceiling of each (figures 9, 10), where an array of geometric configurations recalls patterns on the domes of other royal structures in Gulbarga and Firuzabad. The grand scale and elaborate decoration of the royal hammam at Firuzabad indicates a building intended for courtly pursuits. No doubt these would have pleased the Turkish ladies and other wives of Firuz Shah who were accustomed to such luxuries.

The hammams of Firuzabad, as well as a few surviving paper plans from the early Ottoman period, testify to influences from Anatolia, where bath structures are well recorded. There are, however, certain differences between the hammams in Anatolia and those of Firuzabad, suggesting that plans were adapted to the needs of the Bahmani sultans. The close association of Bahmani hammams with the rectangular, transverse-arched halls that have already been noted indicate that these bath houses may have had more formal functions. Such a usage would have required different spatial arrangements and certain modifications of Anatolian models in order to satisfy the needs of Firuz Shah's court.

Conclusion

The evidence offered by the courtly structures of the early Bahmani period suggests that royal ceremonials of this period were symbolized by the Bala Hisar, an architectural type harking back to the iwan of the Tughluqs in Delhi. This type invariably conforms to a north–south alignment, which by the time of Firuz Shah would be retained for less formal structures – an east–west alignment now seeming to be preferred for the most important ceremonial palace of the dynasty, which was rendered in a monumental configuration in which the four alignments converge under a dome. Expressive of the importance of the Bahmani state, both these building layouts only appear during the reign of Firuz Shah; that is, only after Bahmani power was securely consolidated. Such royal buildings pronounce Firuz Shah's ecumenical ambitions by introducing palace structures related to universal kingship. Nowhere is this better seen than in the Dargah of Khalifat al-Rahman, the cross-in-square plan of which evokes caliphal precedents. As for Firuz Shah's Hazar Sutun in Gulbarga Fort, now known as the Great Mosque, its spiritual overtones clearly express connections to the royal ceremonial edifices of mythical Iranian rulers. Undoubtedly, it is the most significant courtly structure of the early Bahmani era.

BIDAR UNDER THE LATER BAHMANIS AND BARIDIS (1432–1619)

Helen Philon

1 Bidar Fort. Northwest palace zone, Diwan-i Am, here identified as Palace I, after 1443–44. The northern platform has an octagonal pool with dolerite revetments and holes for water jets. At the southern end of the courtyard, the tripartite facade consists of a monumental mandapa framed by rooms with timber balconies.

By relocating his capital from Gulbarga to Bidar in 1432, Ahmad Shah (r. 1422–36) evidently wished to forge a new identity for the Bahmani kingdom and to increase its wealth through natural resources and trade. Situated almost 100 kilometres northeast of Gulbarga, Bidar was located on the edge of an area rich in agricultural and mineral resources that offered an alternative and additional source of revenue to the much-contested Raichur Doab that lay to the south of the original capital, Gulbarga. Bidar was also strategically positioned on the route that led to the ports on the Bay of Bengal – an area that had long been coveted by the Bahmanis, but had not thus far fallen within their domains.

From his new capital Ahmad Shah was able to increase the revenues of his kingdom by adding new resources, as well as profits, from the trans-peninsular trade that linked the Bay of Bengal with the Arabian Sea ports. Furthermore, with this move Ahmad Shah was also able to effectively distance himself from courtly intrigues at Gulbarga, in particular the partisan role played by the now deceased Gesu Daraz (d. 1423) during the last years of Firuz Shah's reign. Under Ahmad Shah at Bidar, architecture, too, had a contribution to make in the formulation of a new identity for the Bahmanis. The military, courtly, and religious projects that he and his successors sponsored at Bidar were strikingly different from those at Gulbarga, in technique, form, and decoration. The new building style proclaimed independence from the Tughluq models that had largely dominated the architecture of Gulbarga. The fresh architectural forms introduced by Ahmad Shah and his successors fused local traditions and symbols of power with others imported from western Islam, and evinced new and direct linkage with Central Asian decorative techniques.

Ahmad Shah did not build the impressive stone-walled city of Bidar with its two intersecting main streets lined with imposing public institutions (plan 13, no. 1), for his reign was too short. This was the work of his successors, inspired by Ahmad Shah's vision of kingship. At the northern end of the city is a fort protected by formidable ramparts, the interior of which is dotted with courtly edifices. The fort occupies a promontory that rises 100 metres above

2 Bidar Fort. Northwest palace zone, Palace I. Jali windows on the terrace topped by merlons. From the terrace, one could ascend to a higher level, where more rooms with balconies were located, on the southern side of the palace. Adjoining Palace I on its northeast corner is the gateway to Palace II (see plan 14). The newly built stone platforms in the foreground are for the use of officials during an annual mela that takes place within this historic site.

the fertile plains watered by the Manjira river, 10 kilometres away. Bidar was the capital of the later Bahmanis; after the disintegration of the kingdom from c. 1500 the city served as the headquarters of the Baridis, rulers of one of the Bahmani successor states. The Baridi kingdom was annexed by Ibrahim Adil Shah II in 1619. In 1656, the city was conquered by the Mughals.

The courtly structures of the later Bahmanis standing inside Bidar Fort differ markedly from those of the early Bahmanis described in the previous chapter. They lack the diversity of forms that distinguished the buildings of their predecessors, and are for the most part confined to the royal enclosure of Bidar Fort rather than being distributed at various sites around the capital. Architectural diversity at Bidar is limited to essentially three building types, the most popular being the tripartite arrangement first noted in Daulatabad and Sultanpur for the more private structures of the early Bahmanis. Later Bahmani palaces are entered through a mandapa framed by rooms with timber balconies, surrounded by a second line of additional rooms on three sides (plan 14). The principal ceremonial space of each palace is to be found to the rear of the mandapa (C in plan 14), creating thus an expanded

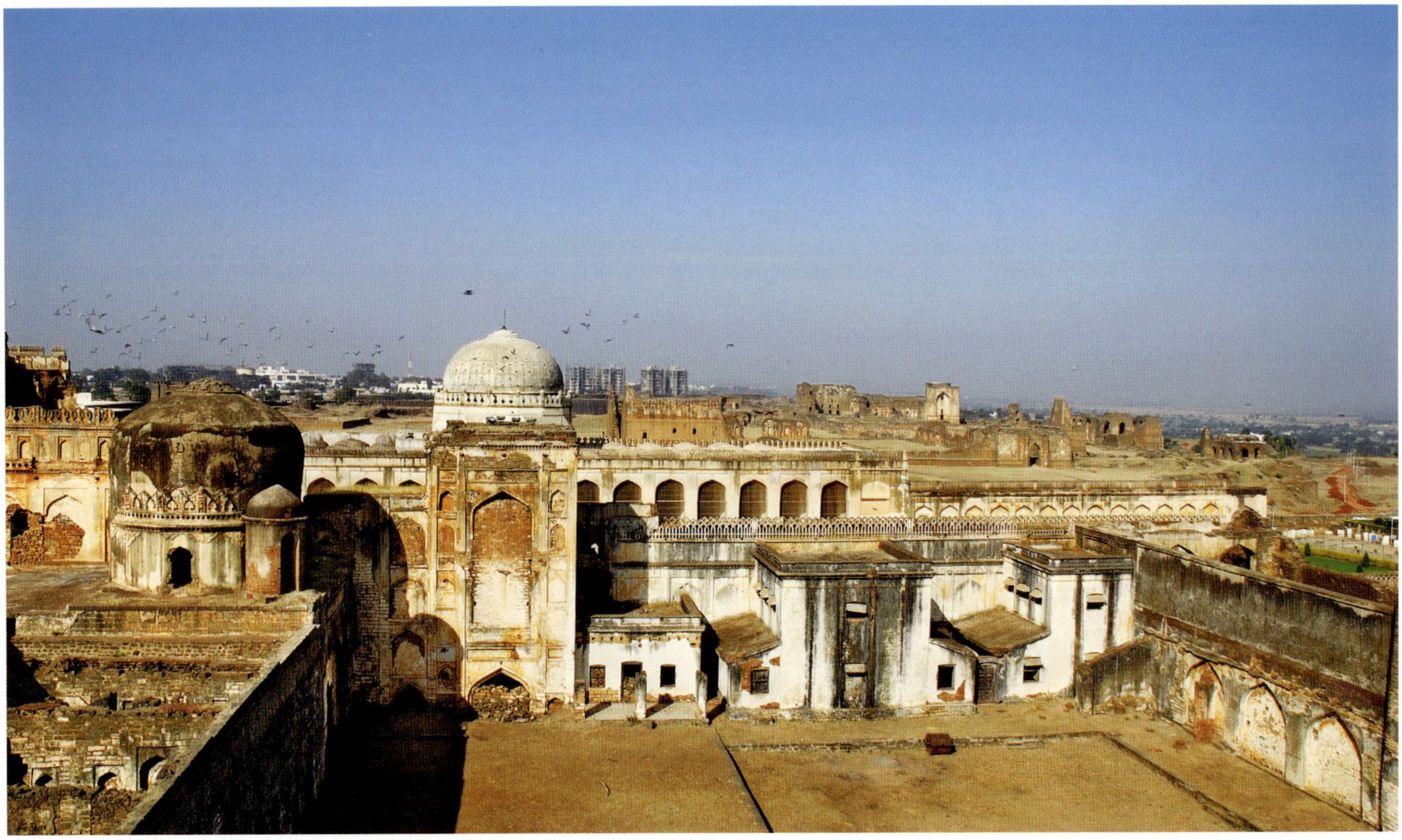

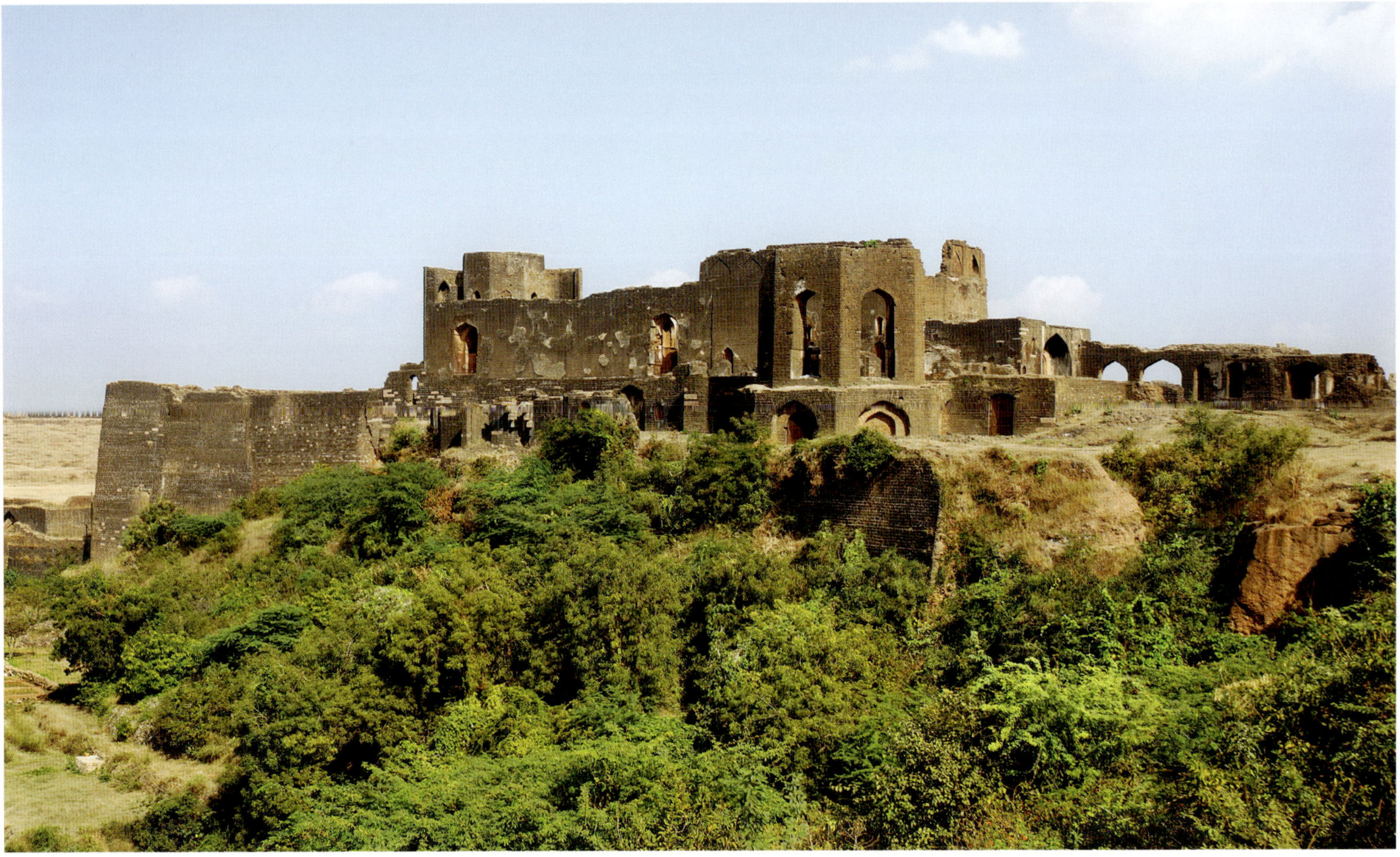

3 Bidar Fort. Southeast palace zone, Prince's Palace, c. 1460. The square tower in the courtyard copies those in Palace II, and is on axis with the domed chamber of the Solah Khamba Mosque.

4 Bidar Fort. Northwest palace zone, western view of Palace III, Palace II, pool house, and cross-in-square pavilion.

5 Bidar Fort. Northwest palace zone, Palace I. Room C is on axis with the fountain and octagonal pool on the northern platform.

tripartite plan (Rooms A, B1 & B2, and C). The palaces have terraces linked to rooms at the upper levels, provided with arched openings and timber balconies that afforded views of the surrounding gardens and/or courtyards. Associated with these expanded tripartite schemes are a number of "cross-in-square-plan" edifices, a type also first attested during the early Bahmani period, which in Bidar was used for pavilions and underground apartments. To these one has to add two-domed pavilions (plans 17, 18).

The ceremonial importance of these tripartite, multi-storeyed structures is signified by a number of features: scale and location; strict axial layout; and the presence of domes, pyramidal vaults, or timber ceilings. As has already been noted in connection with early Bahmani palaces, domes are rooted in Islamic concepts of universal kingship and are, therefore, suitable indicators of majesty. Pyramidal vaults seem to relate to courtly structures without direct connotations of majesty, while flat timber ceilings do not appear to have had direct royal associations. Another feature indicative of royal association, first noted in the palaces of Bidar, is water. This is attested by lotus-shaped and octagonal pools as well as fountains, indicating the influence of local traditions and their role in the architectural symbolism of kingship (plan 14). Water is found in the private areas of Bidari palaces, but also in spaces with ceremonial associations.

Another notable feature of the Bidar palaces is the importance given to changes of level and vertical distribution of spaces. This tendency has already been noticed in the early Bahmani Shah Darwaza at Sagar, where changes of level take on a ceremonial significance. In addition to these tripartite multi-storeyed structures and their associated "cross-in-square-plan" buildings, in which water plays such an important symbolic role, two other architectural forms appear at Bidar. The first is represented by the Gumbad Darwaza, a domed gateway that served as a ceremonial entrance to the fort; the other is the so-called Solah Khamba Mosque, a domed ceremonial pavilion to which hypostyle halls were added and which is here interpreted as a Hazar Sutun (plan 18).

The aforementioned buildings are located in two zones of the royal enclosure at Bidar. Several tripartite palaces are built along the southeastern wall of the fort, overlooking the city and linking the Gumbad Darwaza to the Solah Khamba Mosque (plan 13, nos. 3, 4). This group of palaces constitutes a labyrinthine complex belonging to different historical periods; further research is required to unravel its complicated history. The tripartite palaces in this area to be noted here are the Prince's Palace and the Rangini Mahal (plans 15, 16). Another group of tripartite palace structures is located on the northwestern edge of the promontory. This includes Palace I, previously the Diwan-i Am; Palace II, previously the Takht Mahal; and Palace III, containing a distinctive octagonal chamber and underground apartments with views over the lower garden and the surrounding valleys (plan 14).

In addition to these courtly buildings, at least five wells are located within the upper royal garden and more are in the lower royal garden beneath Palaces II and III, supplying water to the numerous pools and gardens surrounding the palaces. Two qanat irrigation systems supplied a constant flow of water to the royal establishment and its gardens. Qanats are artificially excavated underground water channels, with regularly spaced ventilation holes, to convey water from distant sources into the middle of an arid settlement. This technology was first developed in Iran and was introduced by Persian immigrants into the Deccan, where it makes its first appearance in Bidar.

There are no detailed reports of the Bidar palaces in any of the accounts of historians and travellers; the vague references one finds have been noted in the Introduction. Nor are there any inscriptions mentioning dates or the names of the founders of these palaces, with one notable exception: the Rangini Mahal datable to the reign of Ali Baridi (r. 1543–80).

The absence of descriptions should not be surprising, however, as courtly areas were only accessible to the local elites more interested in the rituals of kingship rather than its architecture which they assumed was grandiose and luxurious. Nor were foundation inscriptions mentioning dates and the

6 Bidar Fort. Northwest palace zone, Palace II, c. 1460. Square tower, with its spandrels decorated with glazed tiles in the mosaic technique.

7 Bidar Fort. Palace II, c. 1460. Walking tigers with rising sun, decoration in spandrel of square tower.

name of the patron necessary, as these were private royal domains where public declarations of patronage were not required. It is on the public monuments that royal munificence had to be recorded. A similar situation is noted in Hampi/Vijayanagar where there is an abundance of inscriptions on temples and in the sacred centre, but none on palaces.

Diwan-i Am (Palace I), Takht Mahal (Palace II), and Palace III

In Bidar Fort there are seven palaces distinguished by a tripartite facade and dating from the mid-15th to early 17th centuries. Each exhibits a symmetrical layout centred on a tripartite facade, which is raised on a platform located on the south side of a courtyard and surrounded by high walls. The two earliest tripartite palaces are those in the northwestern zone of the fort. They were surrounded by gardens and overlooked more gardens at a lower level. Both these structures are provided with terraces. Those of Palace I have openwork jali windows and balconies permitting panoramic views of the gardens and courtyard (figures 1, 2). The terraces of Palace II are enclosed, but large arched timber balconies in three rooms of its western ground-floor facade, allowed views to its gardens.

Other commonalities are seen in the decorative themes and techniques. Carved and painted timber ceilings and columns continue local traditions, as does the use of basalt and green dolerite (plain and sculpted) for architectural elements. Tile compositions in mosaic and polychrome-underglaze painted techniques indicate the influence of Persian and Central Asian traditions, while painted designs of black-outlined vegetal forms confirm the continuing influence of master painters belonging to the reign of Ahmad Shah. To these we must add the now lost woven and embroidered fabrics and carpets that would have furnished these palaces, transforming them into luxurious establishments worthy of the most important Muslim dynasty of the Deccan.

Differences between Palaces I and II may be explained by their roles in Bahmani court ceremonials. The courtyard of Palace I had raised platforms on its northern, eastern, and western sides. These communicated through doors with rooms adjoining its southern platform. On the edge of the northern platform are two water bodies (figure 5): an octagonal pool with water jets and a

BIDAR 49

8 Bidar Fort. Palace II, the "Axis of the Gaze". Along an east–west axis are the gate to Palace II and courtyard D1, with its square pool; followed by the throne-room; courtyard D2; and beyond were the private quarters of the sultan, with views onto the surrounding and lower gardens.

fountain basin. Both are on axis with the wider, central aisle of the mandapa on the southern platform, whose double-height painted timber columns on square dolerite bases once supported a timber ceiling. At the end of this central aisle is a small, beautifully decorated square chamber (Room C). Its ceiling was probably in carved timber supported by engaged timber columns, while its floor shows a radiating geometric pattern of octagons and star-shapes in black-and-white marble. An octagonal concave recess sits in the central star-shape of the floor pattern. This was designed to receive some important, but portable, power-emblem, perhaps relating to fire, to complement the water body with which it is aligned on the other side of the courtyard.

Ghulam Yazdani, the archaeologist who first published the monuments of Bidar, believed that Palace I was the Diwan-i Am of the Bahmanis. The absence, however, of a domed space – that clearest symbol of kingship – and the presence of the richly decorated hypostyle hall preceding Room C suggests, rather, that the palace served as an important administrative centre. It is tempting to imagine that here the most important ministers of the kingdom could meet in the mandapa, with the presence of the absent ruler being signified by the emblem in the room behind. An indication of the date of this palace may be sought in Ferishta. He records that Alauddin Ahmad Shah II, after his 1442–43 campaign against Vijayanagar, decided to leave the governance of the kingdom to his ministers and retire to his new palace outside the capital to follow more pleasurable pursuits.

Originally, the rooms on the southern platform of Palace II projected outwards in two identical, pishtaq tower-like high portal structures marking the sides of this symmetrical structure (plan 14). The towers partly frame an inner courtyard entered by an L-shaped route that linked it with an outer court, where the main gate to this palace complex is located. This gate continues early Bahmani traditions, and could have been the entrance to Ahmad Shah's (1430–36) tented camp, which was replaced by Palace II in about 1450 (plan 13, no. 2).

Only one of the pishtaq or high portal towers survives, K2 (figure 6); the other (K1) is now much ruined (plan 14, Palace II). Both have octagonal internal chambers with arched recesses that recall the internal arrangement of the Gumbad Darwaza (plan 17). Unlike the Gumbad Darwaza, however, they were probably topped by timber octagonal pyramidal roofs with large arched windows on three sides. The spandrels of the pishtaq on the surviving west tower display sunbursts rising behind walking tigers (figure 7). This is a royal emblem with a long pedigree in West Asia as well as Central Asia where it makes a late appearance in the portal of Timur's Aq Saray Palace in Samarkand (1379–96). The occurrence of this motif at Bidar may be credited to Afaqi immigrants from Central Asia and Iran. In the hybrid culture of the Deccan, however, the sun-and-tiger theme would have been endowed with a local symbolism, understood by the various Indian communities. According to the complexities of Hindu mythology, the sun deity, or Surya, is associated with the primeval ocean, at the centre of which is the cosmic tree reaching up to the heavenly firmament. Furthermore, Surya is identified with ferocious animals, such as the lion/tiger, thereby also evoking Agni, the Hindu god of fire.

The public entrance to Palace II was from the steps located in front of Room M rather than from the towers with their semicircular steps (a modern addition) (figure 6 and plan 14). The ceremonial entrance was via the steep steps – each 34 centimetres high, with tiled fronts – which climb to the mandapa (Room A) and throne-room (Room C). This ascending disposition of spaces continued up to the threshold of the throne-room, after which a step descended into the domed space. (The sequence of ascending levels culminating in a threshold recalls the progression through a temple to its innermost sanctum.) From the public entrance, it is possible to reach the private rooms of the sultan (Rooms G, F, and E) after crossing the stellate Room H. This space seems to have functioned as a "distribution centre", since from here one could proceed in three different directions. Chamber F had a unique cooling system, combining air-circulation ducts, within its western wall, and high ceilings, with three arched doorways topped by windows. This chamber led

9 Bidar. Ashtur, the royal necropolis, tomb of Humayun, 1461. This tomb is of exactly the same plan, dimensions, and design to the throne-room in Palace II.

BIDAR 51

10 Bidar Fort. Northwest palace zone, Palace III, c. 1460. Mandapa with dolerite bases for columns.

11 Bidar Fort. Southeast palace zone, the Prince's Palace, c. 1460. Vaulted room with seven-sided apse.

into Courtyard D2. On the western side of Room F is an arched opening with views over the royal and the lower gardens.

Further routes of movement are evident in Palace II (plan 14). The king could enter his throne-room (C) from his private quarters (G, F, E) via Courtyard D2 along an east–west axis. The throne-room was thus framed to the west by the almond-shaped lotus pool in Courtyard D1, and on the east by a square pool with a 14-petalled lotus design in Courtyard D2. In the centre of D1 are four square bases that could have been added later to support a pavilion, or even perhaps a royal seat raised above a water body. The throne-room – with its soaring dome, visible from afar – shares dimensions and wall arrangements with the tomb of Humayun Shah Bahmani (r. 1458–61) at Ashtur (figure 9), suggesting similar dates for both.

From the steps of Antechamber G in Palace II it was possible to reach Palace III (figure 10). This building may have served as a zenana, since it comprises three habitable levels: cool underground apartments; a first floor consisting of a mandapa with four timber columns on carved dolerite bases, leading to an octagonal room with a pyramidal vault; and a roof terrace accessed by steps. The pyramidal vault may have echoed those in the pishtaq towers (K1 and K2) of Palace II. From Palace III, the women of the Bahmani court could enter the underground summer apartments, from which they could enjoy views over the verdant garden and valley with lakes below.

An arched facade and multi-storeyed arrangement is found in the pool house located below the western side of Palace II (figure 4). Here, a rectangular pool is overlooked by three rooms with shallow domes, while underground octagonal pools are embellished with turquoise tiles. The pool house was linked to a cross-in-square pavilion, with an octagonal central pool.

Prince's Palace and Rangini Mahal

These two palaces are located in the southeastern area of Bidar Fort. Here, a number of features relate to the royal complexes that have just been described. Ghulam Yazdani labelled the first of these two palaces as the Royal Kitchen, though acknowledging that it could have originally been the residence of a prince or some important court dignitary. We agree with Yazdani that this must have once been an important palace and would like to propose that the Prince's Palace could have been the residence of the heir to the Bahmani throne. At present, it is possible to distinguish two building periods at the Prince's Palace: an earlier phase dating to the second half of the 15th century, and a later phase belonging to the beginning of the 17th century when Bidar was occupied by the Adil Shahis.

The Prince's Palace has three main levels in its southern section and four different spatial arrangements, probably denoting separate functions, though it is not clear what these may have been (plan 15 and figure 3). The first of these arrangements, according to Klaus Rötzer, includes the building that faces the public space linking the palace to the Gumbad Darwaza and in which the arched rectangular gate that opens to the central courtyard is located. South of the courtyard lies the second group, containing the ceremonial apartments with their tripartite facade. Framing this facade, and imitating those of Palace II, are forward-projecting towers that belong to the third group of rooms. A set of private spaces enveloping the tripartite structure below and above comprises the fourth group.

The oldest section of the Prince's Palace lies on the southern side of its courtyard. Here, at the end of the central aisle of the mandapa, an arch adorned with green dolerite opens into a vaulted room with a deep and broad, seven-sided apse (figure 11). This room is on a slightly higher level than the mandapa, and could be closed off by a large door. The eastern tower is rectangular while the western tower is square and both are

12 Bidar Fort. Southeast palace zone, the Rangini Mahal, 1543–80. Note the tiled mihrab-like entrance.

aligned with the Solah Khamba Mosque. At the ground level of the eastern tower, a seven-sided room is linked along an east–west axis with the central seven-sided arched niche of the mosque. The presence of seven-sided, arched spaces in both the Prince's Palace and the Solah Khamba Mosque suggests similar dates for all these structures. It supports the interpretation proposed here that the mosque may originally have been a ceremonial pavilion associated with this group of palaces.

The Rangini Mahal erected by the Baridi sultan Ali Baridi is much smaller than the Prince's Palace (plan 16). However, it compensates for its diminutive scale by the richness of its interior adornments (figure 12). The rooms on both sides of the mandapa have beautifully carved pyramidal timber ceilings, and probably timber balconies that no longer survive. The virtuosity of the carving of the timber columns and ceiling of this mandapa is the only extant example of decorative themes and techniques that must have been used in all the Bahmani palaces, but which largely no longer survive. Separating the mandapa from the stellate Room C, with its five-sided apse, in which the throne-room of Ali Baridi may have been located, is a square space, D. As in the Prince's Palace, this sequence of ceremonial spaces occupied a higher level than the mandapa and could be closed off by a door.

With its ornate timber columns and ceiling, polychrome-underglaze tiles, and basalt revetments inlaid with mother-of-pearl, the hypostyle hall of the Rangini Mahal is the most complete example of Deccani palace architecture. The decoration framing the doorway that connects Room X with the stellate chamber is unsurpassed in its refinement. It comprises a black basalt revetment inlaid with Persian poetic verses and elegant spiralling scrolls that repeat those on the timber ceiling.

Gumbad Darwaza and Solah Khamba Mosque

The Gumbad Darwaza is the only known Bahmani gateway whose plan comprises an octagon within a square, roofed by a dome (plan 17 and p. 32, figure 8). It is framed on its eastern

13 Bidar Fort. Southeast palace zone, Solah Khamba Mosque, identified here as a ceremonial pavilion (c. 1460), and Hazar Sutun, c. 1470 or later. The dolerite revetment of the almond-shaped pool has been taken from the pool of courtyard D1 in Palace II (plan 14) when this area was turned into a garden sometime in the 17th century.

14 Bidar Fort. Solah Khamba Mosque, domed ceremonial pavilion, c. 1460. The central niche follows a seven-sided form that was repeated on the eastern tower in the courtyard of the Prince's Palace, with which it is aligned along an east–west axis, plan 15.

face by monumental round bastions, which are later additions. The double doors, guarding access to the palace from the city, are found only on this eastern facade. The interior of the dome is painted with motifs similar to those found in the tomb of Ahmad Shah in Ashtur, indicating that the same painters worked in both structures, which were probably coeval (c. 1430). The octagonal space below the dome has tall, pointed, arched recesses on shallow platforms. Each of the arches on the northern and southern sides contains a small, arched window with shutters (E and D in plan 17), possibly originally in openwork jali form. These belonged to a small, square room with pyramidal vaults that could be reached by steps.

A third and similarly shaped window is located on the roof of the Gumbad Darwaza. It is ensconced below the point of the lofty arch of the raised pishtaq portal that adorns its eastern facade, and which faces the Sharza Darwaza, beyond which is the city of Bidar. Between this window and the drum of the dome is a narrow space that could accommodate a cushion or a seat. The presence of this unique opening, together with its east–west alignment under the soaring arch of the facade and the proximity of this gate to the city, suggest that this window may have functioned as a place of darshan, or ritual viewing.

Identified as a mosque, the Solah Khamba within Bidar Fort is usually dated to either 1324 or 1424 on the basis of an inscription found in its debris (figure 13). This early inscription, however, is not contiguous with the building itself. Nor do these dates match with the round columns of its hypostyle hall or with the bracket designs on the sides of its three arched niches – features found only from the second half of the 15th century and later (figure 14). As mentioned earlier, its central domed chamber appears to be aligned with the towers in the Prince's Palace (plan 15). On the western wall of this chamber are three niches; the central and biggest one follows a seven-sided form. Carved into the northeastern and southeastern corners of the chamber are steps to arched openings that were repeated on the other side of the arch. These suggest the presence of balconies with jalis that could have enabled viewers to witness in privacy the ceremonies that took place beneath the dome.

It is here proposed that this original domed chamber of the Solah Khamba Mosque was extended at a later date, possibly in the second half of the 15th century if not later (plan 18). At this time, the hypostyle halls with their massive interior round columns were added, somewhat carelessly positioned in front of the eastern arched opening. The addition of these columns transformed the ceremonial pavilion into a Hazar Sutun, indicating perhaps the changing function of this building that could be related to the new political realities brought about with the death of Humayun Shah in 1461. As early as the reign of Alauddin Ahmad Shah (1436–58), we learn that two seats were positioned on either side of the sultan to accommodate the descendants of two important religious factions. Later, under the infant Nizamuddin Ahmad III Shah (r. 1461–63) and the regency of the queen mother, a political triumvirate is mentioned, while a second such political group governed the kingdom during the reign of Muhammad Shah (r. 1482–1518). It is possible that the three arched niches are a reference to the new political conditions, and that the Hazar Sutun became the audience hall of the Bahmani sultans during the second half of the 15th century.

It is also possible that the ceremonial pavilion, relating to the Prince's Palace and reflecting the political realities of the second half of the 15th century, was turned into a mosque by the Adil Shahis when Bidar became once again a military outpost in the frontier land bordering the kingdom of the Qutb Shahis.

AHMADNAGAR UNDER THE NIZAM SHAHIS (1496–1636)

Pushkar Sohoni

The architecture and the arts of the Nizam Shahi kingdom are the least known and studied among those of the major Deccani sultanates. The rather poor condition of the architectural remains together with the scarce historical evidence are the reasons for this neglect. The kingdom of Ahmadnagar was contained largely within northern and central Maharashtra. It was founded by Ahmad Nizam Shah Bahri in 1490. Ahmad Nizam Shah was at the time the decorated governor of Junnar, controlling key territories and a number of forts like Shivner, Jivdhan, Lohagarh, Kondhana, Jond, Tung, Tikona, Purandhar, Pali, and Danda Rajapuri, which were all vested in his name as a jagir after he had captured them earlier in the name of the Bahmani sultan. He used to mount an expedition from his capital at Junnar every year to try and capture the strategic and affluent fort city of Daulatabad, for which purpose he founded the city of Ahmadnagar between Junnar and Daulatabad. Ahmad Nizam Shah and his descendants tried to assume a distinctly Persian lineage and culture, appropriating symbols and emblems of kingship that were acceptable to the nobility.

Ahmadnagar was the first of the Deccani sultanates to succumb to the Mughal juggernaut in 1636. This would have happened even earlier were it not for the diplomatic and strategic stewardship of Malik Ambar. Following this invasion, the Nizam Shahi territories were carved up between the Mughal empire and the Bijapur kingdom. The northern areas of the kingdom, including Daulatabad and Khidki (Aurangabad) were eventually taken over by the Mughals, whereas the regions to the south and west were annexed by the Adil Shahis of Bijapur and later by the Marathas.

The Nizam Shahis ruled a multi-lingual and multi-ethnic kingdom where different creeds coexisted and a multitude of beliefs were practised. Forging a visual identity was therefore very important to their legitimacy as a unified kingdom. Architecture was a significant medium to express their multi-faceted cultural environment. It demonstrated their status within the Deccan and in relation to other kingdoms, whether local or beyond the confines of the subcontinent. The Nizam Shahis also exchanged embassies with other important kingdoms and formed associations with pre-existent

1 Daulatabad. Palace with tripartite facade, probably 1582. It is now a tomb.

historical and cultural entities, in order to legitimize their position.

The switch to the Ithna Ashari faith (Twelver Shiism) under Burhan Nizam Shah I (r. 1510–53) was due to two important factors, one religious the other political. It is under the spiritual guidance of Shah Tahir Husseini, an eminent scholar, that the sultan adopted this form of Islam. Moreover the acceptance of the Ithna Ashari faith in the 1530s was an astute political move, aimed at neutralizing the power and influence of the other post-Bahmani sultanates. A part of the objective was a strategic alliance with the rising Safavids of Iran and the possibility of attracting to the Nizam Shahi kingdom Iranian emigres of learning and military training thus ensuring faith-based dynastic loyalty and military power. This faith gave the Nizam Shahis a very concrete objective in the architectural and visual imagery they adopted to express their dynasty. The other main source was the existing court culture of the 16th-century Deccan, in large part derived from the Bahmani court.

The nodes of visual culture were the cities and palaces. Strangely, these two entities almost never coincided. All the surviving palaces are in suburban locations or in outlying forts (plan 19). Despite the direct administrative control of the king over the cities, the lack of an urbanism controlled by royalty was probably the biggest failure of the Nizam Shahis. This might have been partly a result of their lack of residence in any urban area. Urban planning and design were largely left to court nobility, many of whom were eager opportunists, ready to switch allegiances and loyalties. The lack of large congregational mosques in Ahmadnagar further illustrates the non-participation of the monarch in the activities of the city, such as weekly presence in a mosque for the Friday prayers.

Thus, architectural expressions of legitimacy and royalty were mainly confined to suburban areas and in some key forts, where the kings built their palaces and gardens. The city of Ahmadnagar does not have any royal palaces, and the fort where the royal presence seems to have resided has not yet been properly examined. The fort of Ahmadnagar is almost a kilometre to the east of the city, and the two entities are not contiguous. It is true that the sultan's absence from the city of Ahmadnagar made the kingdom susceptible to the factional forces at the court in the capital, and no architectural symbols of kingship could have welded the various factions of the elite together. The same was the case in the outlying areas of the kingdom where political and financial power was in the hands of the local hereditary chiefs and where the royal court did not have a significant presence. By establishing architectural symbols of power in the countryside the Nizam Shahis tried to impose the royal presence in these areas, even though all functions at the local level were managed and discharged by the local fief-holders.

2 Daulatabad. Dome above central raised platform of palace, probably 1582. The designs on the dome are formed in stones covered with plaster. The lobed arches of the squinches supporting the dome revive Bahmani examples.

Two types of secular courtly structures survive and these are palaces and hammams. These are all built in stone and timber, a combination of materials that characterizes Nizam Shahi courtly architecture as it did that of their predecessors, the later Bahmanis. Lime mortar and plaster are used to construct and finish the buildings. The decoration is in cut and moulded stucco. In the Daulatabad palace the designs relate to Bahmani examples (figures 1, 2). They were formed out of stones that were subsequently covered in stucco and carved, thus recalling the decorative themes and techniques noted in Firuzabad and the Shah Darwaza in Sagar. Carved stone elements are very rarely used in courtly architecture, but can be found occasionally in mosques and tombs.

The influx of immigrants from West Asia was responsible for introducing into the northern Deccan styles and systems of construction and engineering that had evolved elsewhere. These included water management systems, paper-based transmission of architectural designs, and a whole host of building methods and processes that were unknown in this region before this period. This was possible because the port of Chaul, which the Nizam Shahis controlled, was a gateway to the trade routes of the Arabian Sea. Despite the imported technologies, the importance of pre-existent local building techniques and crafts ensured that the resultant architecture was not just imitative; it was distinguished by the fusion of various traditions.

The systems of water management developed by the Nizam Shahis were the most advanced in the region. They used storage and distribution mechanisms of various kinds – dams, canals, underground pipes, tanks, reservoirs, towers, and many kinds of drawing mechanisms. Equally impressive was their use of water in the context of ceremonial displays. Almost all the buildings associated with the Nizam Shahis integrate the role of water into their use. Palaces often have pools, fountains, and hammams. Mosques have ablution tanks and the mansions of city dwellers have elaborate hydraulic systems to ensure the supply of good water, often from as far as 10 kilometres away. Aside from the availability of water for the city's daily needs it was also effectively used for ceremonial displays in the different palaces of the Nizam Shahis. The number of extant hammams is surprising. There are no less than three free-standing ones, and three more attached to palace buildings. Since hammams were exposed to steam and water for long periods of time, the curing of the lime mortars and plasters on their walls was done well. This might explain the disproportionate number of surviving baths as compared to mansions and palaces. The most impressive of the hammams built in the Nizam Shahi period is one at Daulatabad, which is datable to 1582 by an inscription (plan 24). It would be relevant to mention here that next to this bath is a magnificent palace, with a tripartite facade and an enclosed garden in front (figure 1). The central pavilion has a dome, flanked by two triangular vaults that cover the other two compartments (figure 2). The central chamber has a low platform in the centre. Nothing is known about this building, but its location and its construction strongly suggest its pedigree as Nizam Shahi. It has recently been converted into a shrine, but the overall appearance (particularly the arrangement of the dome and triangular vaults in the composition) leaves no doubt that

3 Ahmadnagar. Farah Bakhsh Bagh, 1583. The palace, on a raised platform, sits in the middle of a pool.

4 Ahmadnagar. Farah Bakhsh Bagh, 1583. Central domed hall.

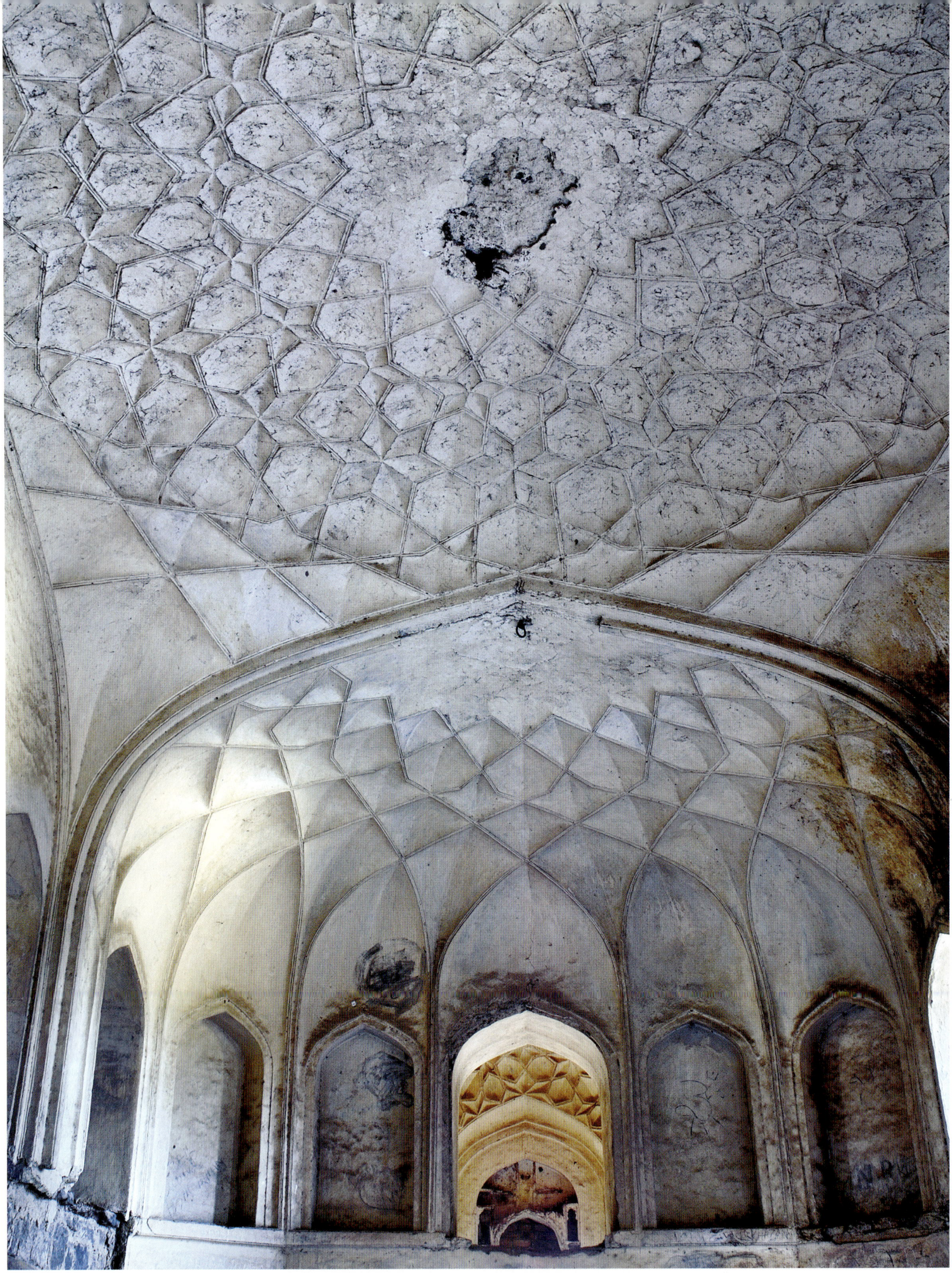

5 Ahmadnagar. Farah Bakhsh Bagh, 1583. Half-domes and domes with radiating geometric designs in plaster.

6 Ahmadnagar. Hasht Behesht Bagh, c. 1525. The octagonal pavilion sits in the middle of a pool.

this would have been a very important building for the Nizam Shahis, for the king himself if not for a very important noble at his court.

Mansions for the Elite and Palaces for the Sultan

Mansions built for the elite are found in the cities while palaces for the sultans were either in the suburbs or in forts. The mansions that survive within the city of Ahmadnagar can be assigned to important court officials. The mansions of Changiz Khan, who was in the early 1570s the Peshwa of Murtaza Nizam Shah I (r. 1565–88), and the owner of Malik Ambar (the famous Habshi slave who later served the Sultan of Bijapur and returned to Ahmadnagar at the time of the Mughal invasion in 1600, to defend his erstwhile rulers with an army of 7,000 men), Qasim Khan, and Neimat Khan Semnani, built sometime during 1570–80, have been transformed into offices and residences for present-day local administrators, but have retained some of their original features.

These mansion complexes were endowed with water courses within them. Even mosques, hammams, and shops are mentioned as part of these estates, typically on the periphery. It is possible to conjecture the layout of a typical nobleman's estate, which formed the basis of a municipal ward in the 20th century. The public institutions that were part of the complex would have been on the outer edges, and through a series of gardens and pavilions, the core would be accessed. This core would have contained the mansion of the court official. Unfortunately, the modern city retains very little of this planning and disparate elements survive bereft of their original context.

Ahmadnagar Fort together with its palaces served as the primary royal residence, and was supplemented by the various garden palaces and pavilions at a distance from the city. In times of distress, the fortified palace complexes at Daulatabad and Junnar served as retreats. Many of the Nizam Shahis' suburban palaces, such as Farah Bakhsh Bagh, Hasht Behesht Bagh, Manzarsumbah, and Kalawantinicha Mahal were designed as pleasure retreats. In a sense, the suburban palaces framed the city limits for the Nizam Shahis. In all these sites, the use and control of water was used to emphasize the importance of the ruler and to impress embassies and important visitors.

Suburban Palaces

Historically, palaces were loci of legitimacy and power, and conquerors and later regimes would almost never reside in the palaces of their predecessors unless the architecture was significantly modified. Here we will consider four palace sites in detail, all of which remained royal resorts as long as they were inhabited. All these were commissioned by the Nizam Shahis, and are located within a radius of 15 to 20 kilometres around the city of Ahmadnagar. They were all built within the 16th century, but only the Farah Bakhsh Bagh can be dated by inscription and supporting textual evidence.

All the buildings show signs of rich decoration in lime-based stucco plasters, which were incised and cut. Unfortunately, only a few fragments of this art now survive. Some other palace

7 Ahmadnagar. Lakkad Mahal, c. 1525–65. View of gate with adjoining hammam.

8 Ahmadnagar. Hasht Behesht Bagh, badgir or wind tower, c. 1525–75. The only free-standing example from the Deccan.

buildings also survive within the fort of Ahmadnagar, but unfortunately they are not completely accessible to scholars. All these sites have extensive remains of water supply systems, not merely for utility, but also for display.

Farah Bakhsh Bagh is less than a kilometre away from Ahmadnagar Fort, and consists of a large garden with an octagonal pool and a pavilion at its centre (plan 20). Neimat Khan Semnani was originally commissioned by Murtaza Nizam Shah I (r. 1565–88) to build the palace. But it was built in its current form due to the efforts of Salabat Khan II, around 1583. An inscription now placed elsewhere (on a wall of the District Court) provides a chronogram for this building. The garden has long since disappeared, but the architectural component survives. The inauguration of the garden was the occasion for a poetry recital by Mukka Malik Qummi (d. 1616), a renowned poet who composed a long panegyric. This poem describes the palace of Farah Bakhsh Bagh in the poetic tropes of the period, but also mentions the specific vegetation of the garden. Qummi describes the cypress, the perennials of the Islamic garden as "standing erect, attentive like the obedient servants to the command of the sultan". The spotless rose is alluded as resembling the "clean heart". "The huge height of the pavilion resembles the sky, the largest ever tent! And the flying sheets of water from your canals are touching the galaxy! The bulbous hyacinths of your garden are like bouquets of joy and celebration just as the sharp thorns of your garden are like the arrows to the eyes of your enemies."

The building itself is octagonal and cross-axially symmetrical with monumental pishtaq portals reminiscent of Persian and Persianate examples. The building techniques are local, but the design is certainly of Timurid inspiration. Yet no palatial structure on a similar scale survives in Iran or Central Asia.

In plan, scale, and monumentality, the Farah Bakhsh Bagh is comparable to the Taj Mahal in Agra, preceding the latter by around 50 years. The building is set on a raised platform, which was surrounded by a large pool of water (figure 3). A series of fountains and connecting pipes carry water inside the building. The water is brought to the site from a few kilometres away through the Bhingar and the Bhandara aqueducts. The centrepiece of the building is a large domed hall with a central fountain (figure 4).

9 Ahmadnagar. Manzarsumbah, 1525–65. Gate and palace.

10 Ahmadnagar. Manzarsumbah, the palace, 1525–65.

AHMADNAGAR 63

The wall construction comprises a rubble core with ashlar masonry on the outer face. Large sections of timber are found in the wall at regular intervals, tying the building together (plan 23). All the openings are framed by large sections of timber, including the lintels. Vestigial traces of shutters are found on these frames in the form of post-holes for hinges. The decorative elements on the ceilings and vaults are beautifully finished in incised and moulded stucco (figure 5).

At a distance of a few kilometres to the north of Ahmadnagar Fort is a second garden palace, the Faiz Bakhsh Bagh or Hasht Behesht Bagh (plan 21). This garden and palace complex was reportedly enlarged, but possibly completely built, under the patronage of Burhan Nizam Shah I (r. 1510–53) on the site of an earlier garden palace called Faiz Bakhsh Bagh. It comprises an octagonal pavilion set in the midst of a similarly shaped pool (figure 6). There are remnants of fountains in front of every arched opening of this pavilion. The octagonal pool is supplied water by means of underground pipes from the Pimpalgaon and Shendi aqueducts. According to some accounts, the eight sides of the pool were planted with different flowers. To reach the pavilion one would either have to wade or cross by boat. The only comparable building from this period in the Deccan is a palace at Achalpur called Hauz Katora, most likely built under the Imad Shahis, if not the Nizam Shahis themselves. On one bank of the Hasht Behesht Bagh pool stands a large building locally known as Lakkad Mahal (wooden palace). There is an additional set of rooms added to the Lakkad Mahal on the eastern side, which includes a hammam (figure 7). According to historical accounts, Hasht Behesht Bagh is where Murtaza Nizam Shah I retired for 12 years, and these chambers would have been constructed as his private quarters in that period. Within the grounds of this palace is the only known example of a badgir, or windcatcher, in the Deccan (figure 8). It is attached to a subterranean bath house called the Shahi Hammamkhane. Unfortunately, this building is now being used as a garbage dump and is inaccessible. It is therefore difficult to conjecture or trace the relationship of this building to the palace.

11 Ahmadnagar. Kalawantinicha Mahal with tripartite facade, 1525–65.

Ten kilometres to the north of Ahmadnagar city, overlooking the pass that controls the old route to Daulatabad, is a hill with commanding views of the surrounding areas, and it is here that the palace now known as Manzarsumbah was built (plan 22 and figure 9). Manzarsumbah is probably a corruption of the word Manzar-i Subah (vantage overlooking the region). On this fortified hilltop is a set of buildings, some of which were probably part of a leisure palace (figure 10). An ingenious system of hydraulic works conveys water from tanks excavated in the cliffs halfway up the hillside. This water is then used to fill up a very large tank beside the palace. A system of fountains and water channels is also seen around the hilltop area. The plan shows the spatial relationships between the various components of the palace complex, including a hammam. From the palace building, one can overlook the plains towards Daulatabad, over a series of water channels, fountain jets, and pools, almost as an act of visually claiming the landscape. The palace building contains an enigmatic fireplace, complete with a smoke flue. Very little is known about this site, but the scanty historical mentions in the *Burhan i Maasir* and Aurangzeb's *Maasir i Alamgiri* indicate royal usage. The construction of this building bears a striking resemblance to two other mansions, the Lakkad Mahal and Kalawantinicha Mahal.

This latter royal suburban site of interest is located about 20 kilometres to the southeast of Ahmadnagar, on the road to Beed. Nothing is recorded about this building site, nor is it mentioned in any historical text. Its name – Kalawantinicha Mahal, or Courtesans' Palace, in Marathi – is commonly applied to many such structures with unknown patronage or ownership (figure 11). This architectural complex served as a palace, and also as a place of martial entertainments, such as

64 PUSHKAR SOHONI

12 Ahmadnagar. Kalawantinicha Mahal, 1525–65. A leaf motif adorns a pendentive in the north pavilion.

fights and military displays and reviews. Though in a ruinous state, it is possible to reconstruct it from the remains. It comprised a large field, bounded by a wall, with pavilions on all four sides. The pavilion to the north is set outside the enclosure wall, and is lavishly decorated (figure 12), suggesting that the king or other important personages used this building. The rooftops of these pavilions command views of the enclosed field, and it is easy to visualize elephant fights or troop displays set in this ground. The fields surrounding the buildings have a number of water tanks, and scattered around are large stones with holes in them. These were used to tether horses, elephants, and other animals. There are some remnants of even larger enclosure walls around the area, but those have not been completely traced.

Conclusion

The palaces of the Nizam Shahis that we have just discussed are remarkable for their variety in scale and design. Stylistically, they share a number of traits but have significant differences in their use. Farah Bakhsh Bagh provided an imposing setting for the entertainment of diplomatic guests, as is suggested by the monumental scale of the building set in a huge pool of water. The poetic contests that took place in Farah Bakhsh and the poetry that was written in its praise stress the importance of this building in the cultural and social environment of the Nizam Shahis. Hasht Behesht Bagh was a palace complex built to suit a more personal, intimate scale. It was used primarily as a residence. Manzarsumbah occupied a strategic vantage point, from where one could observe the important route to Daulatabad. It was a fortified military outpost, with a large palace complex. The palace is set up in such a way that the king would enjoy the views of the plains towards Daulatabad, thus symbolically commanding and appropriating the whole area under his domain. Kalawantinicha Mahal was an arena for military reviews, and perhaps some sporting activity such as elephant fights. The four large pavilions around it were meant for the king and his court to view the events inside the courtyard.

The only feature that binds all these palaces as a group, apart from dynastic pedigree, is the construction technology, which used timber in extensive quantities, though not always for structural reasons. The method of timber construction is reminiscent of that in seismic zones, and its large-scale adoption in this region from the 16th century onwards suggests either that the imitation of an imported construction technology required a significant use of wood, or that expediency of construction was required by a regime keen to raise grand architecture in a short period of time. This was a requirement of the later Marathas as well, ensuring the survival of this technique of quick construction of buildings with wooden frames.

Two of the palaces show unique features in the construction of their roofs. At Manzarsumbah and in the Lakkad Mahal, T-shaped tiles are slotted on the struts between large timber beams. Large bricks are then placed on top of this assembly, and then overlaid with layers of lime mortar and bricks. The top is then finished with a lime plaster to create a flat roof.

This suggests a local idiom of architecture, conveyed either by practice (by trade guilds and generations of workmen) or by the use of paper. The former is more likely, given the absence of any documentary internalization of architecture in this region at the time. It is difficult to state that the Nizam Shahis were executing a well-articulated proposal of regional harmony, thus promoting a conscious melding of regional construction with their imported ideals of kingship and royalty. Many of the building practices were based on accident and convenience, but their success often encouraged the rulers to adopt them as formulas for the good functioning and legitimization of their regime.

All the palaces and other buildings associated with the court are now bare, having lost all their furnishings and the surrounding gardens. It can be quite difficult to imagine what the palaces would have looked like, furnished with rugs, tapestries, and other fabrics that had utilitarian and aesthetic functions. The trees and plants that were consciously planted around the palaces for similar purposes have disappeared as well, and where they have been replaced these are not (in most cases) historically congruous.

BIJAPUR UNDER THE ADIL SHAHIS (1490–1686)

Mark Brand

1 Bijapur, Farakh Mahal or Chini Mahal, 1514 and later. Two-storeyed transverse hall. The sultan's loggia is on the top left.

Of all the Deccan's Islamic courts, the capital of the Adil Shahi Sultanate at Bijapur and its environs provide perhaps the most comprehensive record of a dynasty's palatial architecture and its urban setting. The royal complex at Bijapur was enclosed by a moated citadel in the early 16th century, before its encirclement by the city's walls. This concentric urban plan was refined in the construction of Bijapur's short-lived twin city Nauraspur (c. 1599–1624). Here, an unfortified royal complex stood at the very core of the city's uncompleted walls. These royal centres were dominated by a series of strikingly similar monumental palace-cum-audience halls, which were erected throughout the sultanate's history and provided the principal stages for court ceremonial. Their tall, broad, and flat-roofed masonry structures contained two-storey blocks of apartments preceded by vast porticoes, which roughly doubled their depth. Fronted by arches or columns, the porticoes framed a raised central loggia in the apartments behind – a composition reflected in the waters of the great hauz, or pool, situated before each hall (figure 6 and p. 21, figure 8). Settings for more intimate court gatherings and recreation were provided by slender masonry pavilions constructed from the late 16th century at Bijapur, and at Kumatgi, 16 kilometres east of the capital (p. 108, figure 3). These pavilions had cool and tranquil atmospheres, accentuated by their location beside gardens and artificial water bodies. Taken together, these structures offer an unusually clear picture of the architectural evolution of a later Deccan sultanate court.

Farakh Mahal (Chini Mahal)

Bijapur's earliest Adil Shahi palace is the Farakh Mahal, or Broad Palace, better known today as the Chini Mahal after some Chinese ceramics that were found nearby. This north-facing audience hall was located in the southwestern corner of the newly constructed citadel's ramparts. It was erected in 1514 by the second Adil Shahi ruler, Ismail (r. 1510–34), and extended by Ibrahim I (r. 1535–58), who completed the surrounding citadel defences in the late 1530s. The large courtyard before the palace, enclosed on all sides with arcades and apartments of two or more storeys, was built primarily during the reigns of

Ibrahim and his successor Ali I (r. 1558–80).

The Farakh Mahal has a broad central two-storey chamber, with a closed tripartite facade and interior rear wall articulated by three ogee arches (figure 1). A first-floor walkway runs through the depth of these arches, across the rear of the hall. The central ogee arch opens an alcove and upper loggia on either storey of a polygonal structure protruding from the back of the palace. This structure appears to have been the principal seat of the Adil Shahi throne. This central throne-chamber is set back between blocks of royal apartments, creating a recessed bay which is raised by a stone platform. Large octagonal columns – the imprints of which remain at the front of this platform – created a loggia with a tripartite opening. Although destroyed and unrecorded, the portico before this loggia seems likely to have had a triple-arched facade and preceding hauz similar to those at later north-facing Adil Shahi palaces.

The Farakh Mahal appears to have replaced a Tughluq and Bahmani audience hall on the same site. The profile of the throne-chamber's rear central arch closely resembles those of two early-14th-century Tughluq audience

2 Bijapur. Gagan Mahal, 1558–80. In front of the monumental tripartite facade, there was a pool.

67

3 Bijapur. Gagan Mahal, 1558–80.

axis of this mosque by the location within its courtyard of a tomb traditionally associated with the son of Bijapur's earliest Sufi saint, Pir Mabari Khandayat. Khandayat's dargah in the citadel's southeastern corner was one of several prominent Sufi shrines patronized by the Adil Shahis. Patronage of popular Sufi shrines was central to the maintenance of sultanate authority in the Deccan. The Farakh Mahal would have been specifically associated with Adil Shahi patronage of the dargah linked with Karimuddin's Mosque.

Gagan Mahal and Nauras Mahal

A pair of nearly identical north-facing Adil Shahi audience halls stand within the royal complexes of Bijapur and Nauraspur. The Gagan Mahal lies at the northwestern corner of Bijapur's citadel, while the Nauras Mahal sits at the centre of Nauraspur's royal enclosure (plan 27). The vast Gagan Mahal, or Heavenly Palace, was built after 1560 as the centrepiece of Ali I's redevelopment of Bijapur as a great royal capital between 1565 and 1568. This programme included the construction of Bijapur's walls, a major underground water-supply system, and the new Jami Masjid. The palace acted as the principal hall of royal audience at the centre of the newly expanded city. The Nauras Mahal was constructed after 1599 by Ali's successor Ibrahim Adil Shah II (r. 1580–1627). It was the centrepiece of Bijapur's new twin city Nauraspur, the focus for Ibrahim's cult of Nauras, which presented a synthesis of Hindu and Islamic mystical traditions. The repetition of Bijapur's principal audience hall at Nauraspur re-established royal authority within a distinctive local Indo-Islamic royal cult.

halls: the Khush Mahal at Warangal and another subsumed within the Bala Hisar at Gulbarga. The Farakh Mahal's rear central arch lies on the qibla axis of the adjacent mosque – Bijapur's earliest congregational place of prayer, popularly known as Karimuddin's Mosque, after the governor who supervised its construction in 1320. Specific meaning was given to the Farakh Mahal's position on the qibla

The tripartite facades of these palaces are each dominated by a broad central arch which frames an equally broad raised platform, recessed in the apartments forming the palace's main body (figure 2).

This raised area supported a great loggia rising two-thirds the height of the building and opening into the portico through a pair of columns. Steps led from the portico up to this loggia, which was the central royal seat within the palace. Curtains suspended from iron rings in the portico's ceiling closed the loggia from view. The overall effect of this composition is captured in an early 17th-century miniature depicting Ibrahim II and a companion before exactly such a loggia (Zebrowski, fig. 89). This view emphasizes the intimate and elite nature of the court audiences that were held in these porticos, which brought visitors close to the ruler, while the great hauz before them distanced larger gatherings in front of the hall.

The broad central ogee arch which framed the great loggia in the facade of both Gagan and Nauras Mahals appears to have been a reinterpretation, on a monumental scale, of the distinctive ogee arch which framed the central throne chamber of the Farakh Mahal. This arch's prominence on the facades of the new palaces was accentuated by narrow flanking arches, a roofline canopy, and large medallion-on-bracket reliefs in its spandrels (figure 3) with wing-shaped motifs at its apex. This suggests that the monumental portals of these new palaces were designed to articulate sultanate authority in a way similar to their predecessor: by framing a royal seat whose position in court ritual expressed the ruler's role as a divine mediator.

This certainly seems to have been the case with the Nauras Mahal, which was the setting for the central celebrations of the Nauras cult, of which Ibrahim II was the chief celebrant. The cult involved the synthesis of the most popular Hindu and Muslim mystical devotional traditions in the sultanate – those of the Dattatreya saint Narasimha Saraswati and the Chishti Sufi saint Gesu Daraz – with that of the Prophet Muhammad. The palace lies at the centre of a walled courtyard with nine equal sides, each pierced by a broad ogee arch (plan 27). This composition provided a physical metaphor for the term Nauras, most commonly rendered as the Nine Rasas, or moods, of Indian poetical and musical expression.

Although the Gagan and Nauras Mahals provided audience halls similar to that at the centre of the Farakh Mahal, they lacked this palace's great wings of apartments. Screened upper apartments and roof terraces accessed by narrow stairs in the rear walls of the new palaces allowed members of the royal household

4 Bijapur. Gagan Mahal, 1558–80. Vault imitating timber structures in the private apartments located on the southeast side of the palace. (Compare this to p. 118, figure 3.)

5 Bijapur. Shah Nawaz Khan Mahal, late 16th century.

to remain hidden from, but close to, court audiences. However, the royal household and zenana seem to have remained housed within the Farakh Mahal and its two-storey arcades. This arrangement was duplicated at Nauraspur, where a small triple-arched palace for royal household use lay within a double-height walled courtyard adjoining the southern side of the Nauras Mahal's enclosure. The Farakh Mahal's basic composition was combined with a triple-arched facade in another palace, the Anand Mahal, constructed on a plinth at the heart of Bijapur's citadel for Ibrahim II after 1589. This palace seems to have supplemented rather than replaced the Farakh Mahal as the seat of the royal household.

The tripartite facade with central broad ogee arch seen at the Gagan and Nauras Mahals was repeated in all the principal north-facing royal halls of Ibrahim II's reign, which included audience halls in more public spaces: a now heavily damaged hall between the moats on the east of Bijapur's citadel, and another hall in the courtyard adjoining the northeastern side of the Nauras Mahal's enclosure. Elsewhere at Bijapur, the early 16th-century palace and tomb of Ibrahim's chief vizier Shah Nawaz Khan assumed this royal facade (figure 5), as did the mosque of his successor Mustafa Khan. The distinctive broad ogee arch itself was repeated in the form of a giant frame for a north-facing royal platform at the dargah of Gesu Daraz at Gulbarga. The arch was further repeated in the inner arcade of Ibrahim II's tomb. The broad ogee arch therefore appears to have become a widespread symbol of royal authority during Ibrahim's reign.

Asar Mahal

Located on the eastern edge of the outer moat around Bijapur's citadel, the

6 Bijapur. Asar Mahal, 1646. The northern entrance to the compound is through the Jahaz Mahal, or Ship Palace. The royal loggia is on the first floor.

Asar Mahal, or Palace of the Relic, was built in 1646 for Ibrahim II's successor, Muhammad Adil Shah (r. 1627–56). The palace was originally constructed as a Dad Mahal or hall of public audience outside the citadel. However, this breached the terms of the 1636 treaty which placed Bijapur under Mughal suzerainty. The palace, therefore, became the principal public venue for the veneration of a royal sacred relic, believed to consist of two hairs of the beard of the Prophet Muhammad.

The Asar Mahal followed the same basic design as earlier Adil Shahi audience halls. However, the palace faced east rather than north, and its facade was formed by octagonal wooden columns supporting five bracketed openings, rather than by three masonry arches (figure 6). The most significant development in the Asar Mahal's design was the raising of the central loggia to the first floor, leaving an alcove beneath it. The distance this created between the royal loggia and visitors in the portico below reflected the public nature of audience within the palace. This arrangement recalled that at the Daulat Mahal or Palace of Felicity, constructed early in Muhammad's reign at the northern end of Bijapur's citadel. Here, a raised loggia lay within a south-facing columned portico, suggesting a setting for similarly public audience.

Both the Asar Mahal and the great hauz with shallow flanking pools before it are raised on a masonry plinth above a large walled garden. The main entrances to the enclosure are to the north and south of the palace's portico. The northern entrance forms a central gateway through the broad two-storey structure popularly known as the Jahaz Mahal, or Ship Palace (figure 6, right). This layout suggests that the general mass of visitors progressed from north to south through the palace's portico via its side-doors, without moving into the garden before it, except to access the shallow pools flanking the main hauz. This pattern of movement is suggested by the palace's depiction on a schematic plan of Bijapur and its principal buildings dating from shortly after the Mughal conquest and presently in the Archaeological Museum at Bijapur. Here, the modest doors securing the sides of the Asar Mahal's portico are reproduced in detail and out of proportion to the palace's facade.

A stone viaduct connected the rear wall of the Asar Mahal with a citadel bastion popularly known as the Shah Burj. The viaduct carried walkways from the bastion's arcades and rooftop pavilions, across both moats, onto each storey of the palace as well as its roof terrace. A further viaduct joined the Asar Mahal and the Jahaz Mahal at first-floor level. These walkways allowed the sultan direct access to the upper storeys of the Asar and Jahaz Mahals from the citadel, thus giving the Asar Mahal the character of a royal portal for the citadel as a whole on major festal occasions. The Shah Burj's fulfilment of this role, prior to the construction of the Asar Mahal, was conveyed by

7 Bijapur. Asar Mahal, 1646. The wall is painted with flowering scrolls and the niches with vases.

8 Bijapur. Asar Mahal, 1646. Wall painting of a glass vase with flowers.

BIJAPUR 71

9 Bijapur. Asar Mahal, 1646. A badly damaged wall painting depicting a bejewelled female attendant.

Johan Van Twist, the Dutch East India Company's envoy to Bijapur in 1637; "Thousands of people, both on foot and horseback, gathered to greet His Majesty and to congratulate him .... The Sultan sat, accompanied by some of the most prominent nobles, within the castle by the moat, on a roundel that was lavishly hung with gold drapes and carpets."

In an arrangement similar to that mentioned by Twist, select members of Bijapur's elite appear to have had access to the Asar Mahal's upper storey apartments. The loggia and the four small rooms which flank it appear to have been reserved for the use of the sultan and his household. This is suggested by the rich decoration of the interior, including geometric and floral motifs in gilt and bright colours and, in one room, female groups set in European-style landscapes (figures 7–9). The doors of these rooms were painted or inlaid with ivory and mother-of-pearl. A great hall stretching the full width of the palace behind these rooms is accessed by an antechamber and broad staircase leading up from the portico's southern end. A 17th-century ink drawing published by George Michell and Mark Zebrowski in *Architecture and Art of the Deccan Sultanates* (fig. 133) depicts the veneration of the Prophet's hairs in what appears to be this great hall. The sultan holds a glass tube containing the relics of the Prophet, while surrounded by leading courtiers, religious scholars, and Sufis. Through such ritual the Asar Mahal appears to have acted as a shrine, a function that was reinforced after the Mughal conquest by the relic's permanent placement within the palace. This sacred character would explain the provision of access to the hauz and pools beside it, as water bodies at dargahs and other shrines were generally understood to impart their baraka or blessing to bathers and drinkers.

Beyond settings for public audience, the columned porticos of the Daulat and Asar Mahals did not supersede the triple-arched facades of earlier Adil Shahi audience halls. A modest triple-arched audience hall was constructed at Ainapur after 1651 (plan 28 and figures 14, 15), for the use of Muhammad's wife Jahan Begum, whose unfinished tomb lies nearby. This mimics earlier halls, with its well-preserved loggia giving an impression of how those at the Gagan and Nauras Mahal appeared. The facade's central arch is slightly narrower and those flanking it broader than at earlier Adil Shahi palaces. This distinctive pattern appears to have replaced that

10 Bijapur. Pani Mahal, last quarter of the 17th century.

of the Gagan Mahal's facade as the Adil Shahi architectural regalia – it is found, for example, on the faces of the Gol Gumbad, Muhammad's vast tomb at Bijapur. The same pattern facing the alcove below the Asar Mahal's loggia is apparently a reference to the principal royal halls within the citadel.

Husseini Mahal and Pani Mahal

From the outset of his reign, Ali Adil Shah II (r. 1656–72) ordered the construction of several structures proclaiming the new primacy of Shia devotion at court, in the northeastern corner of Bijapur's citadel. This devotion centred on the Imam Hussein and the Husseini Alam – a Shia standard brought to Bijapur during Ali's reign which, it was claimed, was forged from the armour of Hussein itself.

The centrepiece of this building programme was the Husseini Mahal, constructed in 1656–57, which housed the Husseini Alam. This appears to have been the largely destroyed structure facing east across the hauz before the Daulat Mahal. This structure raised a broad central loggia on a stage with a colonnaded facade between wings of individual large masonry rooms. Central steps at the rear of the loggia lead down to a windowless semi-subterranean room that seems likely to have been the reliquary for the Alam itself.

Another east-facing palace constructed in the same campaign lies a small distance to the east of this reliquary hall, aligned on its central axis. This structure was probably the Ali Mahal, constructed in 1658–59. However, the facade and interior have been damaged

11 Bijapur. Haft Mahal, 1590. Vault imitating timber structures in plaster.

and altered beyond recognition. Its alignment with the reliquary hall and its major central rear entrance suggest that it provided a seat of royal audience directly associated with the Husseini Alam.

This explicit association with the Imamate cult was continued in a pavilion constructed on a small bastion in the citadel wall, just northeast of this audience hall, in 1670–71. Popularly known as the Pani Mahal, or Water Palace, this east-facing pavilion looks out over the citadel's moat, clearly visible from the ground beyond. The pavilion's surviving stone walls form a niche covered with relief inscriptions in devotion to the 12 Shia Imams and related pictorial motifs (figure 10). A central archway opens into the niche from its rear, framing a small fountain or pool. The Pani Mahal's position and structure suggest that it was built as the public face of the Shia cult centred within the citadel.

Haft Mahal and Jalamandir

Rising from the northwestern corner of the Farakh Mahal's courtyard, the Haft Mahal or Seven Storey Palace, was built for Ibrahim II in 1590 as an extension of the royal household (figures 11, 12). A series of intimate apartments with pools and fountains reduce in area as the building rises, providing terraces on each floor. Wall paintings in the apartments depicting male and female companions amongst other themes were recorded in the 19th century, but are now lost.

Seven-storey palaces articulated levels of the heavenly realm in Indian tradition, suggesting royal divine blessing. Despite remaining clearly visible from the city over the walls of the citadel, the Haft Mahal's screened windows and terraces provided for intimate royal relaxation. The palace appears to have signalled the royal household's splendour at the same time as secluding it.

Just to the Haft Mahal's north lies an early 17th-century pavilion traditionally known as the Jalamandir. This very small domed structure stands in the centre of a small but deep hauz surrounded by a low stone wall, offering no ordinary means of access (figure 13). While the Jalamandir is one of few examples of the finely-carved stone construction which epitomized major royal religious structures during Ibrahim II's reign, its heavily shuttered and poorly ventilated single chamber is barely large enough for human entry. In all likelihood the pavilion was originally intended as a reliquary for the two hairs of the Prophet's beard acquired by Ibrahim II.

The Jalamandir lies at the western end of the area bounded by the enclosures of the Farakh and Gagan Mahals and the citadel's western wall. This area was closed on its eastern side by a wall which has since been destroyed, but whose position is indicated by the survival of the great gate guarding entry to the royal household erected for Ali I in about 1560. An Adil Shahi pavilion containing a water tank suitable for a small group of bathers at this area's eastern end suggests that it housed gardens within the inner royal

12 Bijapur. Haft Mahal, 1590. Vaults.

13 Bijapur. Jalamandir, early 17th century.

household. The Jalamandir's location adjacent to both a water pavilion and the Haft Mahal at the heart of the royal household suggests that the relic was viewed as blessing its surroundings.

Water Pavilions at Kumatgi

Several early 17th-century pavilions survive in a former royal garden lying along the northern face of an Adil Shahi dam and immediately west of a contemporary bazaar at Kumatgi, on the main historical route from Bijapur to Gulbarga. The garden's pavilions appear to have been constructed towards the end of Ibrahim II's reign. They are clustered at four sites, progressively distant from the dam with each move west.

The best preserved pavilions stand at the eastern end of the garden (pp. 108–11, figures 3–8). Here, a broad hall opens through five arches onto a large hauz. Steps rising from the side of its facade indicate that the structure had an upper storey. A central fountain and pools in its interior suggest a setting for small informal audiences and recreation. Badly damaged wall paintings depicting natural landscapes, male figures, and recreations, including riders in a polo match, suggest this was the venue for an elite royal male audience.

A two-storey domed pavilion with a single chamber on each level stands on a platform at the centre of the hauz before this hall. Remains of copper shower-roses are visible in the interior, suggesting the creation of a cool atmosphere through the introduction of sprays of water. The pavilion's bulbous dome contains a reservoir for water, pumped into it under pressure from a water tower to the southwest of the tank, close to a sluice in the dam wall. In combination,

14 Ainapur. Palace, after 1651. Built for Muhammad Adil Shah's wife, Jahan Begum.

the adjacent dam, the surrounding tank of water, and the spray mist would have provided considerable cooling.

A similar domed pavilion within a smaller hauz lies to the west of this complex (p. 108, figure 3). This pavilion houses a square pool with seating around its edge sufficient for three or four people. The hauz was screened on its eastern side by a stone colonnade, while a great masonry lifting gear and water pressurization structure stands on its northern edge. The lack of a hall beside this pavilion and its partial screening suggest that it marked the boundary between intimate male royal audience and the zenana.

The two pavilion sites furthest west and most distant from the dam repeat

15 Ainapur. Palace, after 1651. Raised platform with octagonal columns behind the triple-arched facade.

the audience-hall structure preceded by a hauz on a successively smaller scale. The penultimate pavilion group reproduces both hall and water pavilion with bathing pool, while the final site lacks any water pavilion in the very small hauz before its hall. This diminution in the scale and number of structures at successive sites suggests that those to the west accommodated the innermost royal area within the garden complex. In this context, the pavilions at Kumatgi appear to have formed a royal retreat which provided a small and intimate setting for royal audience beyond the zenana.

Summary

The north-facing, triple-arched Adil Shahi audience halls that dominate Bijapur and Nauraspur, such as the Gagan Mahal, appear to have developed as a conscious reinterpretation of the dynasty's Tughluq and Bahmani predecessors. Within this tradition, Adil Shahi authority was increasingly clearly articulated by the association of royal audience with the patronage and veneration of the sultanate's leading religious cults. Halls with upper-storey loggias better suited to mass public audience, such as the Asar Mahal, provided opportunities for the more explicit articulation of royal patronage of mystical cults and royal munificence in making their baraka available. The construction of dedicated royal reliquary and devotional structures, such as the Husseini and Pani Mahals, signalled a yet more explicit royal appropriation of these mystical traditions. The location of structures such as the Jalamandir in and around the royal household would have strengthened these associations. The heavenly imagery and earthly luxury which characterized the royal household at sites such as the Haft Mahal and the water pavilions at Kumatgi provided powerful metaphors for these mystical blessings. In this context, Bijapur and Nauraspur's concentric urban plans may suggest an attempt to articulate Adil Shahi mystical association and leadership through a centrally located seat of royal-sacred authority.

GOLCONDA AND HYDERABAD UNDER THE QUTB SHAHIS (1495–1687)

Marika Sardar

The fortified city of Golconda sits beside a promontory that gently rises from the surrounding boulder-strewn plains; a few kilometres to the east, Hyderabad lies unwalled and on a flat site, within view of the Musi river to its north (plans 29, 32). Both Golconda and Hyderabad served as capitals of the Qutb Shahi sultanate, fulfilling the ceremonial and practical needs of this dynasty. Yet the two cities represent two unique modes of building, having been constructed at different moments and under differing historical circumstances.

From its origins as an undistinguished military outpost established in the 14th century, Golconda was developed into the capital of the Qutb Shahis, who had served as provincial governors under the Bahmanis, gained independence, and then risen in prominence during the course of the 16th century. Throughout its history, Golconda retained its military character; the fort remained in use for defending the kingdom until it was conquered by the Mughal armies in 1687, and even as graceful palatial structures were added to the site, they were confined to the already enclosed areas. Hyderabad, on the other hand, was established as a capital in 1591 when the Qutb Shahis were at the height of their power, and was designed for symbolic purposes. It was planned around two open squares, with large-scale, ceremonial monuments, and was never walled during the Qutb Shahi period. The unguarded palaces were set amongst gardens stretching west and north of the city's centre and up to the banks of the Musi. For this reason, Golconda was retained as the fortified

1 Golconda. Palace area. View from the west, with the northern (public) end, including the gated entrance, first open plaza, and buildings 7, C, and E of plan 30.

2 Golconda. Palace area. View from the west, with the southern (private) end, including buildings 10, 11, and 12 of plan 30.

centre of the kingdom, even after all ceremonial functions had been shifted to Hyderabad.

Like the development of these two sites, the study of the Qutb Shahi capitals today also follows two divergent paths. The palaces within the Golconda Fort are fairly well preserved, but the limited amount of written information about them makes it difficult to determine exactly when they were built and how they were used. In the case of Hyderabad, we have several literary sources if no extant buildings. Poetry by the city's founder Muhammad Quli Qutb Shah (r. 1580–1611) and a chronicle written during the reign of his grandson Abdullah (r. 1626–72) are the primary sources for imagining the buildings that were razed either during the Mughal occupation of Hyderabad in the mid-1680s, or the subsequent Maratha raids of the late 17th and early 18th centuries.

Golconda

The palace area at Golconda is located at the base of the hill known as the Bala Hisar. This hill was first fortified in the 14th century, and the walls that stand near its summit, built of large blocks of granite, studded with rectangular bastions, can be dated to this period (plans 29, 30). The Bahmanis gained control of Golconda in about 1363, and during their occupation of the fort it appears that construction was limited to the original walled area, where there are a mosque and the remains of a few other buildings that may date to the early 15th century. In the mid-1490s Sultan Quli, an emigre from Iran who had joined the Bahmani court at Bidar, was given the governorship of the province of Tilang, with the title of Qutb al-Mulk and the use of Golconda as his headquarters.

As the Bahmani sultanate weakened in the late 15th century, its governors became increasingly independent; as a result, the provincial capitals were expanded as capitals of newly formed kingdoms. At Golconda, Sultan Quli (r. c. 1495–1543) constructed a congregational mosque (1518) and a tomb, and appears to have established the palace area at the base of the Bala Hisar. The mosque is located just outside of the entrance to the enclosed palace area and was therefore accessible both from the palaces and the surrounding town. However, its back was to the palaces, which means that the sultan would have had to circle around to enter through its front gate. Sultan Quli's tomb was built to the north of the palaces, in an area that remained beyond the walled area of the fort, but was only a short distance away and quite visible from the palaces.

Over the following decades, Sultan Quli's descendants made their own additions to the palace area and his son Ibrahim Qutb Shah (r. 1550–80) built a wall around the adjacent town. Each sultan also erected a tomb in the necropolis that developed around Sultan Quli's resting place, except the last sultan, Abul Hasan (r. 1672–86), who was imprisoned by the Mughals and died at Daulatabad.

The entrance to the Qutb Shahi palace area at Golconda is on the northeast side of the enclosure, through a gate today called the Bala Hisar Darwaza. This gives access to a large grassy square, now dominated by an armoury and rows of barracks or stables. To the south is another open plaza, behind which are

3 Golconda. Palace area, tripartite structures around a central court at the south end, 16th–17th century. See plan 30 no. 10.

the numerous Qutb Shahi palaces. These palaces were probably once arranged in specific relationship to one another, but many later structures have been built into and alongside the Qutb Shahi ones, obscuring the original plan. Also confusing is the fact that visitors to the site today are guided from the palace area entrance, past the double row of barracks, and directly to the stairs ascending the Bala Hisar. But it seems likely that in the 16th and 17th centuries, one would have progressed southwards through a series of courts of increasing security, with the broad expanse of the northern first court representing the most public part of the palace area, and the enclosed, smaller spaces of the southern end serving as a private zone reserved for members of the royal family (figures 1–3). The halls located in the middle of the palace area might have been used for holding audience, as they were accessible from both the private and public sides.

The idea that the palace area was partitioned into smaller spaces derives both from observations of the physical remains at the site as well as descriptions by early visitors. For instance, Rafi ud-Din Shirazi, an Adil Shahi courtier who was at Golconda during the reign of Ibrahim, described several distinct "suites" (as translated by H.K. Sherwani) including the royal residence and wardrobe, areas for the fort's commander and the court ministers, and workshops for calligraphers and bookmakers. But the walls that now enclose the buildings at the southern end of the palace area were probably built after the Qutb Shahi period for they block off access to certain buildings and run atop the walls of others. Other features would have demarcated the individual courts in the Qutb Shahi period.

4 Golconda. Palace area, baradari pavilion at the south end of the Bala Hisar, 16th–17th century.

GOLCONDA AND HYDERABAD **81**

5 Golconda. Palace area, tripartite structure in the "Courtyard with Fountain", 16th–17th century. See plan 30 no. 1.

The Bala Hisar would have formed an adjunct to the palace area; the steep climb to its top probably meant that it was not used for official business. Today its most notable feature is a hall called the baradari that sits on a high platform at the southern end of the Bala Hisar (figure 4). On its lower level are several vaulted rooms; at the topmost level is an open-air structure with commanding views over the surrounding countryside, which we might imagine being used for relaxation.

The buildings in the palace area below the Bala Hisar mostly repeat a few simple types. The most common unit consists of a central rectangular platform with enclosed chambers on either side (plans 30 nos. B, 10, 11; 31). The central platform is usually reached by short sets of stairs on its ends; its rear wall is typically decorated with three arched frames into which tiers of smaller arched niches have been set. This platform may have been covered by a roof supported on columns, the bases for which can still be seen in some buildings at the palace area, but no such roofs survive today. These units were typically placed around the sides of an open courtyard with a water feature at the centre. They were constructed in the typical Qutb Shahi fashion, with walls made of rubble stone faced with plaster. In addition, many buildings in the Golconda palace area have supplementary plaster carved into decorative forms to highlight such areas as the spandrels of arches.

This type of building is repeated at least eleven times in the palace area. One such courtyard is located at the southern end of the palace area, at the base of the steps that now descend from the top of the Bala Hisar. Here, there are three similar units on the east, west, and south sides of a rectangular water tank with an octagonal fountain in the middle (figure 5). The fourth side has a blank wall enlivened by five large niches, flanked by stacks of smaller niches. A similar arrangement of units is repeated to the northeast of this courtyard in what is now called the Rani Mahal and in another courtyard closer to the entrance of the palace area, below the stairs on the northern end of the Bala Hisar.

This tripartite building scheme seems to have served as the typical residential structure for much of the Qutb

Shahi period. This general form can be traced back to Bahmani times; it also occurs at Bijapur, though on a grander scale, as in the Gagan Mahal. Because of their location and scale, the tripartite units at Bidar and Bijapur are likely to have been used for official functions. At Golconda, however, the repeated appearance of this form, and its smaller scale, suggest that it was used for both public and residential buildings.

Whereas the tripartite unit is fairly common at Golconda, some buildings appear that are not known at other Deccan sultanate sites. At the southern end of this complex, for instance, is a multi-chambered, open-air structure that once stood on a high platform. This building is now within a court enclosed by high stone walls, although it appears that these walls were added later. This building once had a series of rooms that opened into one another, and to the exterior through large arched openings.

The walls of this building are constructed of plaster over a combination of stone (for the walls) and brick (around the arches), with the substructure in stone. The interior walls are decorated with rows of small niches contained within larger arched frames, one of the hallmarks of Qutb Shahi architectural decoration. Also typical is the placement of segmented bulbs above some arches and the schematic floral motifs over other arches. It is unclear, however, what the function of this building was. Terracotta pipes embedded in the corners of the walls suggest that it was provided with running water, but although hydraulics and raised floors accommodating a hypocaust system are typical of baths, the large openings in the walls of this building make such identification unlikely.

Examples of Qutb Shahi courtly architecture are also found outside the palace area at Golconda, in the gardens that played an important part of life at the court. Although many are described in the contemporary literature, the only preserved Qutb Shahi garden is an early-17th-century example located northeast of the fort, later enclosed within the Naya Qila, or New Fort. This garden originally had a formal plan with a 180-metre-long water channel that ran from north to south through its centre. This channel was once lined with inclined stone slabs that caused the water flowing over them to break into gentle ripples. A row of pavilions, step-wells, and an aqueduct that passed over the eastern wall of the fort create a shorter

6 Golconda. Palace area, pavilion on the south end, 16th–17th century. See plan 30 no. 12.

GOLCONDA AND HYDERABAD 83

east–west axis perpendicular to the water channel. The pavilions in this garden are either rectangular, with arched openings around the four sides (the baradari), or U-shaped. The niches in the rear wall of this structure were supposedly filled with candles at night (figure 6).

A subterranean pavilion near the tombs that was excavated in the 1970s suggests that another garden was located in this area, forming part of a green zone that apparently surrounded the fort. Though these gardens were located outside the walls of Golconda it seems likely that their use was limited to the royal family, but for less formal affairs than those that took place within the fort palaces.

Many other buildings can be observed in the Golconda palace area but they are in a dilapidated state. Great multi-storey halls, some with fountains or water tanks on their upper levels, others with carved stone and tile mosaic decoration, await further investigation. Once studied, they will contribute to a better understanding of Qutb Shahi courtly architecture.

Hyderabad

Unlike Golconda, Hyderabad was built on a site with no prior history. The main reason for its foundation seems to have been a practical one: despite Ibrahim's expansions to Golconda, the old fort was overcrowded and attempts to construct suburbs were unsuccessful. As a result, the sultan seems to have considered moving the court altogether; he ordered the construction of a water reservoir (today's Tank Bund) and a bridge across the Musi (Purana Pul) in order to provide water for the new capital and easy access to and from the old one. Ibrahim died in 1580 without starting the construction of this city, however, and the task was left to his son Muhammad Quli Qutb Shah, under whom Hyderabad was developed in the 1590s.

This capital was quite different in nature from Golconda, where the royal and ceremonial buildings had been placed behind strong fortification walls to one side of the town. At Hyderabad, these structures were located in the heart of the city, some behind walls, others not, and all with areas of access for the public. The city was designed around a central core with monuments arranged

7 Hyderabad. Charminar, with the Charkaman (1590s) visible through the central arch.

on two intersecting axes: a pre-existing east–west road that led from Golconda to the ports on the eastern coast of the kingdom, and a new north–south road that led from the Musi river in the north through the centre of the city and south to the Koh-i Tur, the site of additional Qutb Shahi residences (and later, the Asaf Jahi-period Falaknuma Palace). At the crossing of these axes stood the Charminar, the first structure built in Hyderabad, which was completed in 1591. Immediately adjacent to the north was the capital's congregational mosque, and to the north of that was a large square bounded on each side by a large arch (today called the Charkaman, "four arches" or "four bows"). Directly to the west of these structures was the Qutb Shahi palace area (with an entrance from the west arch of the Charkaman) and a public maidan (aligning with the west side of the Charminar).

Of these features, only the Charminar and the Charkaman still stand (figure 7). The former is an unusual structure with large arches and corner minarets on the first floor, a gallery on the second floor, and a small mosque on the third. This curious mix of elements is typologically unique in the Deccan, but some idea of its original function may be inferred from the fact that it marked the centre of the new city in dramatic fashion, and proclamations were read from its upper gallery. The tall arches of the Charkaman, on the other hand, acted as an entrance point to the palace area: guards were stationed in the north, south, and western arches, while drums were sounded from the eastern arch at regular intervals throughout the day, and to announce the arrival of the sultan and other important guests.

To better understand the courtly structures of Hyderabad that do not survive, we must turn to various written and pictorial sources. Jean de Thèvenot, a French traveller who passed through Hyderabad in the 1660s, provides us with an overall description of the palace area: "The Palace which is three hundred and four score Paces in length, takes up not only one of the sides of the Place [the maidan discussed above], but is continued to the four Towers [Charminar], where it terminates in a very lofty Pavillion. The Walls of it which are built of great Stones, have at certain

8 Hayatabad. Plaster-decorated well, c. 1632.

GOLCONDA AND HYDERABAD 85

9 Qutb Shahi sultan with courtiers, Golconda, 17th-century painting, The British Museum, London, No. 1937, 4-10,01.

distances half Towers, and there are many Windows towards the place, with an open gallery to see the views. They say it is very pleasant within, and that the Water rises to the highest Apartments …." No Man enters into this Palace, but by an express Order from the King, who grants it but seldom …." Other sources, such as Muhammad Quli Qutb Shah's poems, mention buildings like the Sajan, Chandan, and Khudadad Mahals, while the 1644 court chronicle the *Hadiqat us-Salatin* provides such details as the number of storeys some of these palaces had, and describes their decoration with extensive wall painting. Among the list of subjects were likenesses of Abdullah Qutb Shah and rulers from other kingdoms, scenes of hunting and royal sport, and images of the literary couples Yusuf and Zulaykha and Layla and Majnun.

From these sources, we also know a bit about how the maidan functioned. The *Hadiqat us-Salatin* tells us that on the north this square was bordered by the Qutb Shahi palaces and on the south by a nine-storey Hall of Justice, while the east and west sides were marked by the Kotwal Khana (Commander's Station) and the Chowri Thana (translation unclear), respectively. This book also tells us about the festivals that took place here on religious occasions, when the surrounding buildings were decorated and tents set up in the middle of the maidan. The 17th-century French jeweller and diamond merchant, Jean-Baptiste Tavernier, provides the additional information that audiences were held here, with the public assembled in the square and the sultan seated above on a balcony projecting from one of the adjacent palaces. This maidan was also the site of public entertainments, such as the elephant fights mentioned by Jean de Thèvenot.

A more physical grasp of these buildings can be gleaned from a study of paintings produced in the Hyderabad workshops. For example, an illustration now in the British Museum, London, thought to represent either Muhammad Quli Qutb Shah or Abdullah Qutb Shah, depicts a young ruler seated on a platform throne, surrounded by courtiers (figure 9). He is shown in an open hall, the superstructure of which is supported by tall faceted columns. This represents a type of building different from the hall with a central platform found so often at Golconda, but one that is related to the Chihil Sutun type of courtly structure. Although we have no representative palaces, this building type with tall faceted columns can be found in contemporary religious structures such as the Badshahi Ashurkhana (1596 and later), and in the tombs of Muhammad Quli Qutb Shah and the courtier Mian Mishk (d. 1680).

Tall rectangular pavilions with five-sided projecting balconies in a painting depicting Abdullah Qutb Shah in procession (National Library of Russia, St. Petersburg, Dorn 489, fol. 18b) seem to represent yet another type of courtly building that developed in the 17th century. Although no examples of this type remain in Hyderabad itself, a residence constructed by Mian Mishk at Atapur (a suburb of Hyderabad) and a pavilion at the top of the Bhongir Fort (northeast of Hyderabad), both have this distinctive balcony. The so-called Dad Mahal at Golconda also has a pentagonal projection on one end (plan 30D, and shown on the right side of figure 5) as do the "Camel Stables" (plan 30 no. 8), and these were probably 17th-century additions.

Finally, descriptions of the ceremonies that took place in Hyderabad can further enhance our understanding of the city's buildings and why they may have been arranged the way they were. Celebrations of the Prophet's Birthday described in the *Hadiqat us-Salatin* culminated in a procession led by the sultan, accompanied by elephants and his nobles, dancers, and musicians, all dressed in red clothes given to them by the sultan. It started at the Charkaman, continued past the Charminar, and ended at the maidan. Interestingly, such processions were depicted in paintings, of which numerous examples survive from the period of Abdullah.

The Suburbs

Courtly life in the Qutb Shahi period was not confined to Golconda and Hyderabad. The court also travelled to suburbs outside the capitals as the two cities grew increasingly crowded. As mentioned earlier, Ibrahim founded one such settlement, as did Muhammad Qutb Shah (r. 1611–26), and his wife, Hayat Bakshi Begum. These suburbs were not merely royal retreats, but seem to have accommodated official functions. Coins issued by Muhammad Qutb Shah refer to his suburb, Sultan Nagar, as the Dar us-Saltanat – "abode of the sultanate", or capital – and celebrations for Abdullah's shaving ceremony were held at Hayatabad, the suburb built by Hayat Bakshi Begum. This site, 14 kilometres east of Hyderabad, was built up between 1626 and 1632. Although mostly in ruins today, the *Hadiqat us-Salatin* informs us that it once included residential buildings, a garden, and a caravansarai, as well as the mosque and a step-well decorated with carved plaster birds that can still be seen (figure 8). A further study of these intriguing sites – especially Sultan Nagar, whose circular walls can be seen in aerial photographs – would surely enhance our knowledge of Qutb Shahi architecture.

DAULATABAD AND AURANGABAD UNDER THE MUGHALS (1660–1707)

George Michell

After the highlights of Gulbarga, Bidar, Ahmadnagar, Bijapur, and Golconda that have been described and illustrated in the previous chapters, the architectural contribution of the Mughals in the Deccan may appear at first to be of lesser consequence. This impression is, however, deceptive. The Mughals struggled for almost 100 years to conquer the Deccan. Once they had annexed this lucrative region to their imperial domains they set about adapting existing forts and palaces, as well as building new residential complexes where they could conduct the everyday business of governance and enjoy more private moments of relaxation and pleasure. While these courtly complexes were grandly planned and lavishly embellished, they are for the main part poorly preserved, unlike the walls and gateways with which the Mughals strengthened the various cities of the Deccan where they settled, and the great mosques and tombs that they raised for local saintly figures. By far the most famous Mughal edifice in the Deccan is the Bibi-ka Maqbara, erected outside Aurangabad in about 1661 by Prince Azam Shah as a tomb for his mother, Begam Rabia Daurani, queen of Aurangzeb (p. 112, figure 9). Though often compared unfavourably with the Taj Mahal at Agra, on which it is obviously modelled, the Bibi-ka Maqbara exhibits many novel architectural features and is adorned throughout with the finest plasterwork. Similar, high quality decoration was doubtless also employed in contemporary courtly buildings in the Deccan but only the barest traces of this survive.

Daulatabad

Besieged on various occasions by the Mughals, the great citadel of Daulatabad finally succumbed to the invaders in 1633, and over the next 20 years served as their principal headquarters in the Deccan. While the Mughals exploited the existing, formidable military works and the array of courtly structures that stood within the walls, they also erected structures of their own, thereby introducing a new style of architecture into the region.

The most obvious Mughal addition is the baradari pavilion that Shah Jahan is supposed to have constructed in 1636 (figures 1, 2). This is sited beneath the summit of Balakot, the fortified, artificially scarped hill that

1 Daulatabad. Balakot, baradari pavilion, 1636. Interior view. Walls and half-dome decorated with radiating geometric designs.

2 Daulatabad. Balakot, baradari pavilion, 1636.

3 Daulatabad. Mahakot, palace compound, 1653–1707. Dome of small hammam, decorated with a perforated open-flower motif.

forms the dramatic core of Daulatabad. Commanding majestic views over the whole site as well as the roads that wind through the surrounding terrain, the baradari may originally have been built by the Nizam Shahis and later refurbished by Shah Jahan. This is suggested by the construction, which consists of stone rubble and mortar core, pitted timber and facings of basalt blocks (plan 23). Another possibility is that masons trained in Nizam Shahi construction methods were employed by the Mughals. The pavilion presents an east-facing, part-octagonal arcaded verandah, with triple-arched openings on each side, sheltered by a wooden overhang on wooden brackets. Carried high on massive retaining walls of tightly fitting basalt blocks, the verandah opens off an octagonal room that is surrounded by eight arched openings. It is roofed internally with a plastered domical ceiling articulated by diamond-shaped facets that converge on a 16-petalled flower – a typical Mughal motif. This room leads to a long hall with a flat ceiling, with half-domes carried on pointed arches at either end; small octagonal chambers are positioned beyond. Past these rooms lies

4 Daulatabad. Mahakot, palace compound, 1653–1707. Hammam, main hall with pool (see plan 4).

5 Daulatabad. Mahakot, detail of west baradari, showing construction techniques. Pitted wood with rubble embedded in mortar, dressed in stone that was subsequently covered with plaster.

an open court, almost 15 metres square, with long halls on the other three sides.

Whether the generously proportioned central court and side rooms of this complex actually served as a summer residence for Shah Jahan and his son Aurangzeb when the latter was Viceroy of the Deccan, as indicated by the signboard displayed in the court, cannot be confirmed. However, the complex is conventionally Mughal in layout, with its interlocking suite of octagonal and rectangular chambers. That said, the use of plain pointed arches rather than those with lobes indicates that the workmen here may not have been familiar with standard Mughal building practice. The same does not seem to be true of the extensive palace in Mahakot, built up to the fort walls at the base of Balakot, immediately to the north of the hill, now in an advanced state of picturesque decay. Here, Aurangzeb is believed to have been the patron; certainly the configuration of the complex and the style of its architecture are in accordance with Mughal palaces built elsewhere in India during the second half of the 17th century. It is likely this served as the headquarters for the emperor and his court before he permanently shifted his residence to nearby Aurangabad.

The Mahakot palace consists of the usual components of an imperial Mughal residence: formal entrance gate; private mosque; men's quarters with audience hall and residential apartment facing onto a char-bagh; a zenana, consisting of a trio of palaces for women, each with its own private char-bagh; and two hammams (plan 33). These elements are all disposed on a series of ascending terraces, along an approximate east–west axis, with a private male pavilion at the highest level, looking out over the ramparts to the surrounding landscape. The architecture of the palace is for the most part typical, rather than distinguished, though this is difficult to judge since its original decoration is mostly missing. The entrance gate presents the usual Mughal scheme of a central arched portal flanked by double tiers of similar but smaller arches at either side. The open space at the rear (west) probably served as a maidan for parades of troops and animals. At its southwest corner is a small mosque, raised on an elevated walled terrace. Its prayer hall has a simple triple-arcaded facade flanked by slender, non-functional minarets with domical tops. The

6 Daulatabad. Mahakot, palace compound, mardana.

corresponding northwest corner of the complex is marked by a small hammam, of interest for the ornamental vaults and domes, perforated with open-flower and other patterns (figure 3).

A high wall divides the maidan from a spacious inner court at an upper level. Almost 100 metres broad, this area is mostly occupied by a char-bagh, with garden plots divided by raised walkways with plaster-lined water channels in the middle, and a central square terrace with a pool. Clearly this was the mardana, used by the emperor and the male members of the court (figure 6). On the south side of the char-bagh is an audience hall, its north-facing facade marked by a row of lobed arches, its interior now devoid of its flat ceiling. On the west side is a more architecturally interesting building, also with an arcaded facade (figure 7). An arcade of lobed arches gives access to a long chamber with a plastered fountain set into the floor. This leads in turn to the octagonal chamber, roofed in brick and partly surrounded by an arcaded verandah, that looks out over the ramparts. The hammam nearby (figure 4), situated at a much lower level, is reached by a descending flight of steps. More grandly proportioned than the other example just noticed, the bath incorporates three large chambers with perforated domes carried on net-like pendentives, a typical Mughal device. By far the best preserved building of the complex, the hammam suggests the imperial architectural style that was introduced into the Deccan by the Mughals for their royal palaces. From here it is only a short distance to the trio of small residences, now much decayed, that comprise the zenana.

While the hilltop baradari and palace complex just described by no means exhaust the Mughal contributions to Daulatabad, whatever else was added to the fort during this period can hardly be studied, since these remains are in an advanced state of deterioration and thickly overgrown. For a better idea of Mughal courtly architecture of the period it is necessary to turn to Aurangabad, 13 kilometres to the south.

Aurangabad

The city of Khidki served as the headquarters of successive sultans and commanders of the Nizam Shahi kingdom, most notably Malik Ambar, who was responsible for the sophisticated hydraulic system with which the city was furnished, as well as a number of monumental gates and mosques. As successive Viceroys of the Deccan, Shah Jahan and Aurangzeb both resided in Khidki, but the latter eventually shifted the Mughal capital here in 1653, renaming the city after himself as Aurangabad. More than any of the northern capitals of the empire at the time, it was Aurangabad which served as the emperor's principal residence in the later years of his reign. From here he conducted the campaigns against refractory Maratha adversaries that eventually brought ruin upon the entire Mughal enterprise. At first Aurangzeb seems to have had little time for building activities, but after a severe Maratha raid in 1668 he ordered his viceroy Khan Jahan to invest the city with stone walls. Though only portions of these ramparts survive, the gates stand complete. Located at regular intervals, they present a standard Mughal pattern, with lofty arched portals flanked by massive, polygonal buttresses, topped by prominent battlements.

The most elaborate courtly complex to be erected in Aurangabad by the Mughals was the Qila Arg, laid out by Aurangzeb in 1693 as his private residence. This is located outside the walls to the north of the city, on a rise that overlooked a vast lake, with the Kham river beyond. The low-lying area of the lake is still apparent, though it is now known as Himayat Bagh because of the many fruit trees that flourish here. While the site of the Qila Arg is clear enough, it is difficult to make out the layout of the palace itself, since after Aurangzeb it fell into ruin and was partly occupied and more or less rebuilt as the Government School of Art, itself now abandoned and dilapidated. From what remains it is possible to determine that Aurangzeb's residence occupied a series of terraces that ascends from a great maidan, some 250 metres square, now occupied by a multi-storeyed concrete building, under construction at the time of writing. However, the alignment of the palace and great open space with one of the city gates is still evident. Known as the Naubat Darwaza, presumably because it housed the drummers that announced visitors to Aurangzeb's palace, this gate stands about 255 metres south of the complex. Other gates are seen to the east and west, as well as several modestly scaled mosques, one of which is known as the Shahi Masjid, no doubt because it was intended for the emperor's private use. Its exaggerated

7 Daulatabad. Mahakot, palace compound, mardana, west baradari, and white domes of hammam.

lobed arched openings and bulbous domes are typical of the late Mughal style. Of Aurangzeb's pavilions and halls within the Qila Arg only the topmost chamber, with bangla roof and side wings with lobed arched openings, can still be made out, though almost obliterated by the ruinous wings of the Government School of Art. No doubt enjoying splendid views over the lake below, this chamber must have been intended as the architectural climax of Aurangzeb's residence. Beneath, to the south, is a series of terraces at descending levels, one with a central square pool with a cascade at the rear, flanked by flat-ceilinged wings with triple-arched openings.

Compared with the crumbling Qila Arg, now virtually beyond rescue, it is something of a relief to consider the other Mughal courtly buildings of Aurangabad. Most of the palaces that still stand, however, are situated outside the walls of the city, as at Begampura, the quarter dominated by the Bibi-ka Maqbara. That this great garden tomb must also have functioned as a pleasure resort is evident from the baradari pavilions incorporated into two of its outer walls. The pavilion on the east, now serving as an office for the Archaeological Survey of India (figure 11), can be approached from outside the complex, where traces of a small garden with a well and associated

8 Aurangabad. Ismail Rauza, 17th century. Sarai and formal entrance to the baradari.

ramp to draw water can still be seen. Steps within the pavilion give access to a pair of lofty rectangular rooms, separated by a trio of lobed arches. The curving cornices of the flat ceiling and the undersides of the arches are enhanced with muqarna designs; floral medallions are painted onto the ceilings. One room faces westwards onto a small pool with a fountain that feeds the waterway on axis with the tomb itself.

Another palace in Begampura, the Soneri Mahal – so called because of the gilded murals with which the interior was once adorned – is believed to have been erected by a Bundelkhand chief who accompanied Aurangzeb into the Deccan. The focus of the complex is a spacious garden with a single water channel (figure 10); most likely there would have been a transverse channel to create a typical char-bagh, but this no longer survives. The garden is entered on the east through a monumental arcaded gate. On the west is the main building, elevated on a terrace with a small pool, fountain, and cascade descending to the garden. The building itself is disposed on two levels, the upper one set back over a terrace. The somewhat severe exterior and interior suites of flat-ceilinged rooms are relieved only by lobed arched openings; all original decoration has been obliterated by modern restoration.

9 Aurangabad. Ismail Rauza, baradari, at the centre of a char-bagh.

DAULATABAD AND AURANGABAD 95

Gardens

Gardens were a favourite of Aurangzeb's nobility in Aurangabad and this is evident from the series of resorts laid out beside the road that runs northwards from the Delhi Darwaza, beyond the city walls. The best preserved of these is the well-tended garden now within the Dr Rafiq Zakaria educational campus. Known as Ismail Rauza, this is likely to have been conceived originally as a pleasure resort, and only after the founder's death was it transformed into a funerary complex. (Such conversions were popular with the nobility in Mughal times since they ensured that the lands occupied by resorts remained in the ownership of the family, rather than reverting to the imperial estate.) The Ismail Rauza comprises a pair of spacious walled compounds. That to the south was a sarai lined with small domed chambers, which today functions as a college hostel (figure 8). An imposing gateway in the middle of the north side of the sarai serves as a formal entrance to the garden beyond. This finely finished basalt entryway presents a broad arched profile, surrounded by a frame divided into lobed cartouches; a pair of small square chhatris punctuates the rooftop corners. The garden within is contained by high walls, with corner octagonal towers topped by domical chambers in the typical Mughal manner. Four broad walkways flanking water channels, now filled in, divide the garden into a char-bagh. The walkways converge on a square baradari pavilion with a low arcaded elevation, devoid of any central dome, relieved by corner square chhatris topped by fluted domes (figure 9). At the core of the pavilion is an octagonal chamber accommodating the tomb of the founder, surrounded by a suite of communicating rooms.

Nothing can now be seen of the luxuriant planting of this and other gardens in and around the city. However, some idea of their original appearance may be had from the paintings produced for the Mughal court in Aurangabad at the turn of the 18th century, such as the pair of almost matching miniatures now in the National Museum, New Delhi (54.61/7) and Museum and Picture Gallery, Vadodara (Baroda) (P2/86). Each of these depicts a noblewoman reclining on cushions in the company of handmaidens, all on a brightly coloured carpet spread over a terrace sheltered by a textile canopy. The terrace overlooks a

10 Aurangabad. Begampura, Soneri Mahal, 1653–1707.

11 Aurangabad. Bibi-ka Maqbara, 1650–57. Ceiling of baradari in the eastern enclosure wall of the garden.

garden divided into square flowered plots, with fruit trees and lotus pond beyond.

Further examples of gardens are seen in the walled village of Khuldabad, 10 kilometres north of Daulatabad, even though these are mostly associated with the tombs of saintly figures who attracted the patronage of the Deccan sultans from the time of the Tughluqs onwards. Here, next to the mausoleum of Hazrat Sayyed Zainuddin, both Aurangzeb and Azam Shah are buried. Eschewing the ostentatious funerary monuments of their ancestors, father and son chose simple graves open to the sky. Such an avoidance of any building at all is in accordance with Islamic orthodoxy, and no doubt reflects the personal piety of these two figures. Other tombs at Khuldabad maintain the link with pleasure gardens. Lal Bagh, laid out by Aurangzeb's foster-brother and Viceroy of the Deccan, Khan Jahan, for instance, boasts a gateway embellished with brightly toned coloured tiles, while painted designs enhance its corner towers with fluted domes and central octagonal tomb. Such architectural adornments offer a tantalizing clue as to the original splendour of the courtly buildings that the Mughals erected during their occupation of the Deccan, but which sadly can no longer be appreciated.

Note
The author would like to thank Klaus Rötzer and Pushkar Sohoni for their generous assistance in preparing this article.

HYDERABAD UNDER THE ASAF JAHIS (1724–1950)

Alison Mackenzie Shah

The Last Deccan Dynasty

From the mid-18th to mid-20th century, Hyderabad served as the capital of the Asaf Jahis (1724–1950). A provincial Mughal successor dynasty, the Asaf Jahi rulers, the Nizams, rose to power in the course of the 18th-century struggles which propelled the British East India Company to the centre of the South Asian political stage. Because of the depth and detail of colonial sources on the construction of the princely community, Hyderabadis have been perceived only in terms of the policies and treaties that codified their subordinate relationships with the Viceroy and affirmed the hierarchical relationships that linked India's colonial periphery to the centre in Calcutta. Yet, for a century and a half, not only the constraints created by the British empire's visions of governance, but also the opportunities afforded by being on its periphery, shaped the broad axes on which the Asaf Jahis plotted out a political identity.

For more than a century after founding their state in Hyderabad, the two dozen or so families that comprised the Asaf Jahi aristocracy continued to patronize architectural styles and building practices that had developed in the pre-colonial Deccan. The old city deodhis (palace complexes), with their interior courtyards and pairings of three-sided wooden pavilions, provided their elite owners with environments for raising families, commemorating life's rites of passage, and conducting the business of administering jagirdari (rural landholding) estates. These traditional Deccan pavilions with exquisitely carved and painted wooden columns and arches provided the exclusive environments for visual enactments of power in events such as darbars and audiences for this Mughlai aristocratic community in the 18th and early 19th centuries. During the last decades of the 19th century and the first decade of the 20th century, however, noblemen of Hyderabad's aristocratic families looked to the suburbs around the city core and constructed more than eleven grand palaces. These palaces were enormous economic undertakings, with multiple storeys and dozens of grandly proportioned public rooms, furnished with vast amounts of European goods.

While Hyderabadi nobles had a long history of investing in and maintaining suburban pleasure gardens and hunting grounds, these palaces document a new interest in selecting not simply rural areas, but, specifically, rural hilltops as zones to proclaim social status. The hilltop retreats initiated a new palace typology in this Deccan city, with plans, designs, and ornament and furnishings that had originated in Europe. These suburban palaces became the new centres of royal political life and the importance of these palaces in the late 19th century became so integral to aristocratic identity that their styles of ornament and material furnishings came back to the old city deodhis, reshaping these inherited environments with new, mixed architectural styles.

In this article we propose that the addition of European-inspired structures to traditional suburban locations around Hyderabad and beyond, and of European architectural features to old city complexes, did not mark a clash of civilizations, and that the new designs were not foreign impositions designed to please or placate the British officials who represented the Crown in the princely state of Hyderabad. Rather, much like earlier Deccan sultans who adopted Caliphal, Ottoman, or Persian architectural symbols of majesty to claim a position amongst their peers in the world of princes, so did the Asaf Jahis. By embracing the cosmopolitan styles of their era they built a bulwark against the dominance of British colonial power centred in north India.

1 Chowmahallah Palace, pre-Asaf Jahi foundation, 18th-century additions, reconstructions in the 1860s and 1930s. View into the courtyard of the Nizam's throne-palace complex. The plain walled exterior and interior courtyard with its three-sided pavilion represent a standard design of old city palaces under the Asaf Jahis. Photograph: Rajesh Vora.

Palaces were emblems of power and the hilltop palaces of the Asaf Jahis provided a setting for specific kinds of social and political performance tied to the edges of empire rather than its core. And just like with the hilltop palaces of the Nizam Shahis of Ahmadnagar, the enjoyment of views was also a symbolic appropriation of the surrounding domain. The following analysis of the broad urban trends of palace patronage and usage shows how the circuits of elite travel suggested new opportunities for patronage and activated old palace sites as powerful political environments. A study of the Falaknuma Castle (1884), a hilltop palace in which key political rituals took place, presents an example of the complexity with which frameworks of hospitality in these palaces could function in imperial politics.

The Hill Station Travel Circuit and New Palace Designs

Patrons turned to new hilltop palaces to shift not only Hyderabadi nobility, but also Hyderabadi politics out of its bounded and isolated Deccan state identity and into a contemporary urban idiom that developed explicitly to counter colonial political subordination: the hill station. British men and women from the colonial Indian plains, founded hill stations with the intent of recreating English villages. Here, the presence of Indian princes was welcomed because they added an exotic flair to the social environment. The

Nizam of Hyderabad purchased a house called "The Cedars" in the southern hill station of Ooty (Udagamandalam), and spent significant amounts of time there each year entertaining and socializing. For the Nizam, Ooty provided access to a world in which he could mingle with high-ranking British officials in an atmosphere of significant freedom from imperial protocol. The variety of social engagements and the mixing of Indian princes and noblemen with various ranks of colonial officers and their families characterized a season in the hill station. It was a highly personalized alternative to the hierarchies of official life in British India's plains. It was also the very opposite of the succinct and controlled imperial events like the Delhi Durbars, which set strict rules on to whom and in what manner the Nizam was to ritually affirm his subordinate position in relation to the British Crown. As some colonial officials noted with distress, the informal interaction between British officials and Indian princes at the races and at parties in the hills belied the strict political hierarchies through which imperial power was defined.

The Nizam was an active agent in developing the identity of this new community on the edge of empire. These social rituals in which political business was conducted – the dinner banquet, "at home" tea party, or formal breakfast – all required parties to attend. And since the Nizam's party did not include wives, who remained in purdah, he relied on the participation of Hyderabadi noblemen to balance the guest lists. For the noblemen who accompanied the Nizam the hill station's social activities aligned with traditional practices of political negotiation in Hyderabad; the leisure activities and banquets affirmed the values of charm, etiquette, and personal relationships – cultural skills (adab) through which Hyderabad's aristocratic community had long defined itself. Capitalizing on the hill station's new political culture in the princely capital itself offered a strategy to call into question the bureaucratic protocol of the British Resident and the authority of colonial power relations.

In the hill station, social prestige was marked by altitude, and in Hyderabad the new suburban palaces were all positioned on hilltops. Further, the palaces of the highest-ranking noblemen capitalized not only on the scenic vistas, but also on manmade lakes to support boating, public gardens, the racecourse, and well-stocked game preserves for hunting – the very features that defined the hill station's urban morphology. Iram Manzil (1900s), Hill Fort (1900s), and Falaknuma (1884) all looked over the lakes of Hyderabad,

2 Asman Garh, 1885. The grand hilltop palace of Sir Asman Jah, who served as both minister and regent, was a member of the highest-ranking noble family, the Paigahs, and was also a brother-in-law of the sixth Nizam, Mahbub Ali Khan. Photograph courtesy Vikas C. Jain, Fotocrafts.

which were newly equipped with leisure boats. Sir Asman Jah's palace, "Asman Garh" (1885), was perched on the edge of its patron's hunting preserves, and the Nizam Mahbub Ali Khan's "Mahbub Mansion" (c. 1896) overlooked the city's new racecourse.

In design, the palaces follow a clear pattern: activity-focused rooms like billiard halls, saloons, libraries, and banquet halls appear consistently in the designs in Hyderabad and reflect the social activities of the hill station. Further, the new practice of naming palaces in the Asaf Jahi capital reflected current practices of naming homes in Ooty. And much in the way that Ooty was famous for its breadth of historical European architectural styles in its public and grand buildings, Hyderabadi patrons, too, built in a breadth of historic European architectural styles. Pointed Gothic arches appear at Hill Fort, "Asman Garh" showcases a castle-like stone facade (figure 2), Norman crenellations mark the rooflines of Nizam Mahbub Ali Khan's "Mahbub Mansion", and Palladian elements appear prominently in Bashir Bagh (c. 1870s), Bellavista, and Falaknuma "Castle" (figure 3).

This suggests that from interior to exterior, from site to context, these palaces created a trend in which Hyderabadi nobles were active agents in redesigning their capital according to principles that framed a wider architectural discourse used by both the British and by princes to deny the empire's bureaucratic hierarchies. The palaces were not impositions of a British overlord; rather they set a new course for negotiations between Hyderabad's government and the British Resident. As photographs of Asman Jah's breakfast for the British Resident suggest, the palaces provided venues to improve the Nizam's negotiating power with the British Resident over the imposition of imperial policies.

The Europe–India Travel Circuit and New Palace Functions

In the two decades between 1890 and 1910, long-distance travel and life abroad defined a new aristocratic lifestyle from Europe to Hyderabad. The political and titled elite of Hyderabad began to travel to visit the Queen Empress, and during the journey they took ample opportunities to mix in the social world of European dignitaries. Similarly, Hyderabad's Nizam hosted a remarkable variety of international guests, including the Grand Duke of Russia, the archdukes of Austria and Tuscany, princes from Germany, France, and England, an Italian count, a German baron, and a succession of British lords. Titled European visitors, and their accompanying parties, sought out India for exotic adventures. Travelling European nobles would never have visited a hill station – a provincial, colonial social world designed to mimic the British homeland and its traditional aristocratic society. They nevertheless welcomed the comfortable and familiar accommodation provided by the Nizam in Hyderabad's suburban hilltop palaces such as Bashir Bagh and Falaknuma. As Hyderabadis and their visitors forged this new international community, then, the hilltop palaces became settings for a second community that was developing in contradistinction to colonial cultural politics.

As a result of this travel circuit, aristocrats from Hyderabad and Europe began to claim one another's heritage as integral to their own identities. The guests and hosts developed a new ritual of incorporation, held in the pavilions of old city palace complexes, pulling this palace form into new political currency. In a series of posed photographs in old city palaces, the Nizam and his guest sit in the centre, while groups of Hyderabadi and foreign attendants alternate in rows on each side of the central figures. The warp and weft strategy incorporated guests and hosts into a single, international community (figure 7), explicitly outside colonial status. The Nizam and his guest are most notable for their elegant, gentlemanly European clothing, removing any suggestion of a superior power to which this Indian prince owed allegiance. This particular kind of posed photograph ran counter to the incorporative rituals that had ordered Asaf Jahi political life as well as those that ranked imperial elites under Queen Victoria.

These rituals of an international aristocratic incorporation were made possible by the patronage of the suburban hilltop palace, the comforts of which enticed great numbers of high-ranking European nobles to visit Hyderabad. But unlike the highly individualized hilltop retreats, the old palace pavilions where the photographs were taken were almost interchangeable, showing little more in the photos than traditional Deccani styles of columned halls and imported chandeliers. By creating a non-specific backdrop, at once exotic and Europeanate, the old city palaces helped present this community as though it had no specific regional identity or roots. And by receiving more foreign guests than any other princely state, the sixth Nizam's status as an international prince could be repeatedly affirmed outside official policy, denying the exclusive authority of the rituals of colonial subordination to define his stature, prestige, and royal authority. And further, when the viceregal parties visited Hyderabad, formal posed photographs were taken in old city palaces, including the Nizam's Chowmahallah (figure 8). These late-19th-century photographs follow the form of the interwoven, sovereignless, international aristocracy and obfuscate the subordination to colonial status.

Falaknuma as Guesthouse

The grand Falaknuma Castle of Viqar ul Omrah, Hyderabad's minister

3 Falaknuma, 1884. The Falaknuma attracted such attention from Hyderabadis and foreign guests alike that photographs of the palace began to circulate from the moment construction was completed. Photograph courtesy The Alkazi Collection of Photography, 94.101.0022.

4 Falaknuma, the billiard room, 1884. The richly furnished saloon was used for entertaining visiting guests with leisure activities similar to those the Nizam and his noblemen encountered in the hill stations. Photograph courtesy Vikas C. Jain, Fotocrafts.

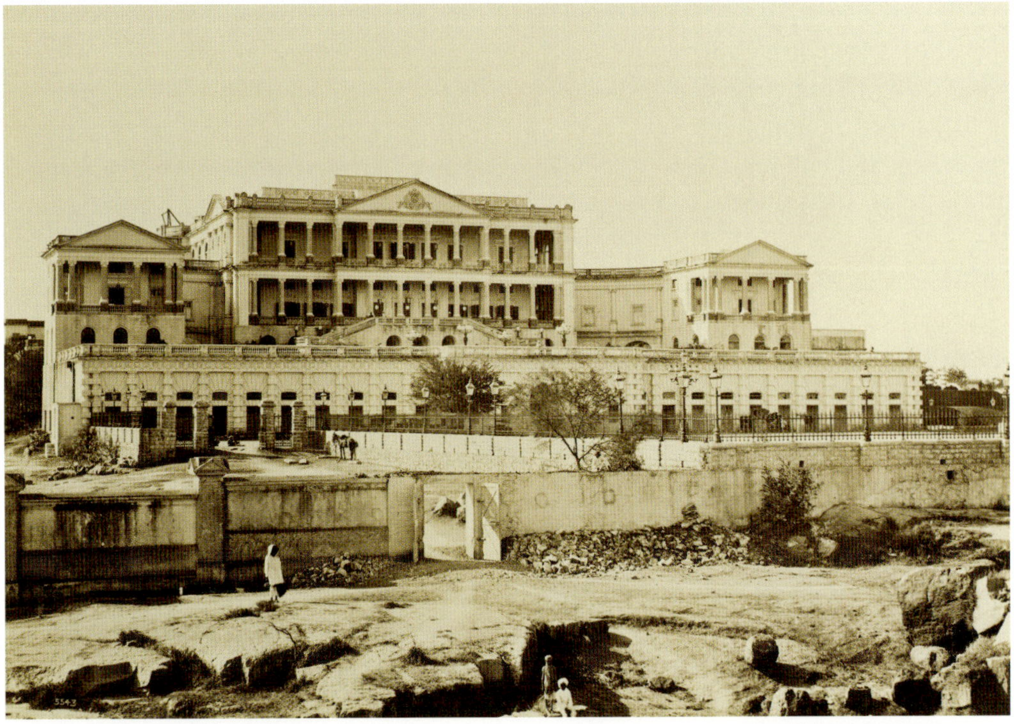

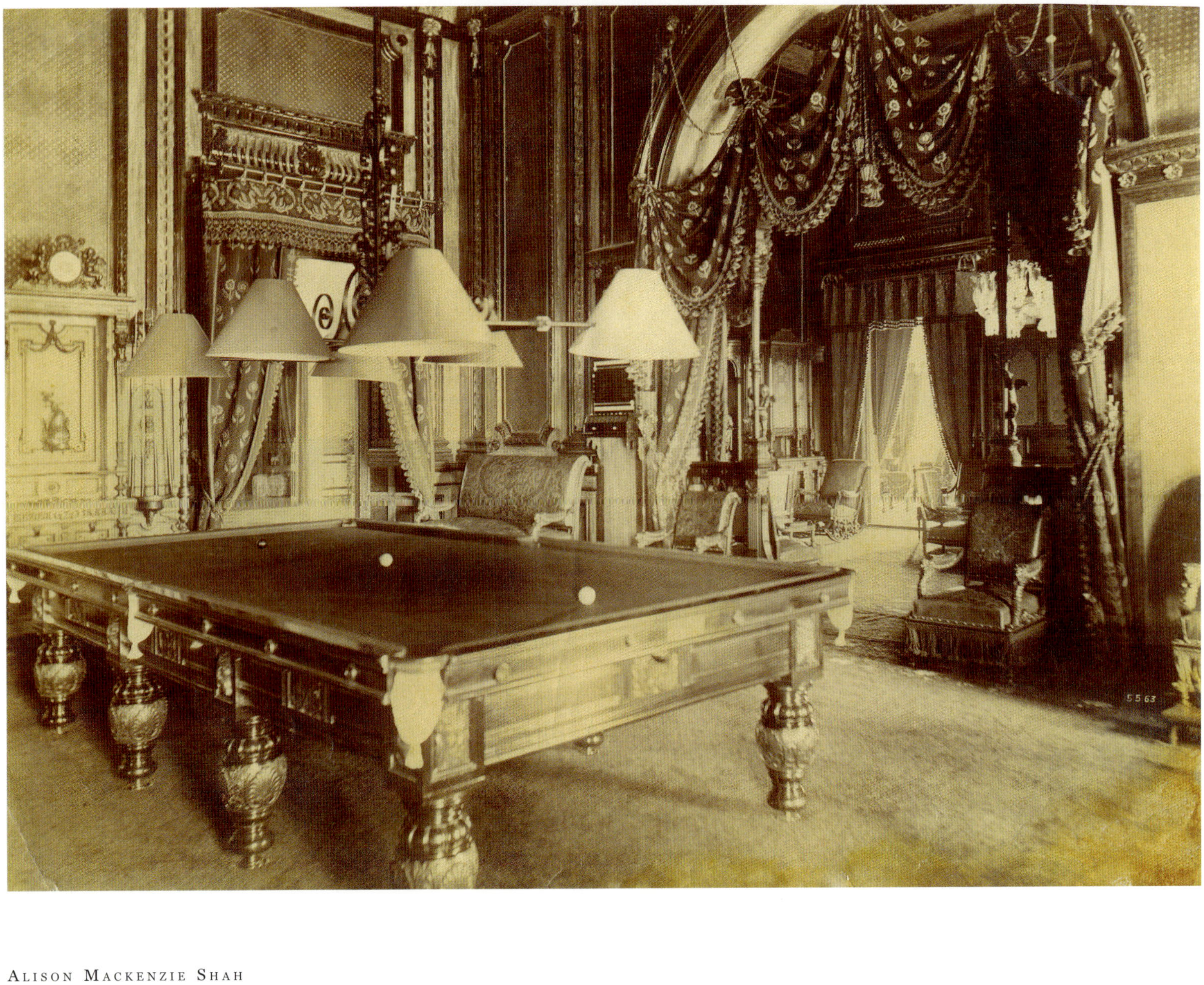

5 Falaknuma, banquet hall, 1884. The grand banquet hall of the Falaknuma palace provided the formal counterpoint to the more casual interactions in the saloon. Photograph courtesy Vikas C. Jain, Fotocrafts.

6 Falaknuma, bedroom suites, 1884. The private suites where foreign guests were accommodated were well-appointed and spacious, though not as lavishly furnished as the public halls. Photograph courtesy Vikas C. Jain, Fotocrafts.

(1894–1901) became the leading symbol of Hyderabad's identity as a princely capital almost as soon as it was built. It was unquestionably a lavish new palace, and it was situated on Hyderabad's highest hilltop (figure 3). The palace had a central building of two storeys and a basement level. Visitors to the palace were met by the grand Palladian facade whose double staircase led to a terrace that provided views of Hyderabad city. All foreign visitors to Hyderabad wished to visit the Falaknuma. The iconic image of the palace as a landmark showcased only the front, Palladian structure, though a zenana and private quarters were added in a courtyard hidden behind the main building. The interior entrance hall displayed not only fountain, furnishings, and frescos of European origin, but offered glimpses of the portraits of the British Governor-Generals that lined the staircase. The interior of the main palace boasted a diversity of styles (figures 4–6), from a formal Italianate entryway and staircase to a 17th-century smoking room, a ballroom, a billiard room, and a library. The capacity to import materials – from the marble floors to the chairs, tables, statues, and even the craftsmen themselves – proclaimed the patron's access to Europe and the long-distance travel that defined this era. But from the moment a visitor entered, it was apparent that the Falaknuma blended a palatial retreat with a Hyderabadi political stage.

The palace was built by Hyderabad's minister, but in 1896 it became the property of the Nizam. The Nizam used the palace not only as his own personal retreat, but more importantly as a guesthouse, particularly for the Viceroy Lord Curzon. The palace is most renowned for its imported styles and materials, but it also resonated with many of the traditional designs of Hyderabad palaces used for political encounters between Hyderabadis and British Residents. The two-storey, columned facade looked similar to the garden pavilions (baradaris) owned by the Asaf Jahis' first ministers in the 18th century, where British officers first gained access to Hyderabadi society. The display of imported goods also had a long history in Asaf Jahi palaces. The mid-19th-century minister Salar Jang entertained the British in his palace, Diwan Deodhi, where the arched niches with Chinese and other porcelains that embellished the surfaces of the 17th-century Mughlai Chini Khana – China Room – had been transformed to walls ornamented with hundreds of English cups and saucers. Similarly, European glass mirrors replaced the mosaic of glass pieces that so much contributed to the halls of traditional palaces with reflecting lights creating a peaceful, relaxed, and poetic environment. Like the palace complexes in the old city, the Falaknuma had a variety of themed rooms for interaction between hosts and guests. Imitating the spatial arrangements found in the hilltop resorts, the focus was on billiards, a library, or a French Baroque hall.

In their individualized identities, these varied rooms were not very different from the various pavilions that characterized the Nizams' and their ministers' old city palaces, whose halls of arms, music, mirrors, and other artefacts, for example, offered discreet visual environments for social and political exchanges between British officials and Hyderabadis. The new fashions and styles were thus embedded into existing architectural practices that developed into political environments in Hyderabad's palace architecture. Unlike the old city palaces, however, the Falaknuma had numerous bedroom suites on the ground floor of the main building, where the living quarters were located. The nature of hospitality was dramatically different, as the suites enabled guests to stay for periods of time rather than just visit for an audience or an evening's entertainment.

As representative of the Crown, the Viceroy undertook tours to visit, and be received by, the Nizam and the other princes of India. These visits were preceded by extensive sets of explicit instructions on protocol. As a member of the British aristocracy, the Viceroy Lord Curzon, on his visit to Hyderabad, expected to be treated as a visiting aristocrat, much in the manner of other travelling European noblemen. As a result, he did not stay at the British Residency, but was instead entertained as a guest of the Nizam (figure 8). In the imperial scheme, Lord Curzon served as a link in the chain toward the ultimate imperial sovereign, but the particular history of usage of the Falaknuma made the politics of subordination less clear. The Viceroy sent directions dictating how the Nizam was to ritually affirm the bonds of empire and the manner by which the Nizam would politely express his allegiance to the Crown by holding a darbar in his old city palace, Chowmahallah. When previously the Nizam had stayed in the Falaknuma, the symbols of the minister Viqar ul Omrah's coat of arms and personal taste could display the alliance between the minister and the Nizam, and display the ultimate sovereignty of the Nizam. But when used as a guesthouse for the Viceroy, these very symbols took the direct subordination of the Nizam out of the political setting. The Viceroy stayed in a palace with the coat of arms of a subordinate Hyderabadi noble. And in the banquet hall, the crucial site of formal ritual where the Viceroy played host to Hyderabadi guests, the chairs and plates were still inscribed with the initials V.O. The Viceroy's status as higher-ranking political official was delimited by the use of the minister's plates and his initialled chairs in the rituals of hospitality through which the Viceroy hosted the minister's master, the Nizam.

7 In a series of group photographs, the Nizam and his entourage developed a ritual that incorporated guests and host into a single international aristocratic community. Photograph courtesy Vikas C. Jain, Fotocrafts.

8 Group photograph of the parties of Lord Curzon and Mahbub Ali Khan at Chowmahallah. Viceroy Lord Curzon stayed in Hyderabad as a guest of the Nizam and was photographed in a group portrait similar to those of other visiting dignitaries. Photograph courtesy Vikas C. Jain, Fotocrafts.

Conclusion

The suburban princely palace, with its contemporary European designs and historical European ornament has long been used to showcase the cultural impact of subordination to British imperial power and the dependence on the hegemonic European civilization of the Raj. Recent studies of the integration of new communities within imperial society through visual culture offer little revision of agency for India's princely patrons. David Cannadine (2001) brushes off the princely patronage style as one defined by "flamboyant confections". Like the earlier judgement of mimicry, descriptors such as fantasy and confection suggest that in the world of high imperialism, princes are not to be taken seriously as patrons. In the world of high imperialism, however, cultural politics were the best weapon that the demilitarized prince had to manipulate power relations and secure sovereignty within his borders as well as beyond them. In the context of Hyderabadi circuits of mobility and rituals of hospitality, the palaces provided a rich environment in which the Nizam could manipulate complex practices to suggest his independence. The potency of these palaces in the new political rituals explains in some measure the political capital offered by extravagant palace patronage.

Note

This short study is based on an extensive analysis of Hyderabadi palaces in my dissertation. For specific citations and primary source records, please see, Alison Mackenzie Shah, "Constructing a Capital on the Edge of Empire: Urban Patronage and Politics in the Nizams' Hyderabad, 1750–1950" (PhD thesis, University of Pennsylvania, 2005).

HYDRAULIC WORKS AND GARDENS

Klaus Rötzer

On the Deccan tableland rainfall is scarce and occurs essentially during the monsoon from June to September. In this dry region people regard water bodies and luxurious vegetation as marks of divine intervention. The ruler was not only the guardian of the country, he was also expected to make the rain fall, and the ground water fill wells and baolis. In such a context, gardens were good omens and signs of heavenly protection. The ideal world that everyone dreamt of was a verdant garden full of fruits and flowers, with flowing water, baolis, pools, and fountains.

In the Deccan, from the middle of the 14th century until the end of the 17th, many gardens were laid out at the foot

1 Sultanpur. Royal villa, baoli, Yadava and Bahmani, c. 1420.

2 Aurangabad. Panchakki, 17th century. The water conveyed from distant sources is forced up into a tank by ventilation towers, and then down again. Like a mist it rains down from a fountain to a pool over a surface covered with small niches for the lights.

of dams, inside royal enclosures, and on the outskirts of towns and cities. None of them have preserved their original plant life. Only the architectural frames, more or less well conserved, testify to their bygone existence.

Waterworks

The water required to irrigate the gardens was provided essentially by wells, baolis, and man-made lakes. Under Persian influence a system of irrigation called the qanat was introduced by the middle of the 15th century at Bidar, and later applied in basaltic regions. It could be described as a horizontal well sourcing the water collected in lateritic formations or in the fissures of basaltic rocks. Manholes were dug at regular distances for the upkeep of the qanat and to allow people who lived nearby to draw water from it. At the end of the qanat a sluice regulated the outflow.

The water-lifting device consisted generally of a pulley fixed at the top of a masonry buttress overlooking the well. Behind the buttress, a slope made of earth extended the construction and enabled a draught animal to move along. The water was lifted in a bag fixed to a rope pulled by the

3 Bijapur. Kumatgi, water pavilion with "Kumatgi device", 17th century.

draught animal. This process seems to have been the only one in use till the middle of the 16th century. Later in Bidar and Bijapur, another device, generally termed the "Persian wheel", was introduced and applied at some water bodies. In this case the water was lifted in small earthen or metal buckets fixed on a kind of girdle moved by a wheel. Instead of going up and down a slope, the draught animal here moves around an axis on a platform. A third device was also invented during the 17th century at Bijapur. We here term it the "Kumatgi device" because the best preserved examples are found at Kumatgi near Bijapur. We do not know exactly how it functioned. What is left of the structure shows a high wall built on one side of a well or reservoir; on top of the wall there are corbels to fix the lifting mechanism and small tanks; earthen pipes set in lime mortar linked the tanks to fountains. How the water-lifting device was set in motion cannot be established. For certain, this device was invented to bring water under high pressure to fountains.

During the second half of the 16th century another innovation was introduced in the Deccan to supply water to a palace or city over long distances. Daulatabad, Bijapur, Ahmadnagar, and their palaces or gardens were partly provided with water from reservoirs or springs located some kilometres away. The water source, reservoir or spring, had to be at a higher level than the area where the water was needed. The runoff collected behind a dam or the spring water filling a storage tank was conveyed through a sluice into the earthen pipes of a masonry aqueduct. In order to ensure low pressure inside the pipes, manholes were set at regular intervals. Where the aqueduct is underground, these manholes have the shape of a square masonry well; where it reaches the lower ground, they look like towers.

Gardens

In a dry region like the Deccan, gardens are entirely dependent on water supply. As would be expected, there would often be a garden at the foot of a dam. The upper surface of the dam was a perfect camping ground, placed as it was between the water expanse of the reservoir and the plant life of the garden below. Banyan or tamarind trees were

4 Bijapur. Kumatgi, "Kumatgi device", 17th century.

5 Bijapur. Kumatgi, eastern group of pavilions, 17th century. At the centre of the lotus flower that adorns the dome, are openings for spraying mist.

6 Bijapur. Kumatgi, eastern group of pavilions, 17th century. Pipes frame the base of the pavilion, and connect to stone brackets in the shape of ducks, out of which water streamed into the pool that surrounded the pavilion.

7 Bijapur. Kumatgi, rectangular pavilion in northeastern group, 17th century. Wall painting depicting a sultan conversing with a Sufi, one of the few surviving paintings on the walls of this pavilion, which closely resemble, in both subject matter and style, manuscript paintings of the period.

8 Bijapur. Kumatgi, rectangular pavilion in northeastern group, 17th century. See figure 7.

planted on the dam: their shade added to the comfort of visitors and their roots strengthened the structure. The earthen dams of this region were very broad, for two reasons. First, the available earth, especially the black cotton soil of the basaltic region, was not a good waterproof material, and in consequence a broad dam was more efficient. Second, if the garden were to be used as a camping ground for a royal retinue or an army, much space was needed.

The best preserved example of this category of garden is located at Kumatgi village, outside Bijapur, laid out in the 17th century. Leisure pavilions were built in the garden, on the sluices, and on an artificial island in the middle of the lake. Three water-lifting structures fed fountains set up inside and around the pavilions. The garden displays a typical Deccani layout: there being no symmetrical arrangement, with a mix of working and leisure structures. For example, one sluice is topped by a pavilion from where one could take pleasure in the vista around and supervise the flow of water below.

However, most gardens in the Deccan were not situated at the foot of dams. At Bidar, for instance, the Bahmani palaces inside the fort were sited at the top of a cliff, between two gardens. The first garden was on the

9 Aurangabad. Bibi-ka Maqbara, 1650–57. Water courses run along the walkways.

112 KLAUS RÖTZER

same level as the palaces, the other one at the foot of the cliff. The upper garden was irrigated by five wells, which also supplied water under pressure to fountains and pools inside the palaces; the lower garden included a dam and its reservoir. The greenery was upstream, between the cliff and the reservoir; the water was provided by two qanats, two wells, and two baolis. The sluice of the dam was enlarged so as to compose a hidden leisure space with stairs leading down to the water and up to the top of the dam. The layout of both gardens ignored any rectilinear outline; the wells and their water-lifting devices were situated inside the gardens so that work and leisure were located in the same space. These features are typical of the Deccani garden. As viewed from the valley of the Manjira river, the royal residence at Bidar rose out of luxuriant vegetation. It was obvious to every onlooker that the Bahmani sultan was in command of the fertility of the country.

However the majority of the gardens of the Deccan are to be found in the surroundings of towns and cities, forming a green garden belt that belonged to the social elite of the region. Inside this belt the main idgah was situated, and sometimes even a polo-ground as at Bidar. With the expansion of urban life in recent years the remnants of most of these gardens have disappeared. The only examples that are still preserved have a funerary character. The domed building inside the garden could have been originally a pavilion transformed later into a tomb so as to keep the garden in the ownership of the family of the deceased. However some gardens formed part of a funerary compound from the beginning. Two examples are worth describing.

At Bidar the funerary compound of Ali Barid Shah (r. 1543–80) was laid out in 1576 (plan 37). It is composed of a square walled garden, a char-bagh, with the domed tomb at the centre; four walkways forming a cross each lead to a gate. Located outside the boundary walls of the garden was a residential unit that included a two-storeyed residence, a pool, and a mosque. Three wells outside the garden supplied water to the compound. The garden was used as a leisure centre and visited by the royal family, and the water-lifting devices were not admitted into this green "paradise". The layout of the garden was strictly orthogonal and symmetrical; it also showed a precise sequence of six distinct levels, from the beds filled with plants at the lowest level, to the platform that sustains the green dolerite gravestone of the tomb at the uppermost level. In its main features, this Baridi garden illustrates a fundamentally different approach to the earlier Bahmani garden, focused on a water body and its lifting mechanisms. In contrast, the formal Baridi garden displays a clear separation between work and leisure.

The other funerary garden of the Deccan that needs to be discussed here is that of the Bibi-ka Rauza at Aurangabad, which may be considered the masterpiece of garden architecture of the region. Here we find, at the end of the 17th century, a perfectly geometrical layout. This consists of a walled rectangle, with octagonal towers at each corner and an edifice in the middle of each wall; a high platform in the middle of the garden, on which the white tomb is raised; four main walkways forming a cross, and eight octagons with fountains at the intersections of secondary walkways. The wells supplying water to plants, water courses, and fountains are located outside the boundary walls. The typical features of this late Mughal garden are the same as those which we have already noticed in the Baridi garden. The formal type was the expression of a desire for order and cultural evenness.

Conclusion

The evolution of water storage and lifting techniques and gardens in the Deccan from the Yadava period (850–1334) up to the 17th century may be summarized here. Until the 15th century water bodies were set within architectural frames made of dressed stone. This water architecture is exceedingly impressive, but it does not mean that the water storage and lifting techniques were truly effective. However, fetching drinking water and taking a bath were religious activities; any water body was sacred and a respectful attitude towards it was usual. During the 15th century certain changes are noticeable. At that time the Deccan became a cosmopolitan and multi-ethnic region. Sultanate rule attracted peoples from other Muslim countries. Water specialists coming from Iran and other regions introduced novel techniques with an almost scientific approach to geological and physical realities. These specialists already had experience in obtaining more water from renewable sources. The use of lime mortar allowed them to build waterproof dams and to transport water over long distances. New lifting mechanisms enabled the water experts to stage water displays in gardens, pavilions, and palaces. As the religious attitude of the people towards water had not essentially changed, such displays impressed audiences, reinforcing the belief that the ruler also had command over water and fertility. On the other hand, the substitution of the more informal Deccani garden layout by a formal one, as took place during Baridi and Mughal times, shows a greater desire for geometric order and the rule of law.

ARCHITECTURAL DECORATION

Helen Philon

The Deccani palaces that have been surveyed by the different writers in this volume display varying decorative techniques, schemes, and themes expressed in plaster, ceramic revetments, timber, stone, and painting. Bahmani and Baridi courtly structures show a predilection for combining different materials and techniques within the same building, and even on the same wall surface (p. 53, figure 12). In the palaces of the Adil Shahis, plasterwork and stone carving prevailed, as did wall paintings, although only fragments of these survive in Bijapur and at Kumatgi (pp. 71–74, figures 7–12; p. 111, figure 7). The palaces of the Qutb Shahis and Nizam Shahis seem to display a more limited repertoire of decorative materials and techniques, mostly plasterwork (pp. 57, 60, 61, 65, figures 2, 5, 6, 12), but there are references to the existence of monumental painting under the Qutb Shahis. However, conclusive evidence is lacking as the remains are in a poor condition, either through re-use or neglect. The Mughals would seem to have continued local building traditions, with plasterwork and painting as their favourite decorative media (pp. 88, 97, figures 1, 11).

Plasterwork or stuccowork was probably introduced to the Deccan after the Tughluq conquests, and was continued in use by the Bahmanis and their successors for the adornment of all their structures, both religious and secular. Remains of painted stuccowork on Bahmani funerary examples suggest that the interior spaces were probably coloured and that exterior surfaces were left white with colour highlighting specific architectural features. Bijapuri palace structures were probably left white as indicated by the buildings depicted on Bijapuri miniatures. By the 15th century, the adoption of carved grey-black basalt and/or dolerite for columns, pilasters, column bases, chhajjas, and door frames – a technique borrowed from local traditions – added a colouristic effect to otherwise plain white exterior plastered surfaces (pp. 44, 48, 50, 52, figures 1, 6, 8, 10). To the same local traditions we must also credit the elaborately carved and painted timber columns, flat ceilings, and pyramidal vaults that are recorded in the palace inside the Kalakot enclosure of Daulatabad (p. 35, figure 2). This combination of decorated stucco, basalt, and timber continued in the Deccan throughout the 15th and first half of the 16th centuries, with the new ceramic techniques imported from the Turco-Iranian world of Central and Western Asia claiming equal importance (pp. 48, 49, figures 6, 7). The coloured-tile revetments in both mosaic and underglaze techniques found in the Bahmani and Baridi palaces of Bidar also belong to this imported tradition (figure 6; p. 53, figure 12). The few, but important, examples of wall paintings at Bidar and Bijapur reveal that immigrant and local artists working for the Deccani sultans were attuned to the prevailing artistic trends of their time, both in Asia and Europe (figure 7; pp. 71, 72, figures 7–9). We may, therefore, argue that the tendency to harmonize local materials, decorative techniques, and designs with those imported from both northern India and abroad is noticeable in Bahmani and Adil Shahi monuments, but less evident in those of the Qutb Shahis, Nizam Shahis, and Mughals. Mention must also be made here of textiles and carpets; though the survival of such luxury items is rare, their use in the Deccan is attested both by historians and artists of surviving miniature paintings. Their presence would have added yet another texture to the already rich, versatile, and colourful decor of these palaces.

Plasterwork

In this decorative medium, four themes prevail in Deccani examples: geometric, knotted, floral, and figural, the last being fewest in number (pp. 34–36, figures 1–3) as are also inscriptions. Although painted plasterwork has not survived in the courtly context, other Bahmani monuments preserve plasterwork with red, black, charcoal-grey, yellow, sage-green, and aquamarine colours.

During the early Bahmani period, decorative themes in plaster are realized in two techniques: designs were imprinted with carved blocks into wet plaster and subsequently incised or enhanced with colour pigments for further definition; alternatively, designs were created from stones or bricks set in mortar (pp. 34–36, figures 1–3; p. 2).

Examples using the second method are found mostly on vaults and domes where broad geometric or floral patterns were created in relief, and then covered in plaster (p. 3; p. 36, figure 4). Of the two methods, only the first persisted into the 18th century (figure 1); the second method prevails during the Bahmani and Adil Shahi periods and occasionally reappears under the revivalist trends of the Nizam Shahis (p. 57, figure 2). As the study of the decorative techniques of the Deccani sultans is still in its infancy, this assessment can only be tentative. Inscriptions on funerary monuments, gates, baolis, and other civic structures are noticeably absent from courtly

1 Bijapur. Haft Mahal, 1580–1627. Banana bud and scrolls.

2 Bijapur. Anand Mahal, 1589. Imitating timber structures is this pyramidal vault supported on brackets with overhanging banana buds in plaster.

architecture with a few rare exceptions such as the Shah Darwaza in Sagar and the Rangini Mahal in Bidar. Figural representations – especially those of birds, leonine creatures, and elephants – though rare, are attested on Bahmani and Adil Shahi royal monuments (p. 42, figure 11; p. 49, figure 7; p. 68, figure 3).

Moulded and incised plasterwork or stuccowork covers the interior surfaces of domes and vaults in Deccani architecture (figure 2; p. 23, figure 10). Medallions with different adornments decorate the spandrels of arches: others mark the apex of an arch while bands outline its profile. Beehive or honeycomb designs reminiscent of muqarnas decorate the base of domes as do bands with foliate designs and vegetal forms (figure 1; p. 35, figure 2).

Geometric and floral designs are found alone or combined on the same arch or wall surface. On jali windows made of bricks or stones bedded in mortar, or carved out of basalt, geometric designs prevail. On Bahmani buildings, knotted designs are often associated with floral themes especially the lotus. Flowers fill a triangular leaf on a thick trunk to become an imaginary vegetal form, the lotus tree, found in Firuzabad and on royal and elite tombs, or schematized to a surface for decoration; alternatively, flowers can be used as a scroll or vine (p. 2). They can be depicted alone, or are associated with banana buds that recur in all manner of decorative formations. Those on the apex of the arch tend to follow a winged movement, which was further emphasized during the Adil Shahi and Qutb Shahi periods when tendrils and intricate arabesques expanded outwards in a symmetrical movement (figure 1). To these vegetal themes we must add leaf forms, which could be arranged in a geometric configuration in order to fill a medallion or roundel, or repeated on a vault. Indeed, domes, semi-domes, apses, and vaults provided excellent opportunities for the display of various decorative themes that are otherwise unknown in other locations. Vaults were often decorated with repeated bands, which imitate timber structures, as do flat radiating bands on apses (figures 2, 3; pp. 69, 73, figures 4, 11). Indeed, the imitation of timber structures in vaults is one of the recurrent themes in Bahmani and Adil Shahi plasterwork, as also in carved stonework; such designs are among the finest examples of stucco ornamentation we have from the Sultanate period. Designs comprising radiating lines are known in Bahmani and later monuments, while curving rays are found both on Adil Shahi and Mughal domes. Open-flower motifs and fanlike or cobweb designs in an undulating movement can be seen both on Bahmani and later examples, while geometric configurations recalling muqarnas or beehive arrangements, often interspersed with open-flower motifs, appear on Nizam Shahi, Qutb Shahi, and Mughal buildings (pp. 60, 88, 97, figures 5, 1, 11).

Two vegetal themes in plasterwork are found on Nizam Shahi monuments; both are distinguished by austere abstract forms. The first theme appears to be an abridged rendering of the lotus tree with a stylized triangular leaf on a thin, long stem that fills kite-shaped pendentives, as in the Kalawantinicha Mahal (p. 65, figure 12). The second theme consists of broad, slightly curved, cobra-like leaves, used to smooth the angular crossing from one surface to another, as in the facade of the Hasht Behesht. Yet a third theme is the chain with a hanging lotus or medallion, rendered in different sizes and shapes. This last theme is first attested on the mihrabs of Bahmani funerary monuments, crossing over to the courtly domain at some date during the second half of the 15th century, as attested at the Prince's Palace in Bidar (p. 52, figure 11).

Plaster was used to highlight specific areas of Bahmani architecture, usually arches and domes, thereby enhancing the robust appearance of buildings. During the 15th century, however, there was a tendency to unify spaces by using overall decorative themes in different techniques,

116 HELEN PHILON

thus obliterating form in favour of texture. To this array of decorative themes, the vase with a tree-shaped ornament was introduced during the same period. This is rendered in stucco, on ceramic panels, and also painted in a vibrant palette on the walls of Ahmad Shah's tomb in Ashtur, outside Bidar. A further attestation to this tendency to stress texture over form is the adoption of the arched theme to decorate the walls of the palace of the Qutb Shahis in Golconda and later those of the Mughals in Daulatabad (pp. 82, 83, figures 5, 6). Here, wall surfaces have numerous niches of different sizes in order to create a "fictive" space. The Nizam Shahis adopted this same pattern at Farah Bakhsh Bagh near Ahmadnagar. Here, arched forms with rectangular openings are combined with differently sized arched niches, creating an interplay of light and shade (p. 59, figure 4).

In the courtly domains of the Adil Shahis, decoration reverts to a traditional emphasis of architectural forms, and designs are used to highlight specific architectural features. On the spandrels of the monumental arch of the Gagan Mahal in Bijapur, figural motifs form part of an elaborate composition consisting of a medallion on brackets. The sinuous movement of these brackets that can take the form of an upside-down fish is repeated in other bracket designs in Bijapur, Ahmadnagar, and Golconda. This bracket motif is yet another design that is recorded on Bahmani tombs from c. 1500, suggesting that, like the chain motif, it too migrated from funerary to courtly architecture (pp. 67, 68, figures 2, 3). The other birds and quadrupeds on the Gagan Mahal brackets are modelled in high relief, while the medallions are decorated with deeply carved intersecting axial designs. The latter repeat fleshy vegetal forms, and echo the influence of themes found on textiles and Chinese porcelains. The deep and delicate, lace-like plaster carving on the medallions recalls examples in stone, suggesting an interaction between the two materials. This is further corroborated by a second style shared by both plasterwork and stone, in which vegetal and other motifs are rendered in a broad flat manner (p. 72, figure 10).

Plaster figural motifs in high relief would seem to continue early Bahmani traditions, as a similar rendering is found on the large, leonine creatures that adorn the spandrels of the arched gate in Firuzabad (p. 42, figure 11). Aside from leonine animals, which were also depicted together with elephants on stone-carved elements, birds too were represented. These were rendered in either a naturalistic style, as attested in Bidar and during the Adil Shahi period, or in a more stylized linear fashion, as recorded in Sultanpur.

Woodwork

Sadly, little remains of the timber architecture of the Deccan, but the elements that contributed to it – columns, pilasters, capitals, brackets, chhajjas, vaults, and ceilings – were so often imitated in stone and plaster that the memory of timber construction remains very much alive. During the early Bahmani period, a combination of timber and stone was used for buildings of a more private nature, which were distinguished by simple tripartite layouts, while an architecture of solely stone construction was the prerogative of important ceremonial structures, such as the Hazar Sutun in Gulbarga. The introduction of the expanded tripartite format for buildings of overarching ceremonial importance during the later Bahmanis reintroduced the usage of timber and stone as the paired materials worthy of courtly structures.

The earliest surviving examples of timber decorative elements in the sultanate palaces of the Deccan are the remains of the engaged columns, capitals, and ceilings in the Bahmani palace in Daulatabad (p. 56, figure 1). Plain pilasters support tiered capitals with carved, overhanging banana-bud motifs, framed by four leaves, which adjoin brackets supporting the beams of the timber ceiling. Temple-type engaged columns framing arched doors and niches consist of cuboids alternating with long-necked, bulbous vase-forms.

The best-preserved example of woodwork in the expanded tripartite palace format can be seen in the Rangini Mahal in Bidar Fort (figure 3; p. 53, figure 12). The free-standing square timber columns of the mandapa support round, tiered capitals carved with varied motifs on which rest brackets with overhanging buds that support coffered ceilings. The ceilings are decorated with dense, leafy, spiralling scrolls that expand outwards from central flowers. These same scrolls are also present on the sides of the brackets, while others show a sinuous stem on which a fleshy lotus and peony flowers have been carved. Remains of blue, black, and yellow pigments suggest that the woodwork in this mandapa was once painted in various colours. On both sides of the mandapa are rooms with pyramidal timber vaults carved with arabesques in a flat style and square Kufi inscriptions (figure 3). They constitute the only surviving evidence of the timber vaults that inspired the many plaster examples that we have from Bahmani and Adil Shahi palaces.

From the Adil Shahi period, we have only isolated examples of timber elements. The best known are the columns and ceiling of the double-height portico to the Asar Mahal, the originals of which are now lying in the courtyard adjoining the palace.

Carved Stonework

A particularly distinctive feature of the

3 Bidar. Rangini Mahal, 1543–80. Timber pyramidal vault carved with leaf motifs, foliate designs, and "Muhammad" in square, Kufi writing.

Deccan palaces is the use of black basalt and dolerite. These hard, unyielding stones were carved into geometric, foliate, knotted, and vase-shaped designs in either a crisp or a flat, bevelled style (figure 4). Those responsible for these carvings were craftsmen brought up in the age-old traditions of local temple structures. However, inscriptions in the fluid, elegant, but bold style of writing peculiar to the Deccan are rare in Bahmani palaces, and thus this extraordinary calligraphic virtuosity did not contribute to the artistry of Bahmani palace architecture at all.

In Bahmani palaces, stonework with carved designs frames arches and adorns the temple-type pilasters that flank arched entrances (often in a recession of planes); dolerite footings serve as bases for timber columns. A totally new use of basalt, first recorded in Palaces I and II in Bidar, is represented by strings of carved or plain basalt, which outline the ceramic panels that once adorned the walls (p. 49, figure 7). On the capitals and bases of faceted pilasters, deeply carved, crisp arabesques, floral and knotted patterns can be seen (figure 4; p. 52, figure 10), while on the thick rounded courses that frame architectural elements, a flat bevelled carving has often been applied. This latter style is probably modelled on decorative themes from Seljuq-period Anatolia. The plausibility of this hypothesis is suggested by the immigrants from Rum (Anatolia), who were responsible for introducing into the Deccan the hammam and "cross-in-square-plan" audience hall, such as in Firuzabad.

One of the finest examples of stone-carved revetments can be seen in the Jalamandir in Bijapur (p. 75, figure 13). This multi-storeyed miniature pavilion sits in the middle of a square pool. It is raised on a podium with sinuous bracket supports, and culminates in an onion-shaped dome surrounded by stone petals and framed by four fluted, guldasta pinnacles. Moving upwards, each design is repeated at a smaller scale on the facade, the ascent being marked by two chhajjas carried on elaborately carved brackets. The basalt revetments that cover the stone surface of this building are carved with arched niches. Each of these niches has a chain and a hanging ornament motif, as well as open-flower lotus patterns and brackets with overhanging buds – exactly as in the wood-carved examples of the Rangini Mahal in Bidar, thus further testifying to the influence and interaction of different materials throughout the Sultanate period. In Bijapur, the crisp carving of the Jalamandir is replaced by a flat depiction of scrolls, cyprus trees, bottles, and fruits at the Pani Mahal (p. 1; p. 72, figure 10).

Inlaid stonework in the Deccan is rarely found prior to the Mughal period. There are, however, two examples that allow us a glimpse at the virtuosity of Deccani craftsmen. The first and oldest example is in Room C of Palace I in Bidar, which has a pavement consisting of a radiating pattern of octagons and star shapes (p. 47, figure 5). The other example is in the throne-room of Ali Barid in the Rangini Mahal. This is the only known occurrence of mother-of-pearl set into polished basalt, a technique that, according to Klaus Rötzer, may have originated in the inlaid designs that decorated the cannons of the Baridis (figures 5, 6). The spiralling foliate scrolls that originate from beneath a leaf shape on the spandrels of the arches here resemble those on the brackets supporting the coffered wooden ceilings, offering yet another example of decorative motifs shared between different materials. In this luminous and sumptuous inlaid mother-of-pearl panel are inscribed poetic verses evoking in mystical terms the grandeur of Ali Barid, the founder of the palace.

Glazed Tilework

Surely the most spectacularly colourful example of decoration in any of the Deccani palaces is that created by glazed tilework. A variety of themes is found

4 Bidar. Palace II, c. 1440. Knotted and foliate themes carved on stone engaged columns.

5 Bidar. Rangini Mahal, 1543–80. Mother-of-pearl inlaid on basalt.

ARCHITECTURAL DECORATION 119

here: vases displaying flowers within arched forms; geometric compositions; cloud motifs with enclosed flower designs, evincing the influence of Chinese patterns; and quatrefoils laid out within a grid that extends both horizontally and vertically. These motifs on underglaze, polychrome ceramic panels are among the patterns that once embellished the wall panels of the Bahmani palaces in Bidar and those of their successors the Baridis (figure 6). Other designs show square Kufi calligraphy aligned between parallel lines, and vertically disposed oak leaves. All these motifs were painted in blue, green, white, and yellow underglaze colours, with occasional strokes of a red pigment. Yellow is not a colour that is known in the ceramics of western Islam, but the red pigment has a long history in both Syria and Iran; it is also recorded on Syrian-Egyptian ceramics inspired by Chinese designs, and rendered in a local palette. The designs on the tiles in Bidar are preserved solely in the photographs in Ghulam Yazdani's monograph on the city: they have otherwise mysteriously disappeared. Their decorative repertoire testifies to the international contacts of the Bahmani rulers, who must have encouraged gifted artists and artisans from West Asia to settle in the Deccan.

Although underglaze painted ceramics, to which the colour red is occasionally added, may be traced to West Asia, the mosaic technique employed to model the sun-and-tiger motif on the spandrels of the pishtaq towers in Palace II at Bidar has antecedents in both Iran and Central Asia (p. 49, figure 7). In Palace II, hexagonal or rectangular tiles in blue, yellow, and turquoise glazes have been skilfully assembled to create an emblem of royal power. Responsibility for encouraging the introduction of this technique from Central Asia could lie with Mahmud Gawan (1458–82), prime minister in the later Bahmani period, especially as this technique is also attested on the walls of his madrasa in Bidar.

6 Bidar. Rangini Mahal, 1543–80. Polychrome-underglaze painted tile panels framed by engaged basalt colonettes inlaid with mother-of-pearl.

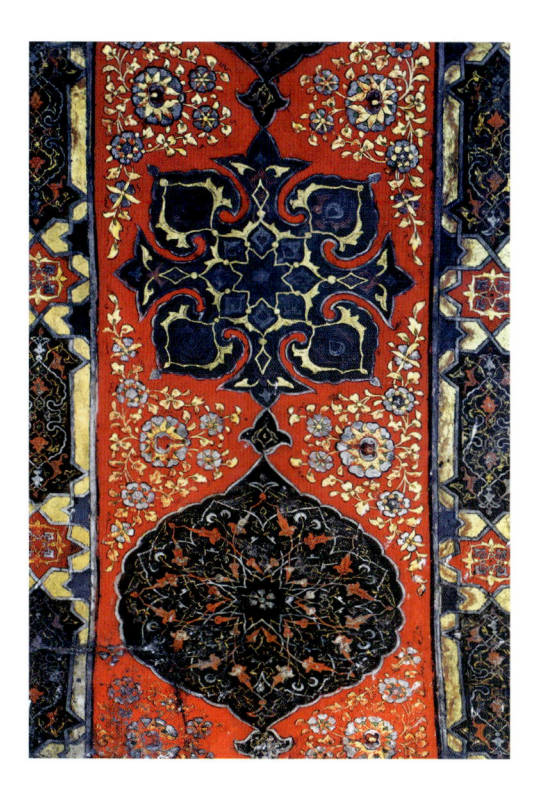

7 Bidar. Tomb of Ahmad Shah, 1436. Detail of painting of star-shapes and lobed medallions on arch.

Ceramic compositions also survive in the rooms that adjoin the mandapa in the Rangini Mahal in Bidar. Here, the colours are mostly blue, green, yellow, and white. Intersecting ribbon-like lattices in white and mustard enclose fleshy flowers that grow on sinuous tendrils. Together with the mother-of-pearl-inlaid designs in the throne-room of this palace, they evoke the luminous and sumptuous world of the Deccani sultans.

Murals

The only surviving painted decorations in Bidar are the faint remains of the designs on the dome of the Gumbad Darwaza and the numerous drawings in black in Palace II. The leafy forms seen on these walls recall murals in the tomb of Ahmad Shah, as do the painted designs on the dome of the Gumbad Darwaza. The latter are closely related to the ornaments embellishing the dome of Ahmad Shah's tomb, suggesting that the same artists probably worked on both monuments (figure 7). The painted compositions in Ahmad Shah's tomb and the Gumbad Darwaza can be linked to the Timurid school of painting. The dispersal of artists from the royal kitabkhana of Samarkand following the decree of Ulugh Beg in 1411 – and later from Shiraz, Iran, after the death of Iskender Sultan in 1414 – contributed to the spread of artistic forms and designs throughout the Islamic cultural sphere. It was painters from these schools who, in search of patrons, reached the Bahmani kingdom as well as that of the Ottomans in Turkey. These artists established new schools of painting with shared visual styles and repertoires, as is suggested by the star ornaments found in the murals of the tomb of Ahmad Shah and the Star Ushak carpets from Anatolia (figure 7).

There are no surviving murals on the palaces of the Qutb Shahis or Nizam Shahis, although there is an abundance of paintings from both courts. According to Marika Sardar (p. 87), the entrances to the iwans in the palaces of Golconda were painted with likenesses of the ruler and his peers during the religious festivals in Hyderabad. There are, however, murals from the Adil Shahi period. These are found in the Asar Mahal in Bijapur, originally built as an audience hall before its conversion into a sacred reliquary in 1646. Compositions of bejewelled, rotund courtly ladies in transparent garments caught in various activities with their attendants allow us a glimpse into the private life of the sultans (p. 72, figure 9). According to Mark Zebrowski, the crowded scenes and shaded limbs of the figures in various postures should not be credited to European artists, as had once been proposed. The Asar Mahal murals are more likely to have been the work of Deccani painters familiar with European examples, thanks to prints or other visual documents that reached the Bijapur court. (The existence of European models is further implied by the trompe-l'oeil, relief, and painted representations of books depicted on the mihrab of the Jami Mosque in Bijapur.) In another chamber of the Asar Mahal, the decorative scheme is less ebullient, but perhaps more elegant. Chinese-looking vases and glass containers, painted in gold and filled with luminous flowers, are contained within arched niches. The niches are surrounded by flowering creepers, though these motifs are probably much later, perhaps even dating from the 19th century (p. 71, figures 7, 8).

Further evidence of mural paintings is seen in one of the pavilions at Kumatgi; these, however, are in a poor condition and difficult to comprehend. Here, again, courtly scenes are depicted, a theme perfectly suited to the recreational activities that must have taken place in this garden resort, and which closely relate to examples in contemporary painting (p. 111, figure 7).

PLANS

Klaus Rötzer

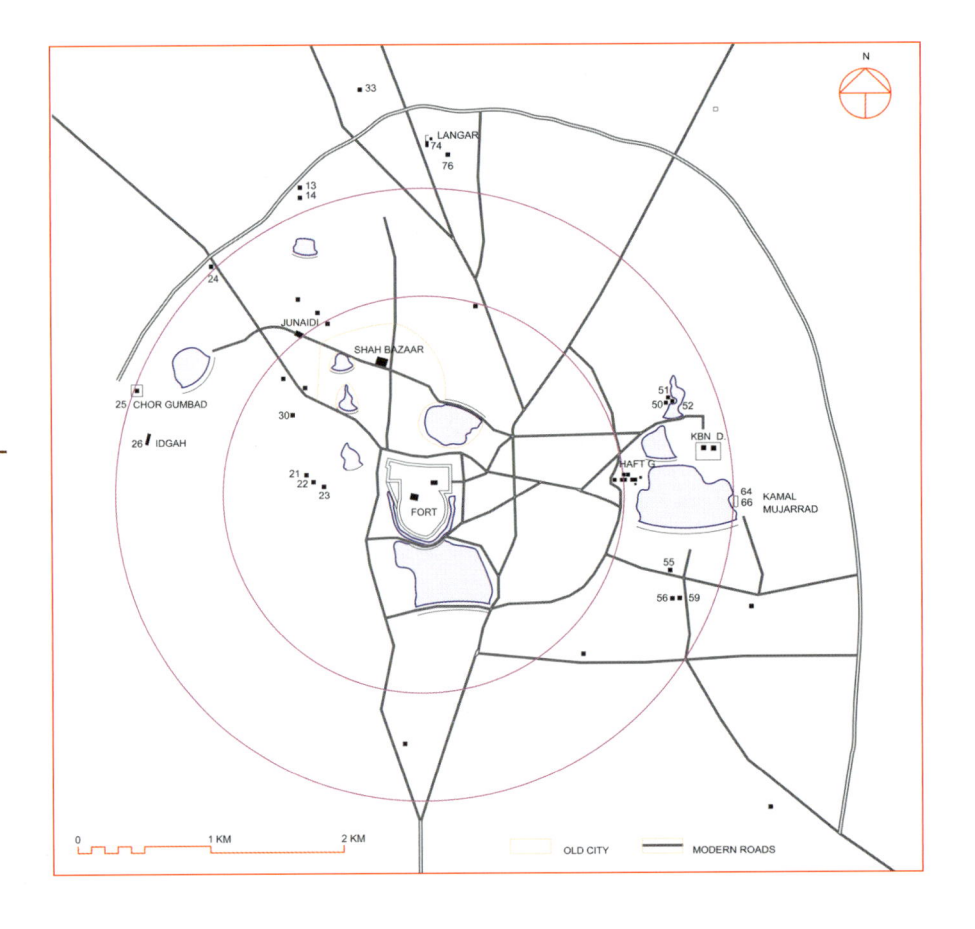

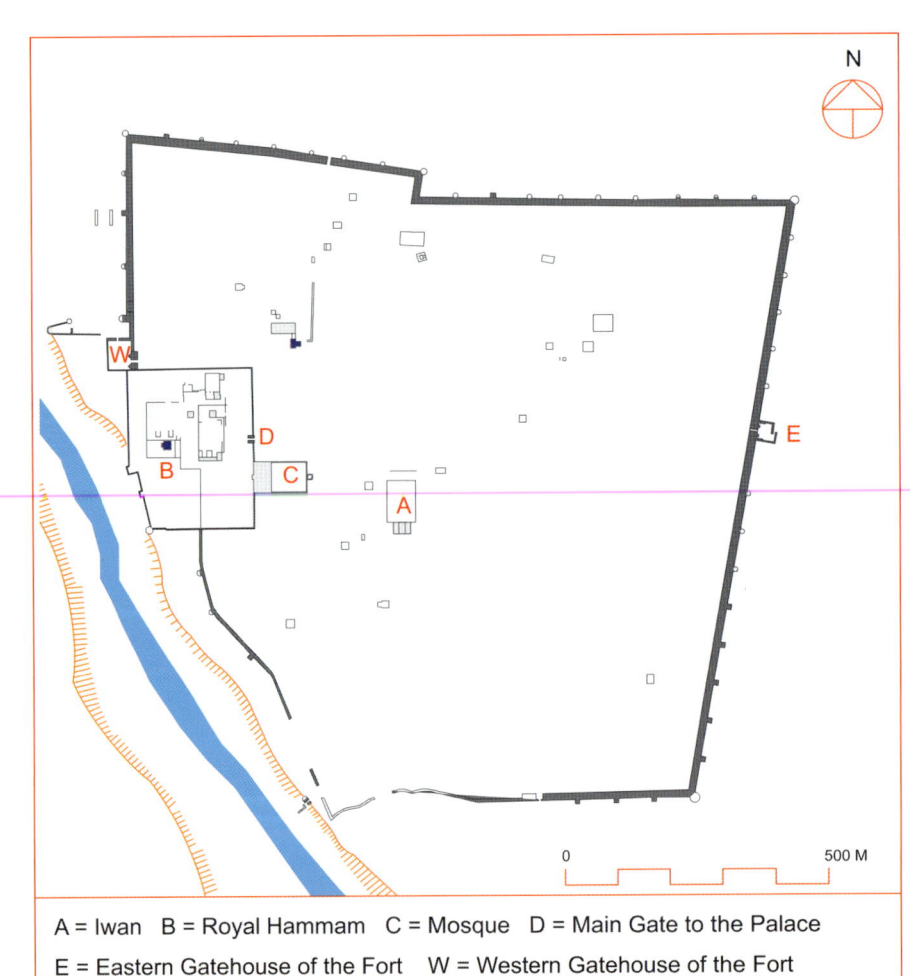

Plan 1 Gulbarga, capital of the Bahmani kingdom, 1350–1432.
The grid indicates the two townships of Gulbarga: northwest is Gulbarga I and east of the fort is Gulbarga II. On the periphery of the circles are the dargahs of Sheikh Junaidi (d. 1380), Kamal Mujarrad (1400s), and Gesu Daraz (c. 1410), KBN, and the royal necropolis of the sultans, the Haft Gumbad.

Plan 2 Firuzabad, the secondary capital of the Bahmanis on the Bhima river, 1400 and later.

A = Iwan   B = Royal Hammam   C = Mosque   D = Main Gate to the Palace
E = Eastern Gatehouse of the Fort   W = Western Gatehouse of the Fort

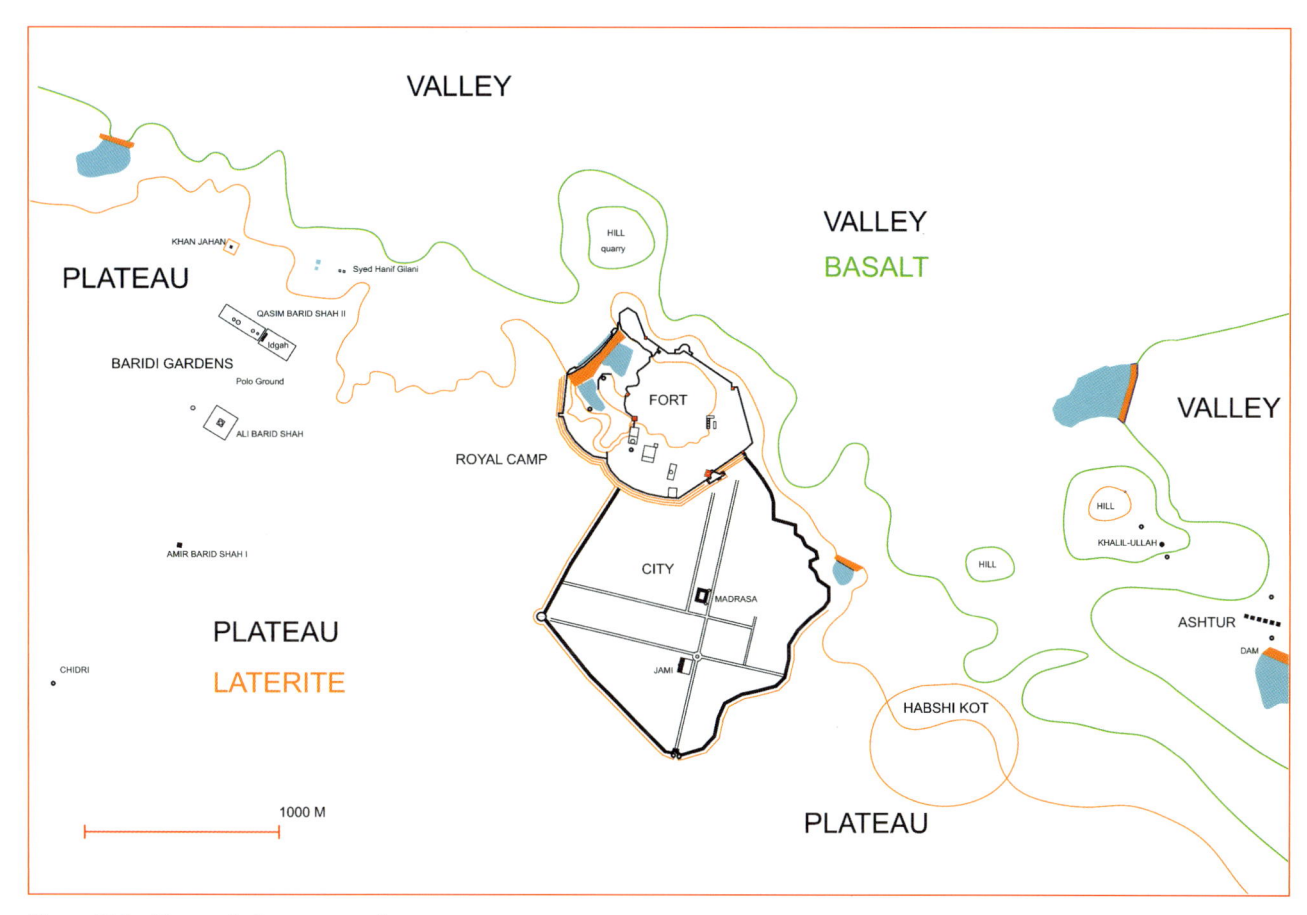

Plan 3 Bidar Fort and city, 1432–19th century.

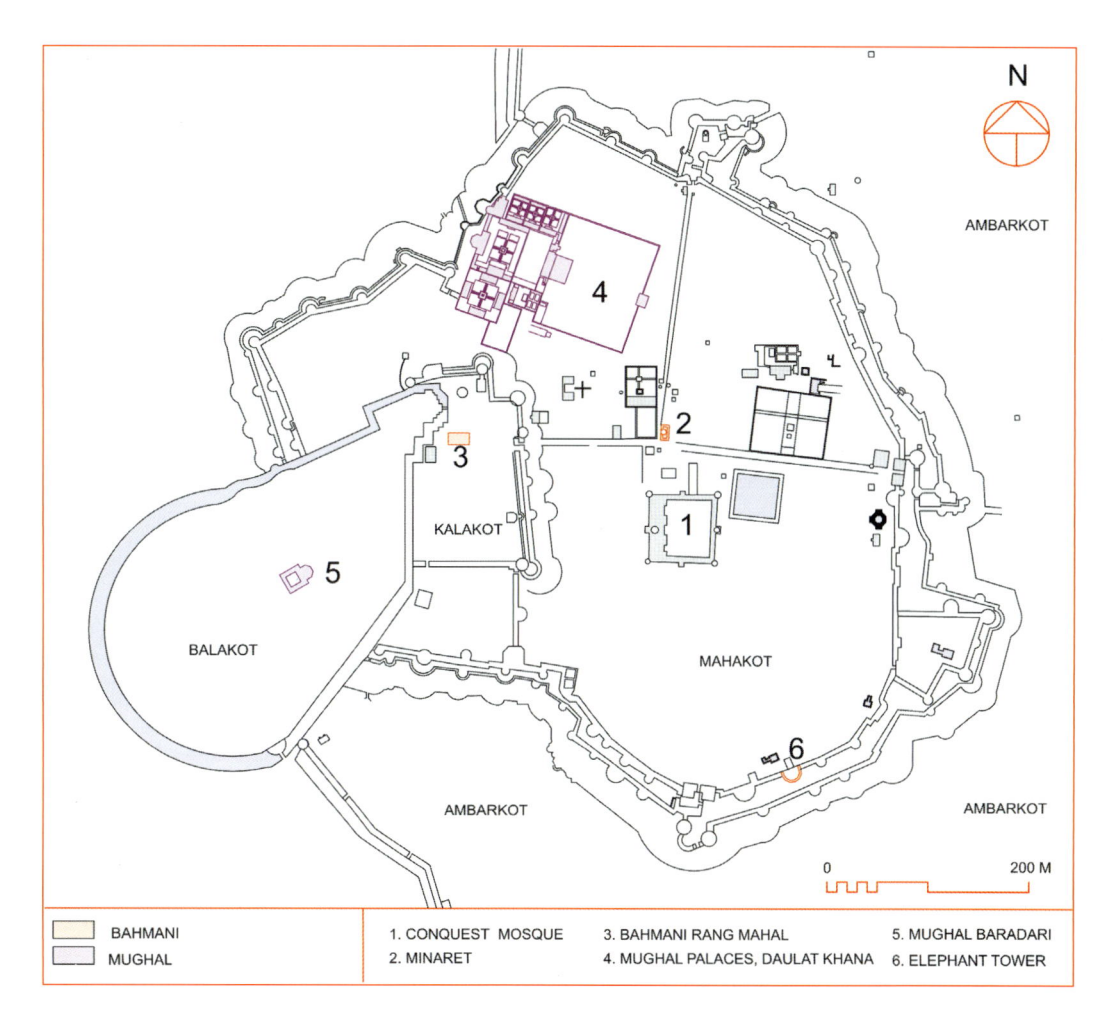

Plan 4 Daulatabad. Fort in blue outline.

BAHMANI
MUGHAL

1. CONQUEST MOSQUE
2. MINARET
3. BAHMANI RANG MAHAL
4. MUGHAL PALACES, DAULAT KHANA
5. MUGHAL BARADARI
6. ELEPHANT TOWER

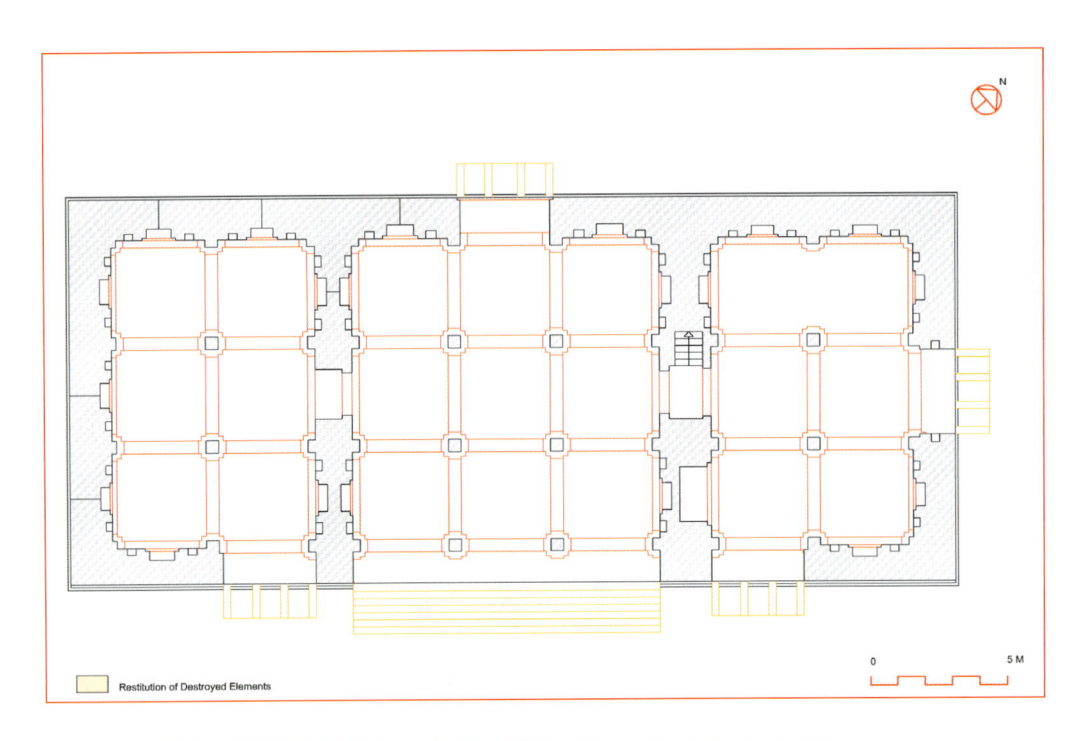

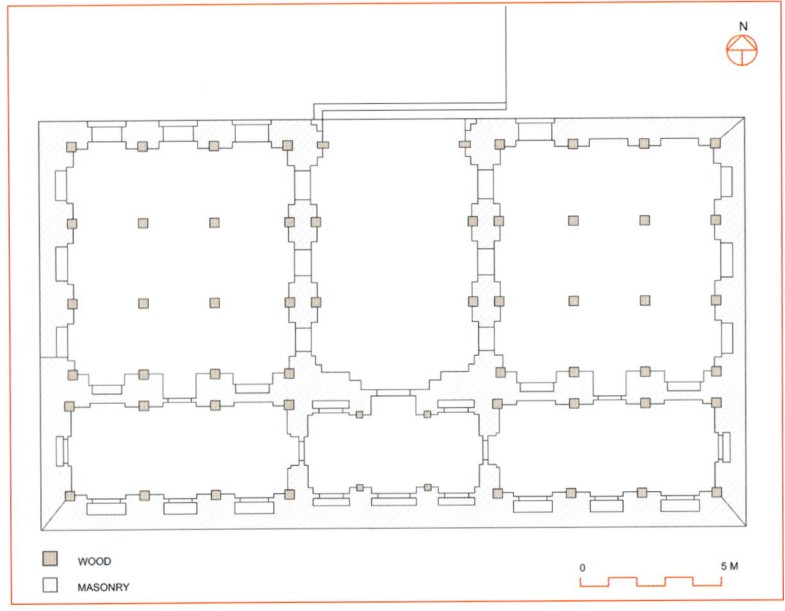

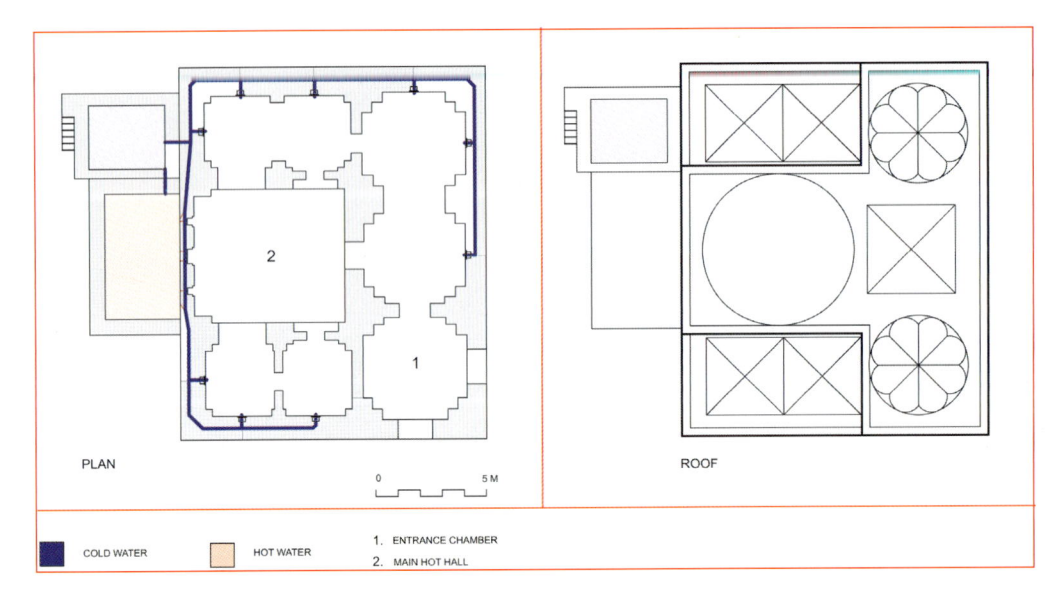

Plan 5 Sultanpur, royal country villa, c. 1410, with balconies in wood on the northwestern, northeastern, and southeastern sides.

Plan 6 Daulatabad, Kalakot, Rang Mahal, c. 1400, see plan 4.

Plan 7 Firuzabad, royal enclosure, hammam, c. 1400.

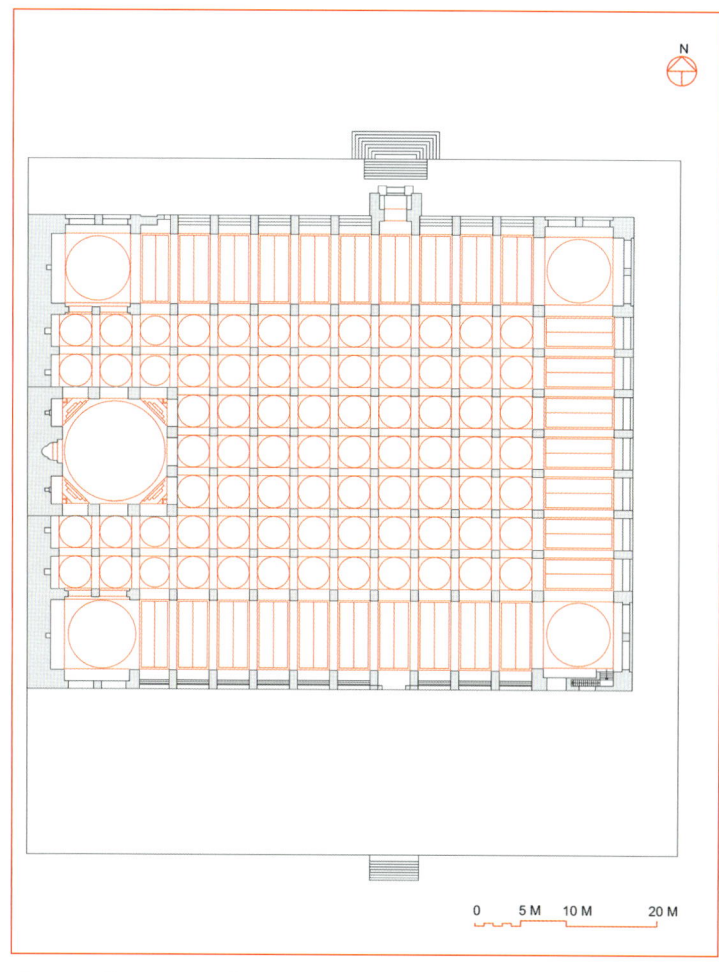

Plan 9 Gulbarga Fort, the Great Mosque identified here as Hazar Sutun, after 1407.

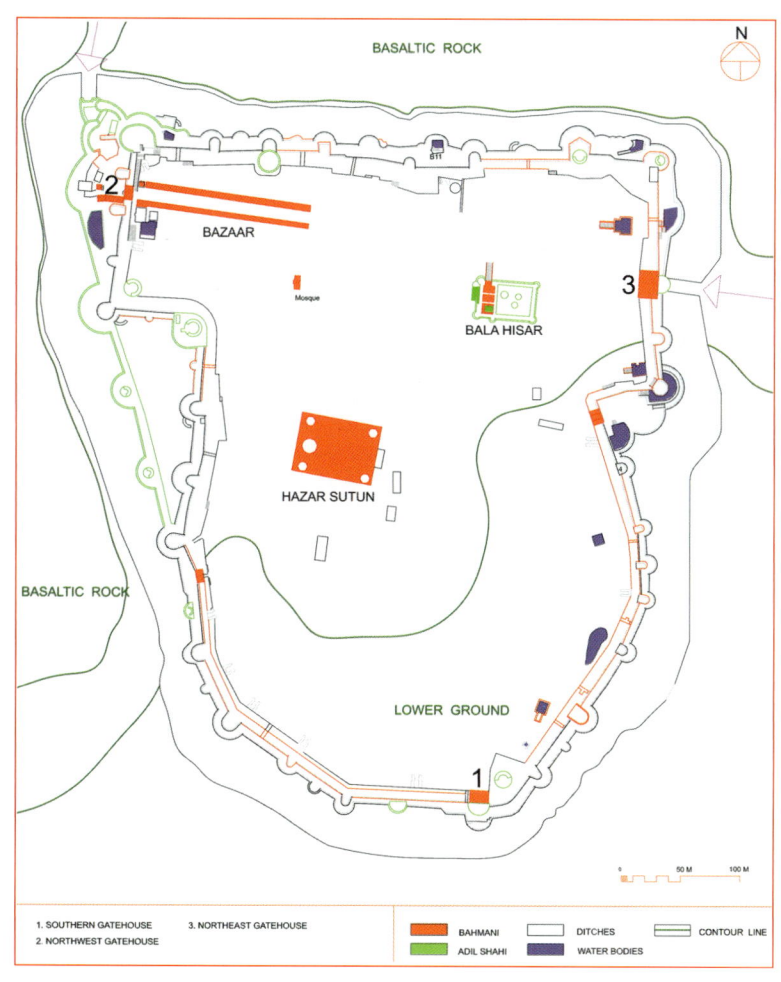

Plan 8 Gulbarga Fort.

PLANS **125**

Plan cut at the level of the guards' platforms

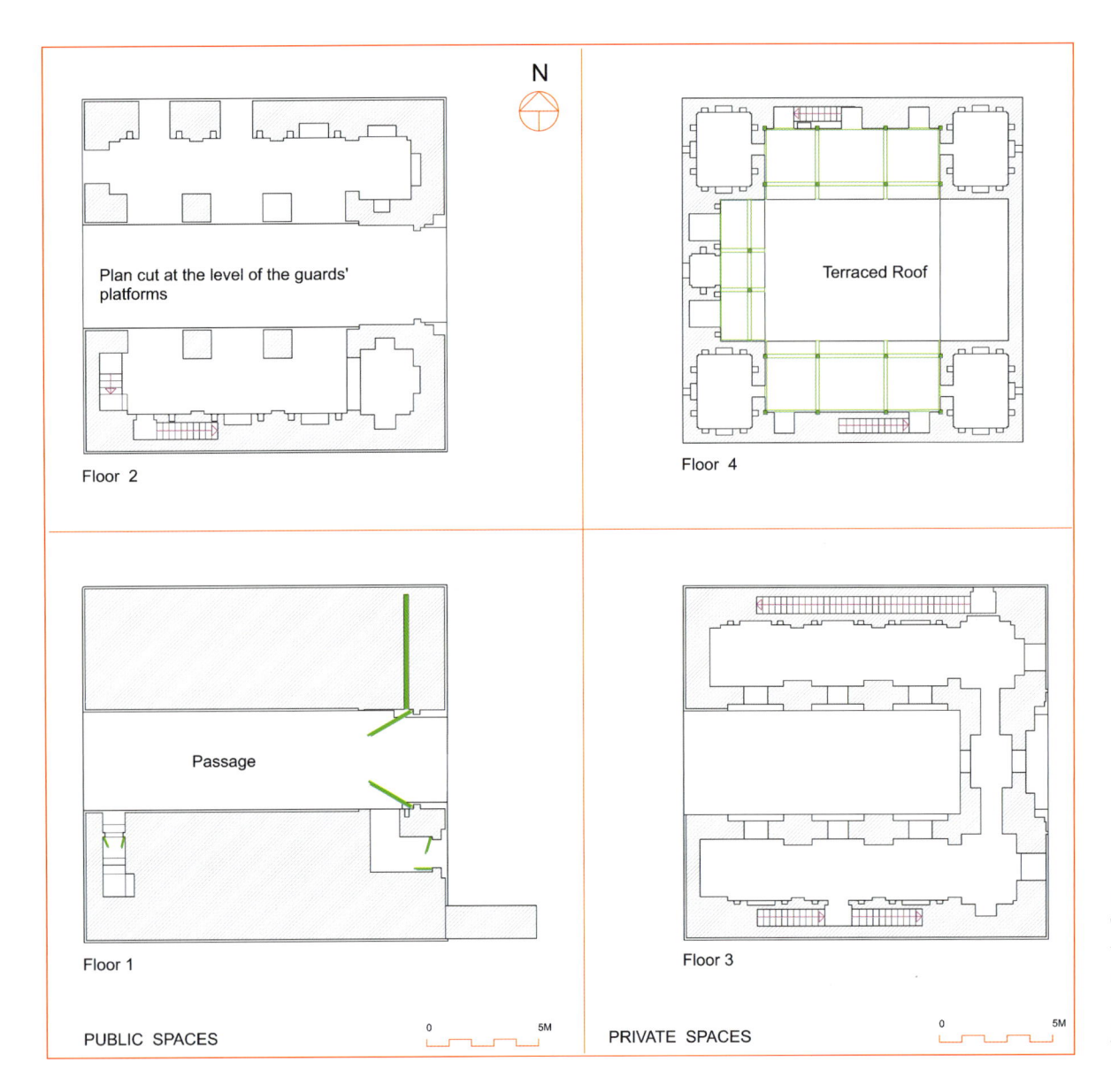

Floor 2

Floor 4 — Terraced Roof

Floor 1 — Passage

Floor 3

PUBLIC SPACES

PRIVATE SPACES

0 5M

Plan 10 Sagar, Shah Darwaza, 1407. On the southeastern corner of the southern platform on floor 2 an elevated cross-shaped area suggests the ceremonial space.

Plan 11 Firuzabad. Dargah of Khalifat al-Rahman, c. 1400. The congregational mosque with adjoining burial chamber is separated from the cross-in-square structure identified here as an audience hall, by a water body.

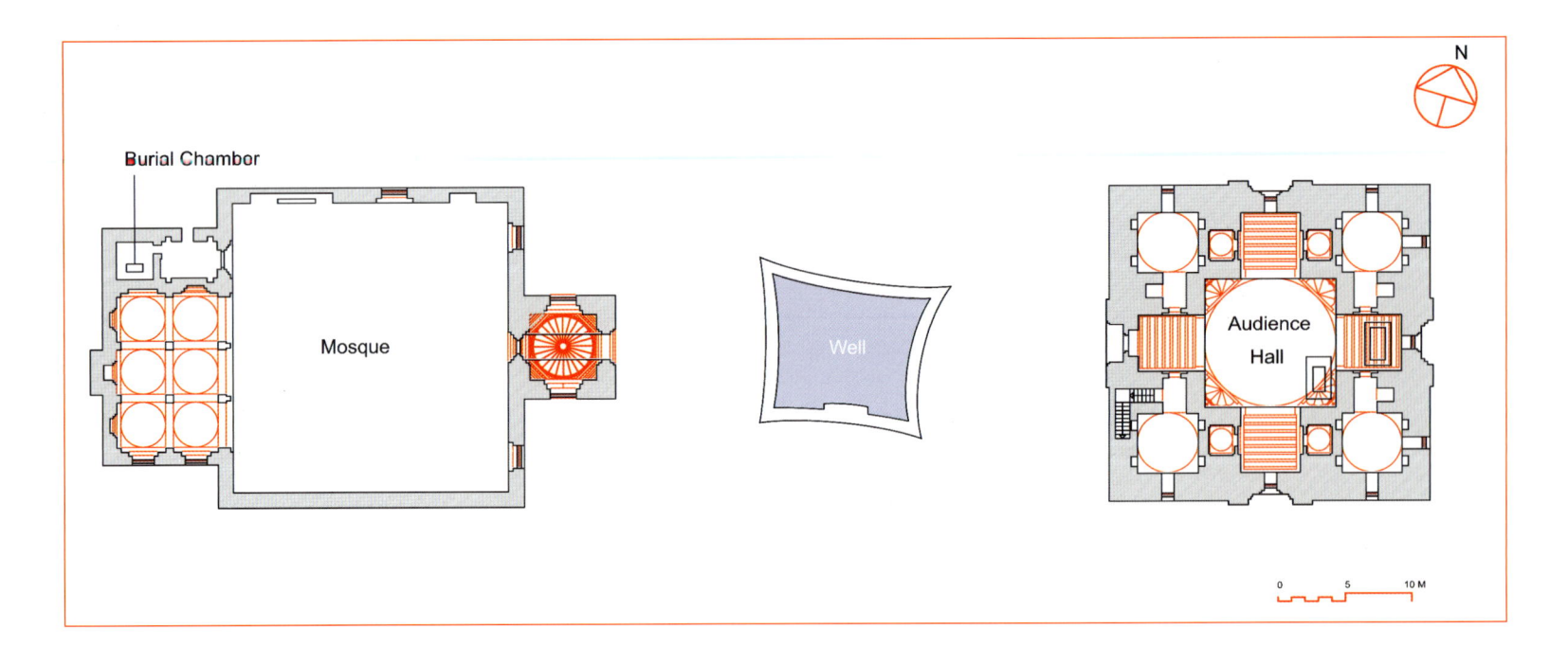

Burial Chamber

Mosque

Well

Audience Hall

0 5 10 M

126 PLANS

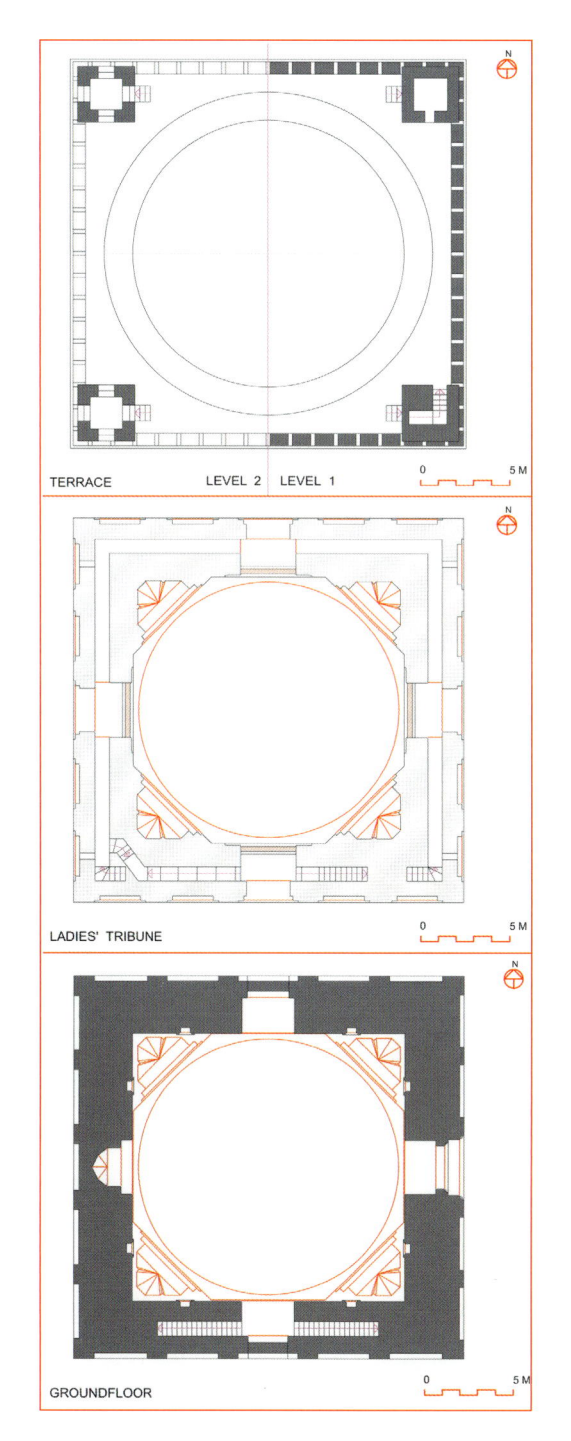

Plan 12 Gulbarga, Chor Gumbad, c. 1430. The corridor that runs around the building is located on the second level, or Ladies' Tribune.

Plan 13 Bidar Fort, the royal enclosure, 1430–80.
1. The fort and the city.
2. The fort at the time of Ahmad Shah Wali (1430–36).
3. The fort at the time of Alauddin (1436–58) and Humayun (1458–61).
4. The fort, c. 1500–c. 1600.

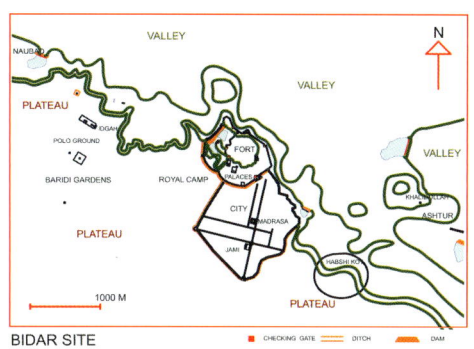

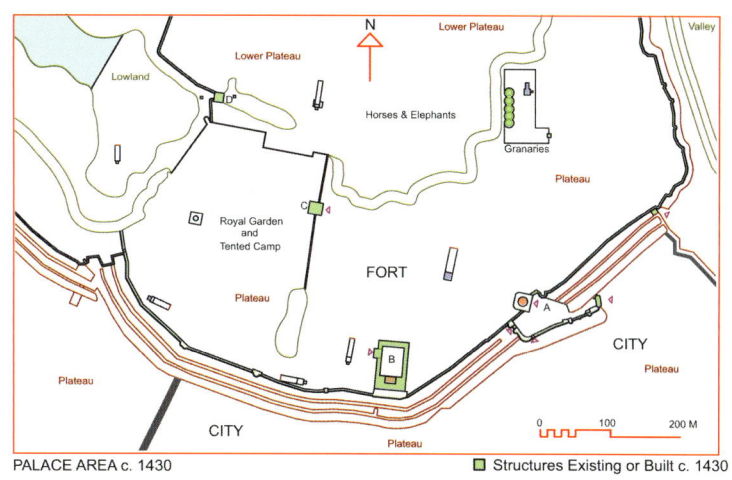

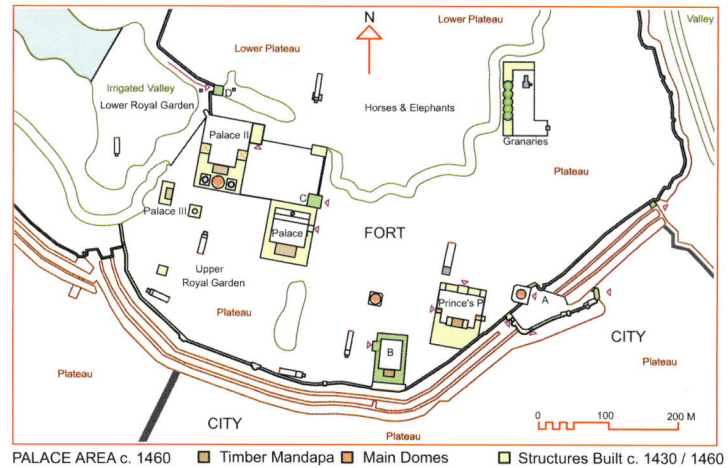

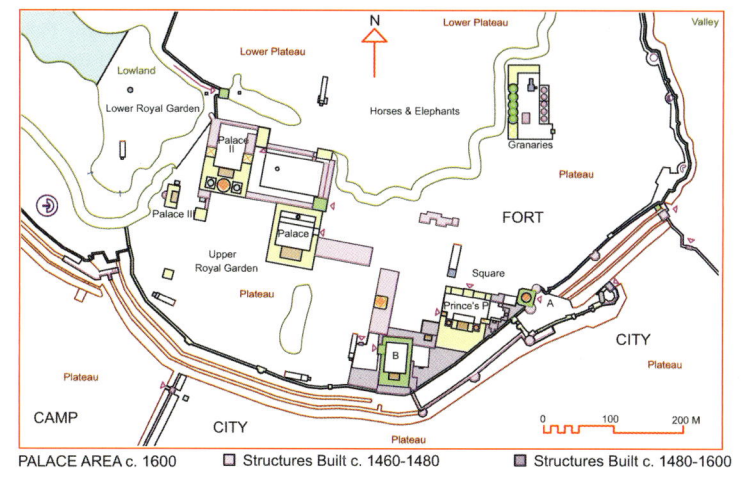

PLANS 127

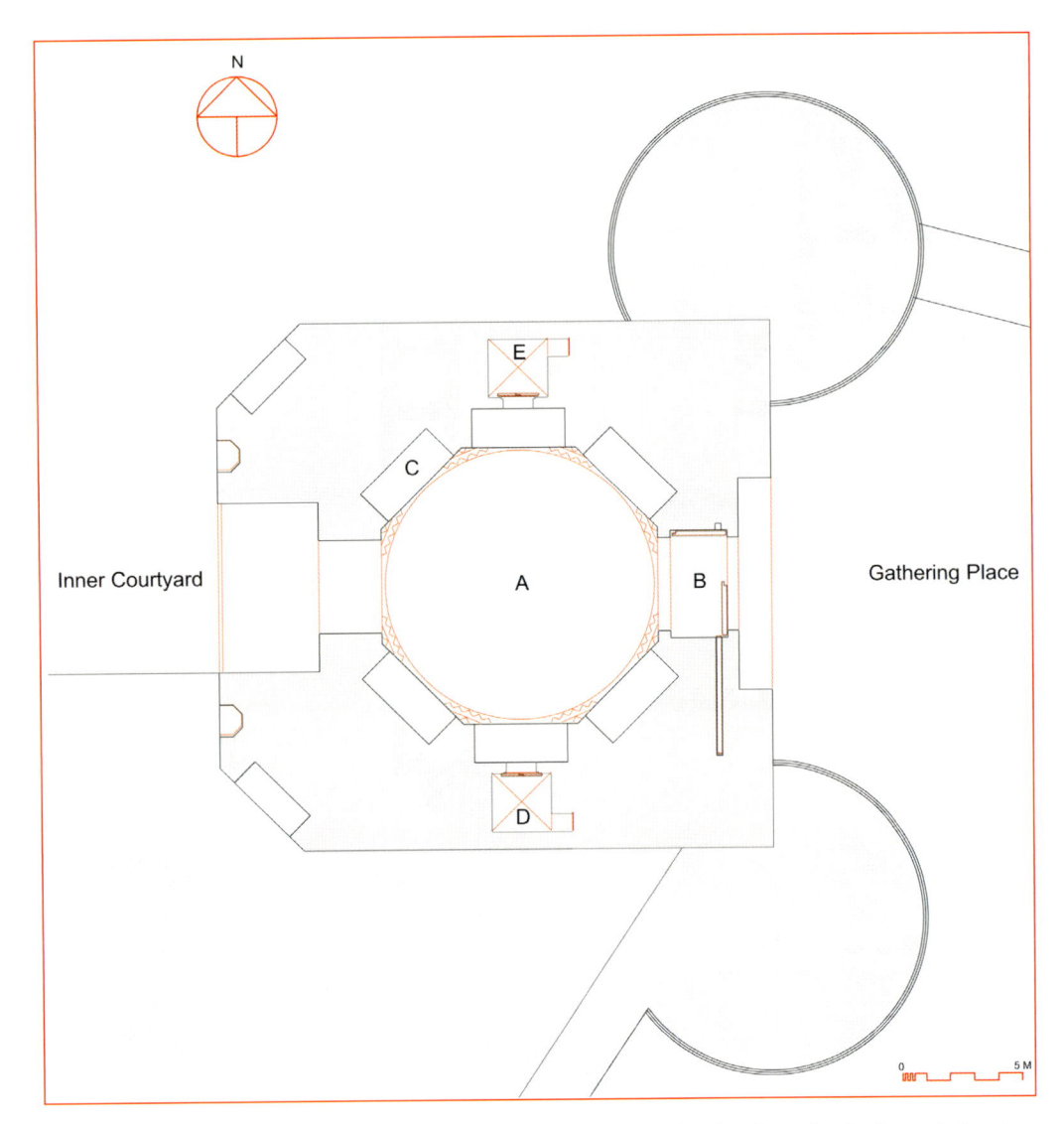

Plan 17 Bidar Fort, Gumbad Darwaza, c. 1436. B is the east-facing facade where the darshan window is located. E and D are two small rooms with pyramidal vaults.

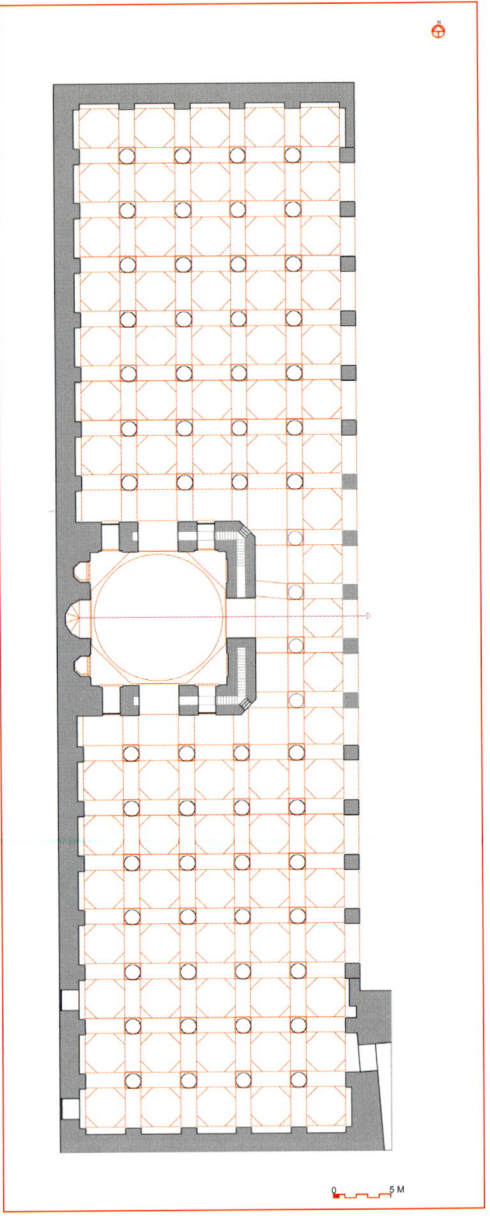

Plan 18 Bidar Fort, southeast palace zone, Solah Khamba Mosque, identified here as a ceremonial pavilion, c. 1460, to which hypostyle halls were added later.

130 PLANS

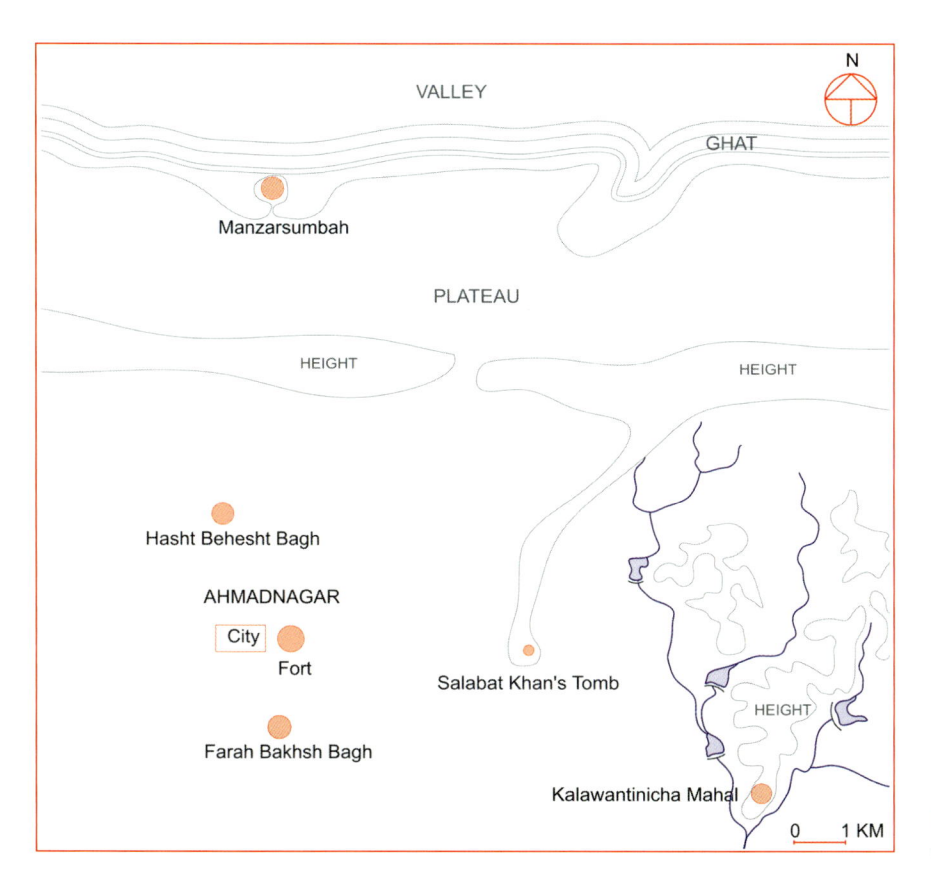

Plan 19 Ahmadnagar Fort and city with royal suburbs, 1490–1636. © Pushkar Sohoni.

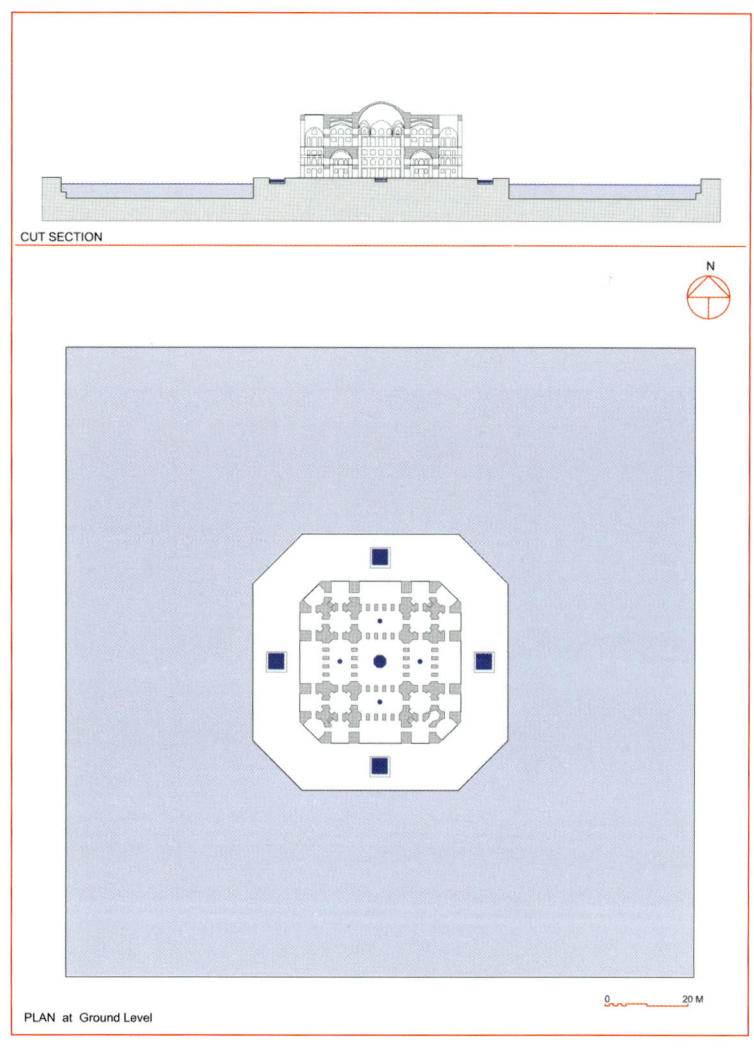

Plan 20 Ahmadnagar, Farah Bakhsh Bagh, 1583. © Pushkar Sohoni.

PLANS **131**

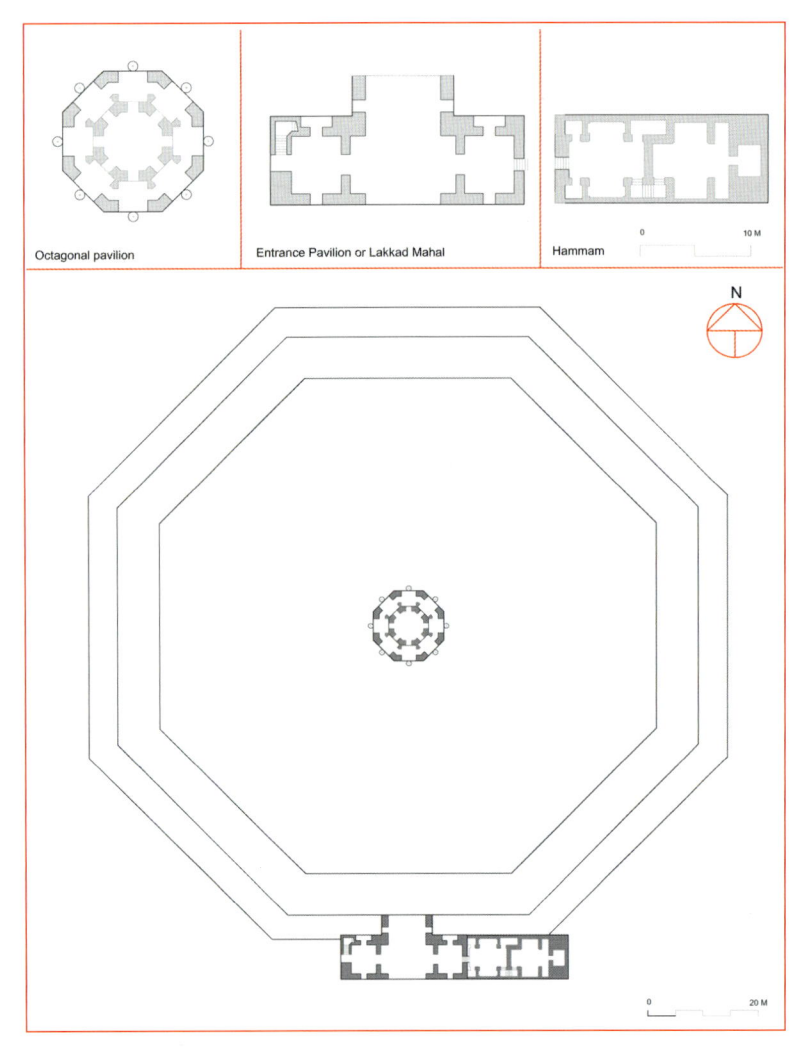

Plan 21 Ahmadnagar, Faiz Bakhsh Bagh or Hasht Behesht, c. 1525–65. © Pushkar Sohoni.

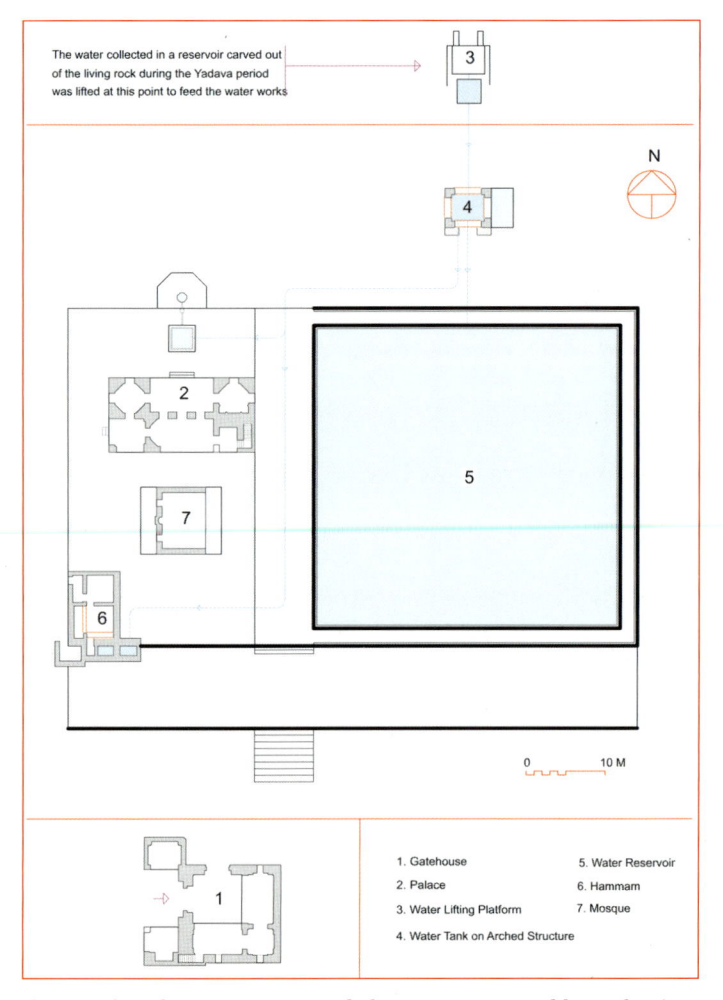

Plan 22 Ahmadnagar, Manzarsumbah, 1525–65. © Pushkar Sohoni.

1. Gatehouse
2. Palace
3. Water Lifting Platform
4. Water Tank on Arched Structure
5. Water Reservoir
6. Hammam
7. Mosque

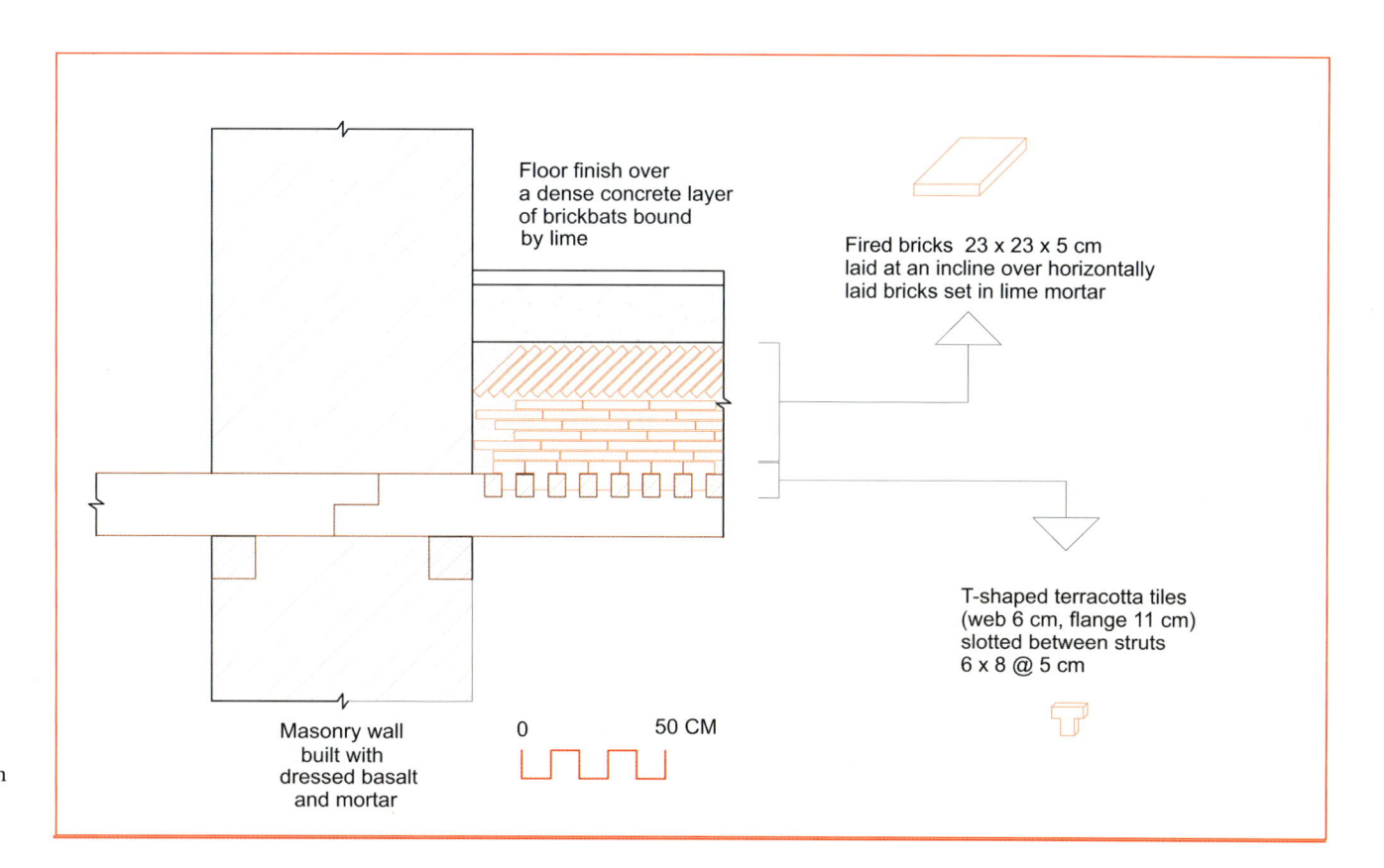

Plan 23 Wall construction, Nizam Shahi period. © Pushkar Sohoni.

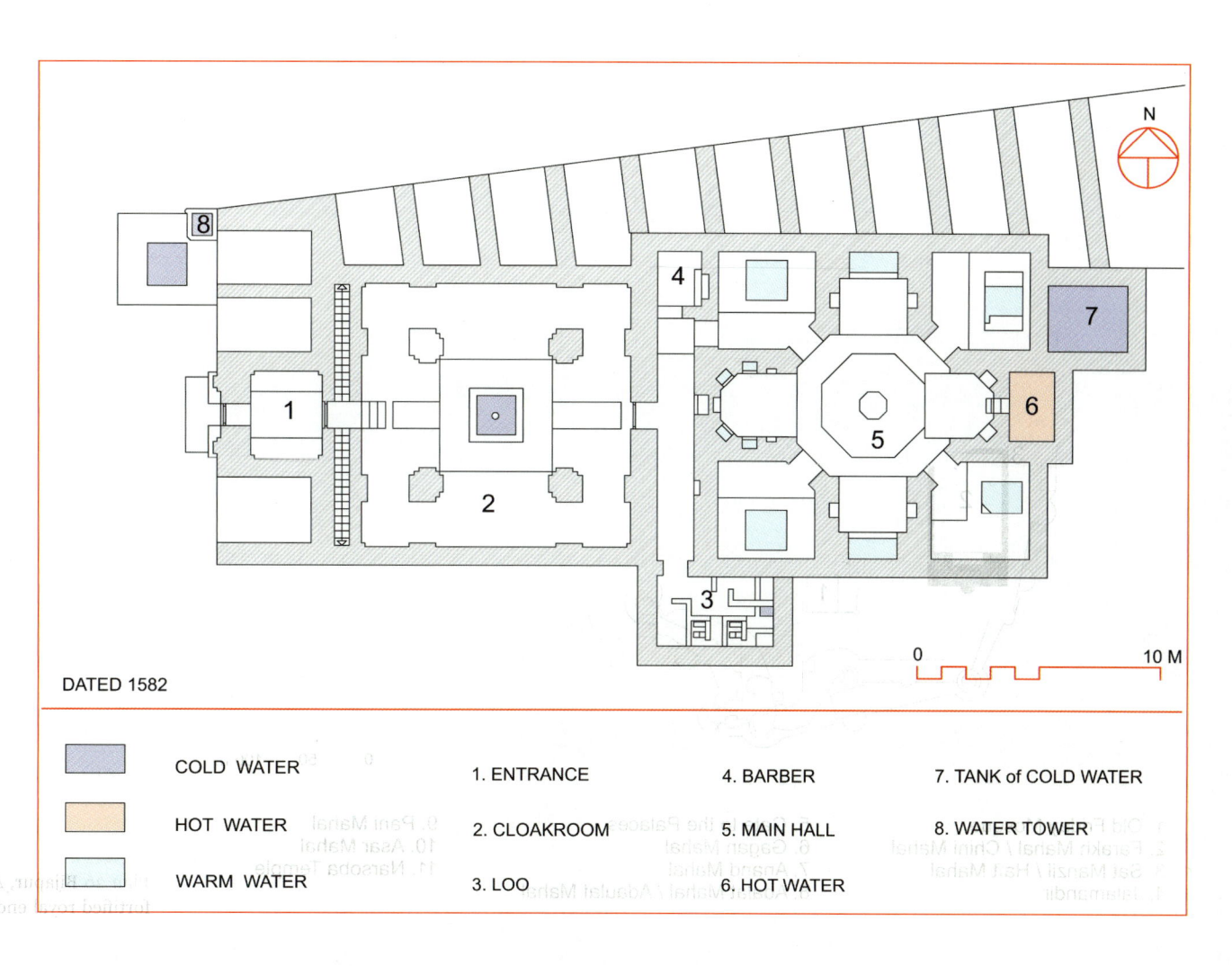

Floor finish over a dense concrete layer of brickbats bound by lime

Fired bricks 23 x 23 x 5 cm laid at an incline over horizontally laid bricks set in lime mortar

T-shaped terracotta tiles (web 6 cm, flange 11 cm) slotted between struts 6 x 8 @ 5 cm

Masonry wall built with dressed basalt and mortar

0   50 CM

Plan 24 Daulatabad, hammam, 1582.

DATED 1582

0   10 M

COLD WATER
HOT WATER
WARM WATER

1. ENTRANCE
2. CLOAKROOM
3. LOO
4. BARBER
5. MAIN HALL
6. HOT WATER
7. TANK of COLD WATER
8. WATER TOWER

PLANS 133

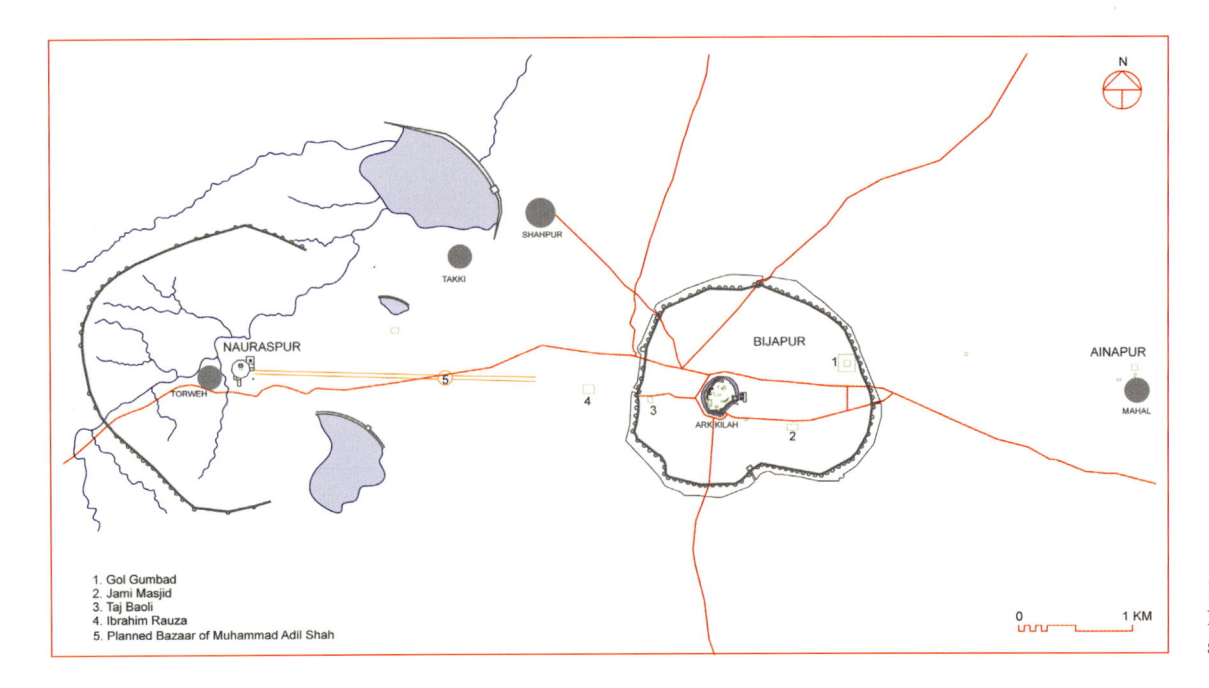

1. Gol Gumbad
2. Jami Masjid
3. Taj Baoli
4. Ibrahim Rauza
5. Planned Bazaar of Muhammad Adil Shah

Plan 25 Bijapur, its secondary capital Nauraspur, 1599–1624, and the royal suburb of Ainapur after 1651.

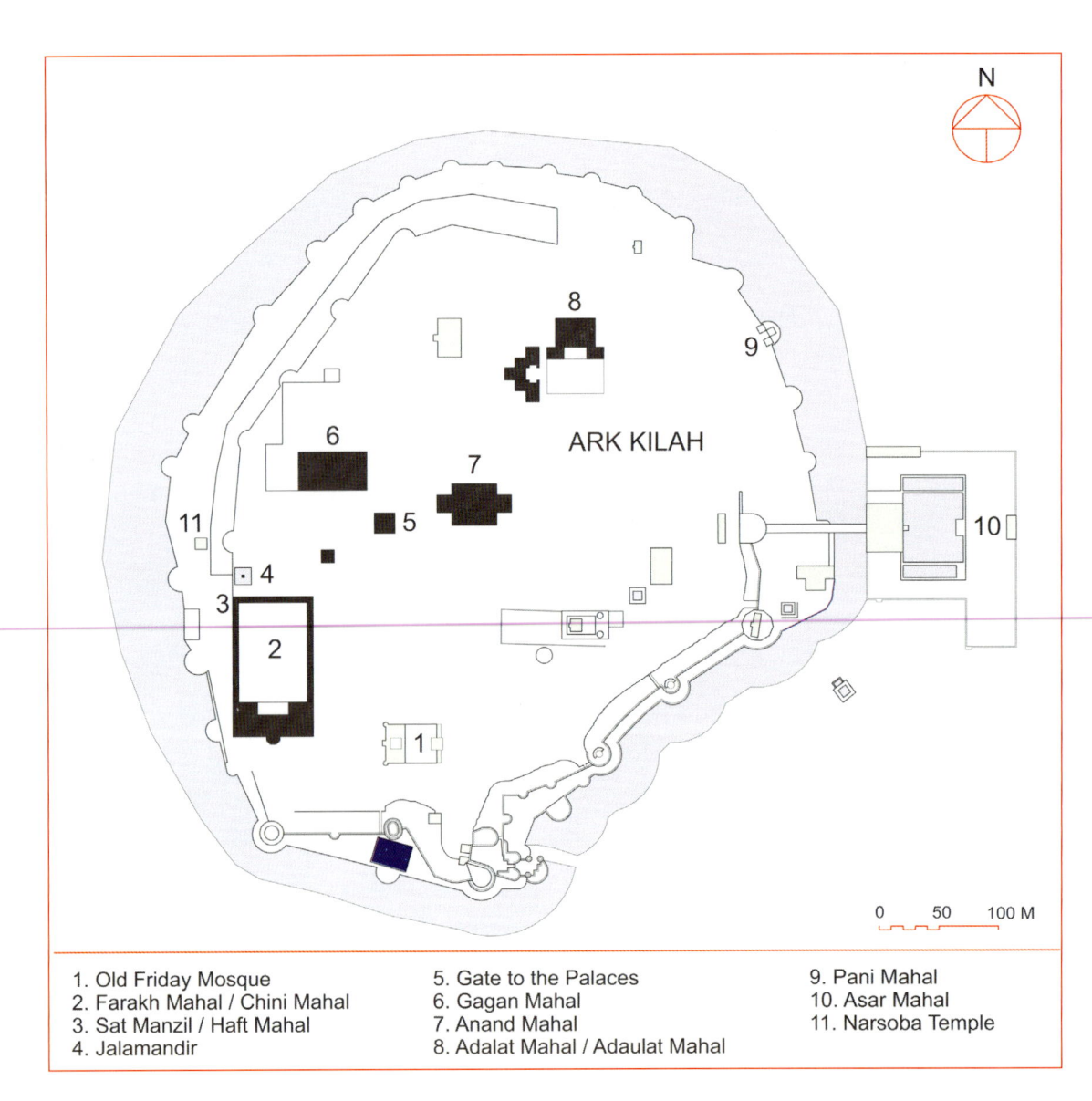

1. Old Friday Mosque
2. Farakh Mahal / Chini Mahal
3. Sat Manzil / Haft Mahal
4. Jalamandir
5. Gate to the Palaces
6. Gagan Mahal
7. Anand Mahal
8. Adalat Mahal / Adaulat Mahal
9. Pani Mahal
10. Asar Mahal
11. Narsoba Temple

Plan 26 Bijapur, Ark Kilah, the fortified royal enclosure and palaces.

134 PLANS

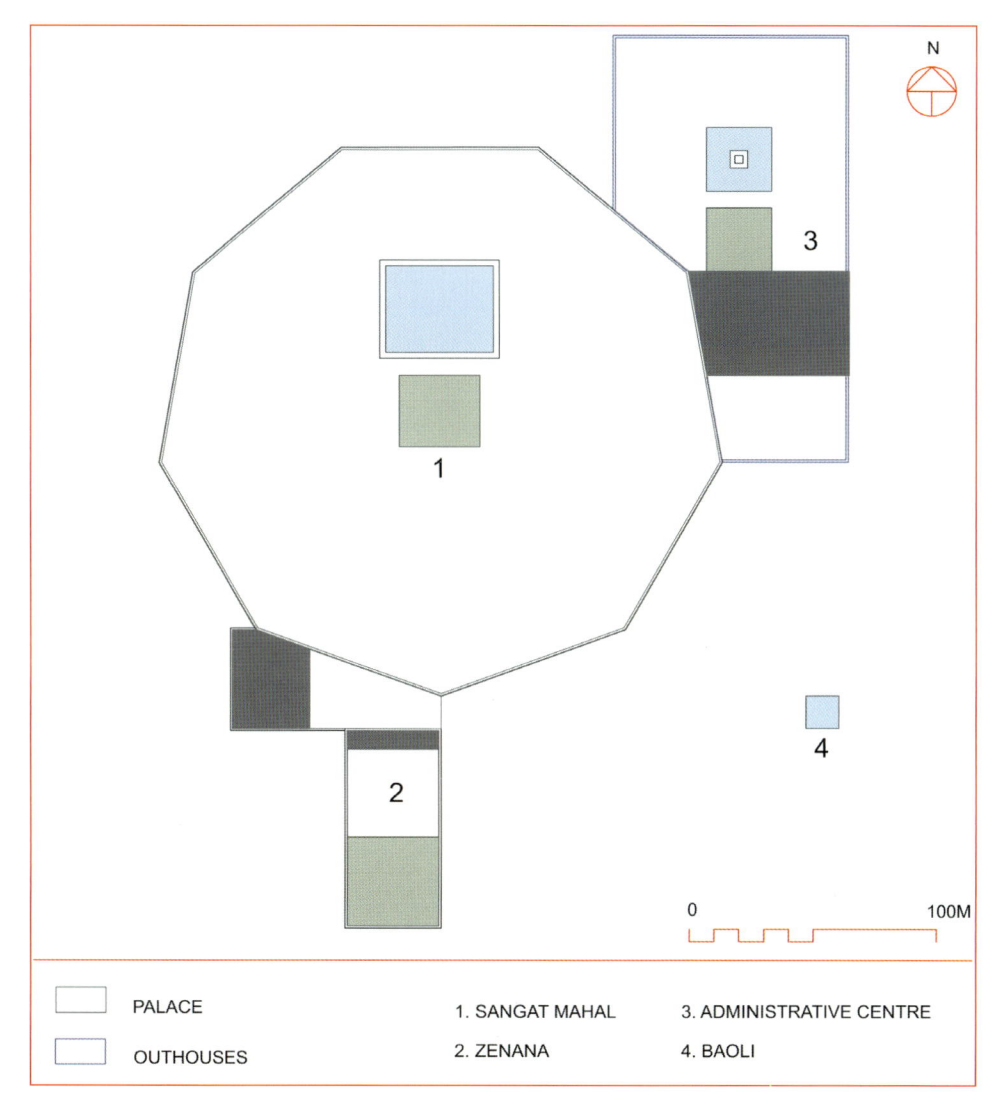

☐ PALACE	1. SANGAT MAHAL 3. ADMINISTRATIVE CENTRE
☐ OUTHOUSES	2. ZENANA 4. BAOLI

Plan 27 Nauraspur, the palaces, water bodies, and hydraulic system, 1599–1624.

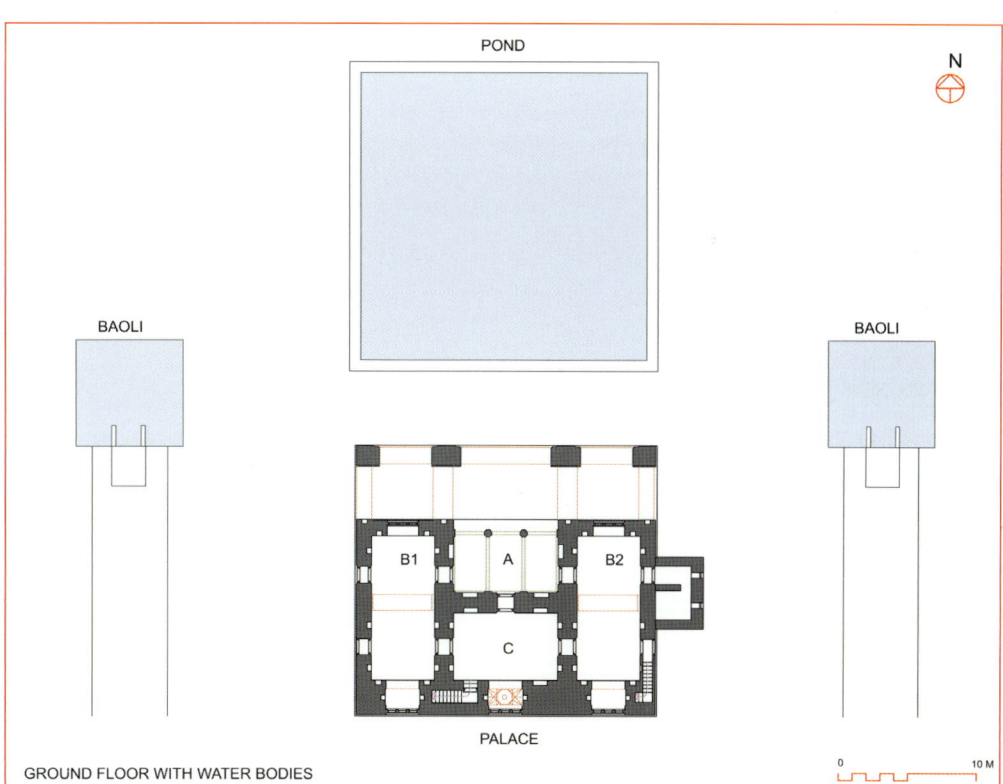

Plan 28 Ainapur, tripartite palace, after 1651. The palace has a large pool on its northern side and is flanked by two baolis.

PLANS **135**

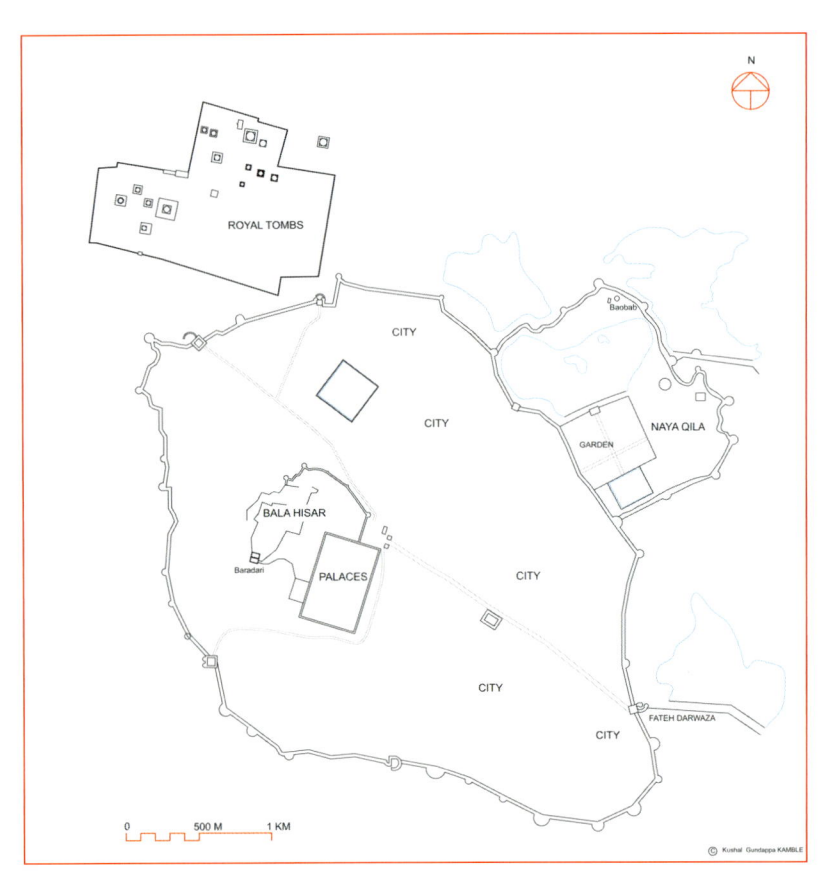

Plan 29 Golconda, Fort with palace area, city, Naya Qila, and the royal necropolis. © Kushal Gundappa Kamble.

Plan 30 Golconda, palace area. © Kushal Gundappa Kamble.

1 ENTRANCE PAVILION
2 ENTRANCE PAVILION
3 BARBICAN
4 GATEHOUSE
5 HAMMAM
6 BAZAAR
7 SECRETARIAT (?)
8 CAMEL STABLE
9 MOSQUE
10 TRIPARTITE STRUCTURE
11 COURTYARD with FOUNTAIN
12 PAVILION

A ROYAL KITCHEN
B TRIPARTITE STRUCTURE
C GRANARY II
D DAD MAHAL IV
E RANI MAHAL III

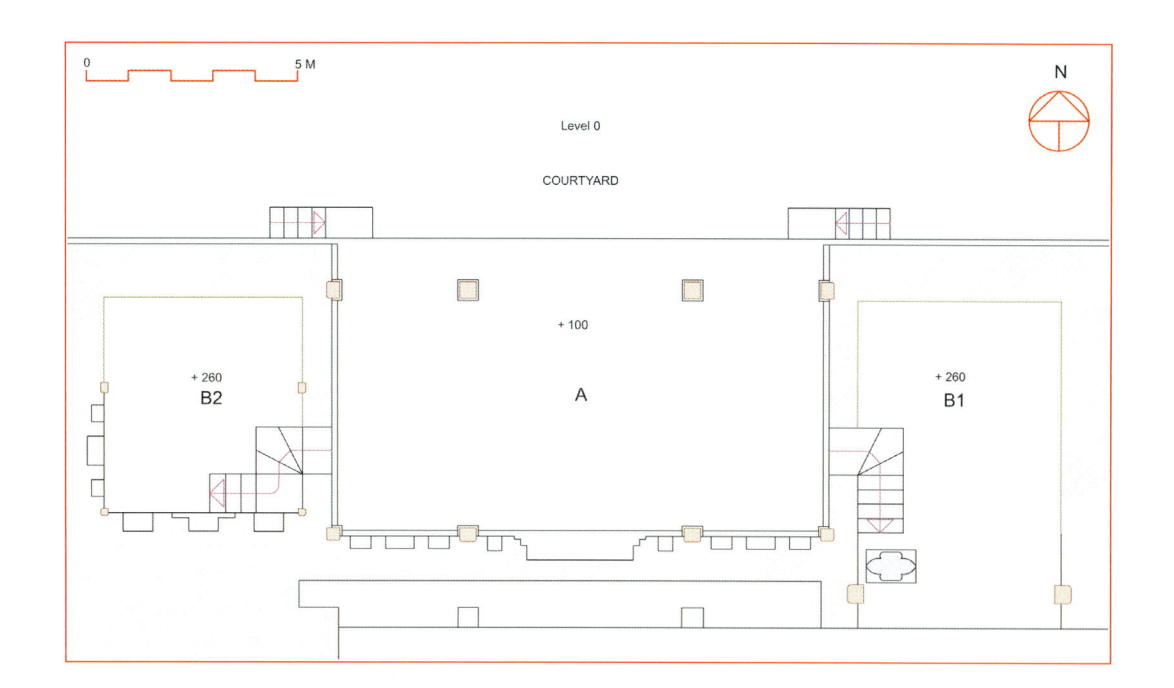

Plan 31 Golconda, tripartite palace.

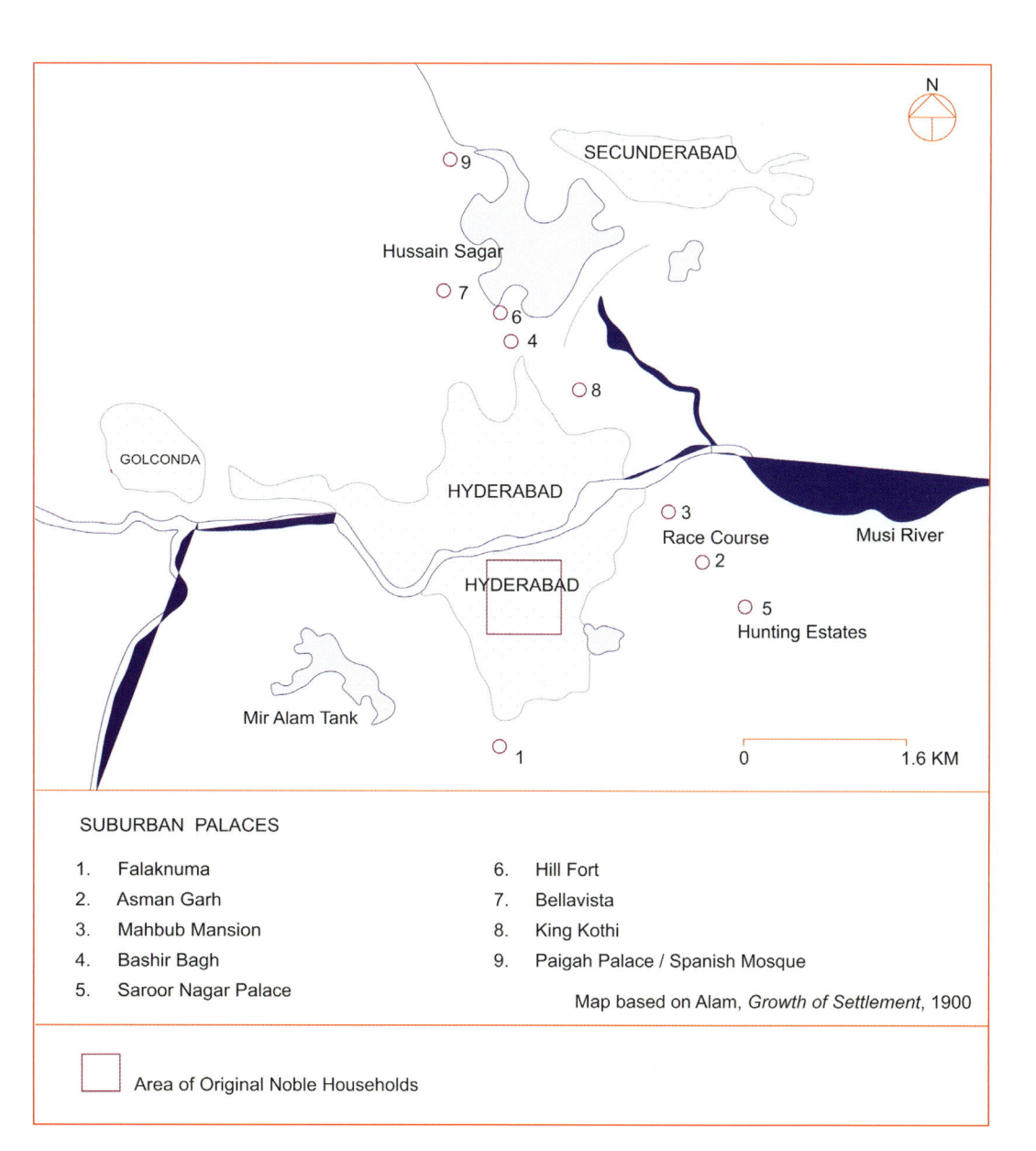

Plan 32 Hyderabad, the city and the suburban palaces of the Asaf Jahis, 18th and 19th centuries. Source: Alam, Shah Manzoor. *Hyderabad-Secunderabad, Twin Cities: A Study in Urban Geography*, New York/Bombay, 1965.

SUBURBAN PALACES

1. Falaknuma
2. Asman Garh
3. Mahbub Mansion
4. Bashir Bagh
5. Saroor Nagar Palace
6. Hill Fort
7. Bellavista
8. King Kothi
9. Paigah Palace / Spanish Mosque

Map based on Alam, *Growth of Settlement*, 1900

Area of Original Noble Households

PLANS **137**

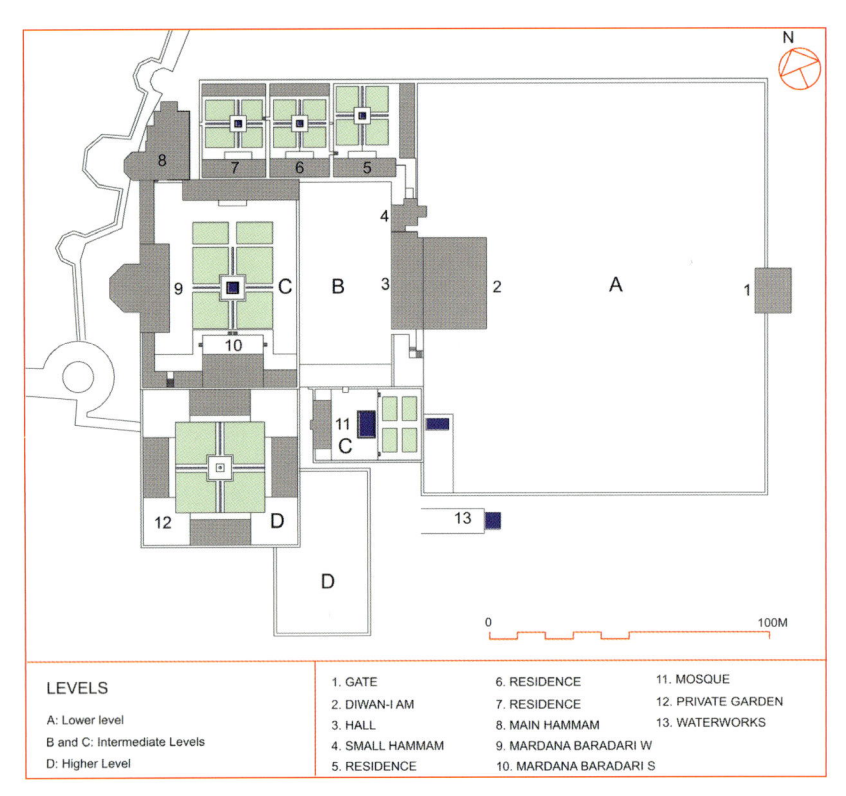

LEVELS
A: Lower level
B and C: Intermediate Levels
D: Higher Level

1. GATE
2. DIWAN-I AM
3. HALL
4. SMALL HAMMAM
5. RESIDENCE
6. RESIDENCE
7. RESIDENCE
8. MAIN HAMMAM
9. MARDANA BARADARI W
10. MARDANA BARADARI S
11. MOSQUE
12. PRIVATE GARDEN
13. WATERWORKS

Plan 33 Daulatabad, Mahakot, palace compound, 1653–1707.

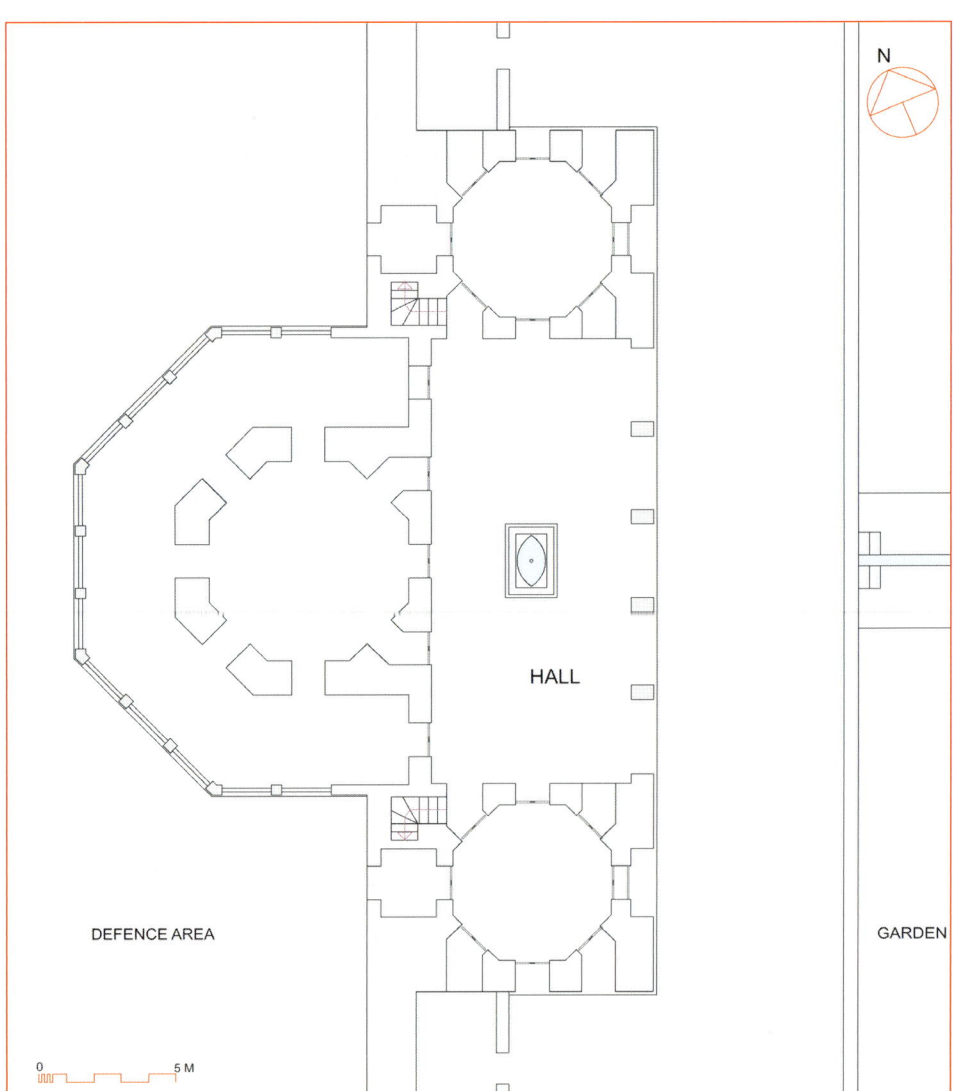

Plan 34 Daulatabad, Mahakot, mardana, Nizam Shahi pavilion, 1653–1707, see plan 33 no. 9.

138 PLANS

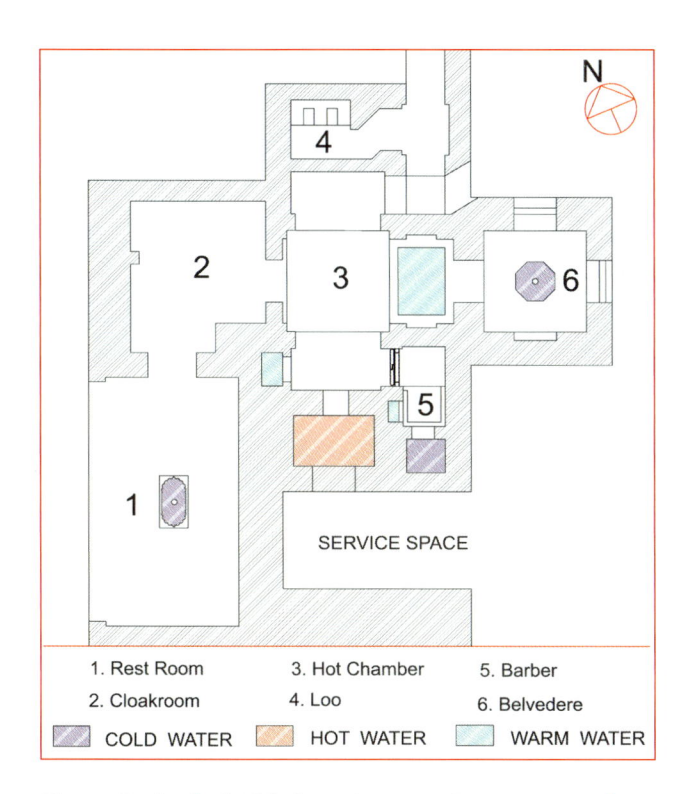

1. Rest Room
2. Cloakroom
3. Hot Chamber
4. Loo
5. Barber
6. Belvedere

COLD WATER   HOT WATER   WARM WATER

Plan 35 Daulatabad, Mahakot, 1653–1707, hammam, see plan 33 no. 4.

Plan 36 Daulatabad, Mahakot, palace compound, 1653–1707, hammam, see plan 33 no. 8.

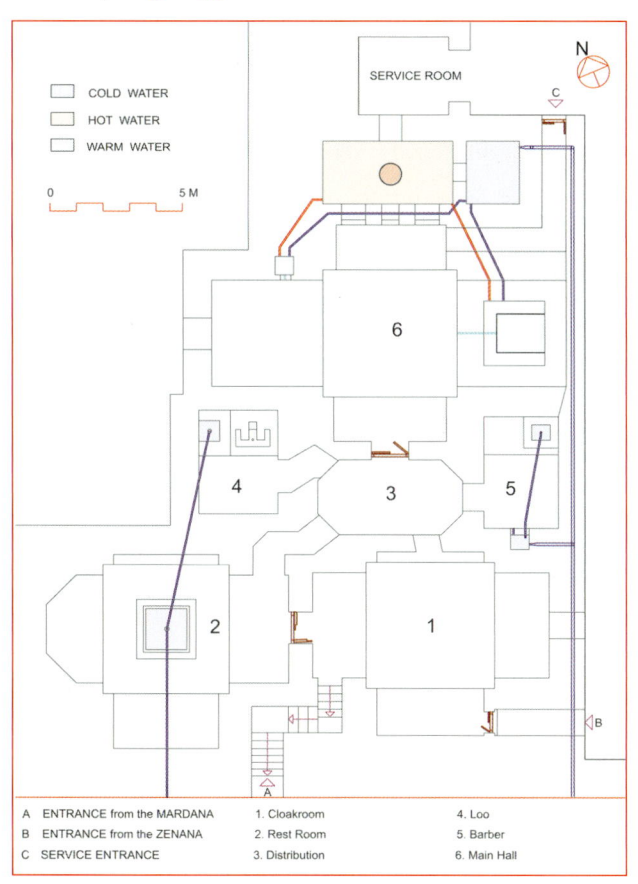

COLD WATER
HOT WATER
WARM WATER

A ENTRANCE from the MARDANA
B ENTRANCE from the ZENANA
C SERVICE ENTRANCE
1. Cloakroom
2. Rest Room
3. Distribution
4. Loo
5. Barber
6. Main Hall

Plan 37 Bidar, Tomb of Ali Barid, 1576. The tomb sits in the middle of a symmetrical garden. The wells to water the garden are outside the enclosure wall. On its southern side are the residential buildings and a mosque.

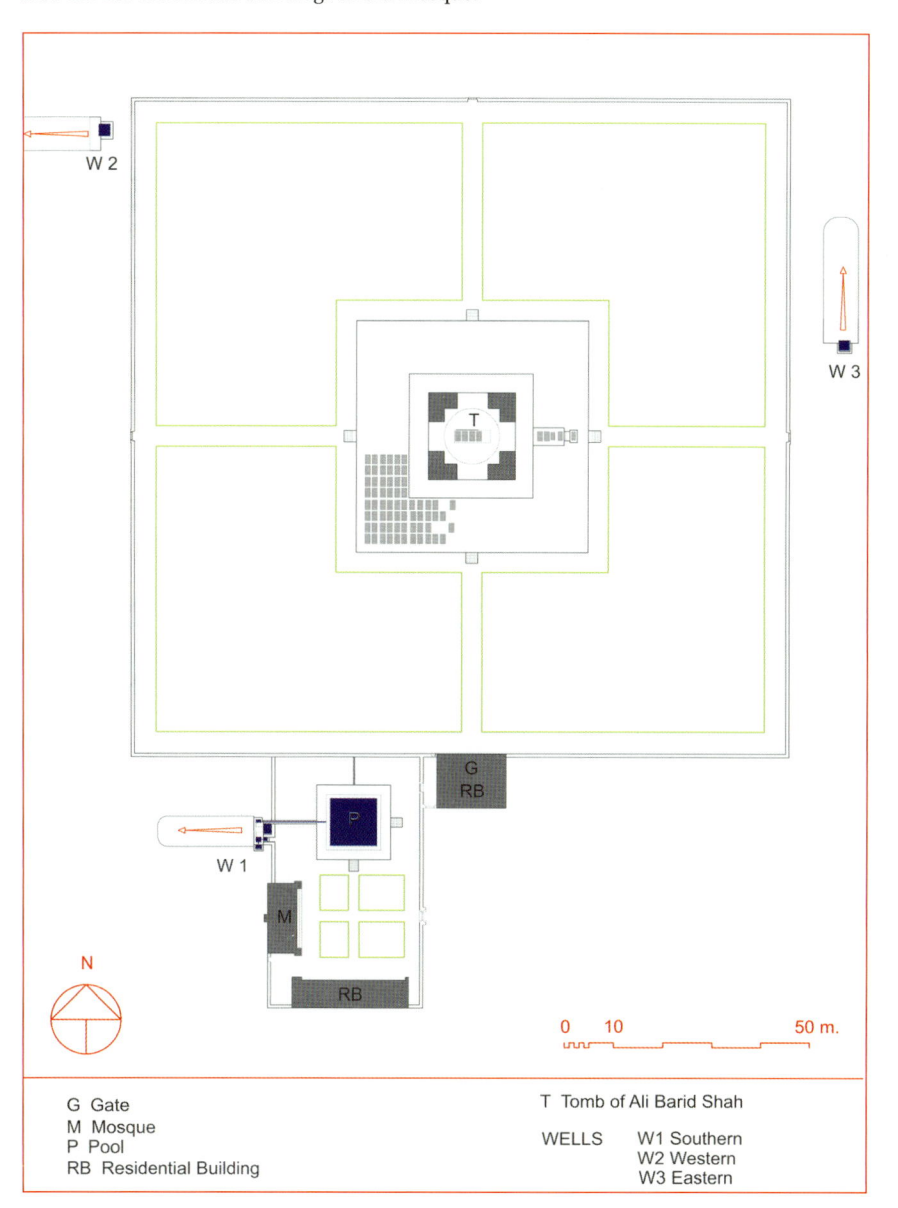

G Gate
M Mosque
P Pool
RB Residential Building

T Tomb of Ali Barid Shah
WELLS W1 Southern
        W2 Western
        W3 Eastern

PLANS 139

Glossary

adab: cultural etiquette, skills.

afaqi: immigrant from Iranian and Central Asian lands.

alam: Shia commemorative standard in metal.

asma al-husna: the 99 names of Allah.

badgir: wind tower of Iranian origin.

bangla: curved roof derived from the Bengali hut. Two types exist: the do-chala, with curves on the two longer sides, and the char-chala or chau-chala with eaves curved on all four sides.

baoli: step-well.

baradari: rectangular or square pavilion with a colonnade on each side.

baraka: sacred Muslim blessing.

barbican: wall protecting a gateway by blocking direct access to it.

bombard: late medieval cannon to hurl large stones.

brattices: in fortifications, structures that crown the wall.

char-bagh: literally four-fold garden. It is a walled garden subdivided into four (or a multiple of four sections) by paved paths or water canals.

chhajja: a sloping projection from a wall, supported on brackets.

chhatri: open pillared domed kiosk.

Chihil Sutun: forty pillars – a reference to the numerous columns of the hypostyle hall or mandapa. See also Hazar Sutun.

Dakhini or Deccani: from the Deccan, peninsular south India. An important political faction composed of local Muslims, the descendants of early immigrants and Habshi slaves.

darbar: formal audience.

dargah: literally "court" – tomb of a Sufi.

darwaza: gate or gate-house.

deodhi: urban palace complex in Hyderabad.

guldasta: bouquet; ornamental pinnacle on a building.

hammam: bath house.

haram: forbidden, the women's apartments. See also zenana.

hauz: pool or tank.

Hazar Sutun: one thousand pillars, reference to a multi-columned hall or mandapa. See also Chihil Sutun.

Ithna Ashari or Isna Ashari: the majority sect among Shias, which accords special veneration to Ali and the Twelve Imams.

iwan: vaulted or flat roofed hall, open at one end.

jagir: country estate or farmlands.

jagirdar: the state official who has the power to control land and its revenue. At the official's death the land reverts to the crown.

jali: perforated screen of stone or other material.

jilukhana: guards' square.

latifundia: great landed estates, from the Latin "latus", spacious and "fundus", farm, estate.

maidan: open ground.

Malik at Tujjar: Lord of Merchants, title given to high-ranking officers during the later Bahmani period.

mandala: sacred diagram.

mardana: rooms for men in the palace or mansion.

merlon: battlement.

mihrab: niche located on the wall facing Mecca, the qibla wall in a mosque.

minbar: pulpit in a mosque from where a sermon or khutba is delivered.

muluk khana: in a mosque the enclosure for the royal family.

muqarnas: honeycomb-like ornamentation composed out of individual cells and found on pendentives and the transitional zone between a dome and its support.

nauras or noh ras: nine rasas – flavours or moods – in Deccani Urdu poetry and music.

nazr: gift, offering.

necropolis: city of the dead, a cemetery.

ogee: S-shaped curve.

Paigah: the family name of the senior Hyderabad aristocracy. The Paigah nobility were considered next only to the Nizam of Hyderabad.

pendentive: in architecture, a triangular segment of a spherical surface that forms a support for a dome.

Peshwa: prime minister of the Marathas, ruling from Pune.

pir: elder, Sufi preceptor, the teacher to the spiritual path.

pishtaq: high portal consisting of a lofty arch framing an iwan.

purdah: screen or veil.

qanat: horizontal wells found in laterite formations on basaltic rock with regularly spaced vertical ventilation shafts with holes for drawing water.

qasida: poetic form.

qibla: orientation of mosque towards Mecca.

rasas: flavours or moods.

sarai: palace, or place of recreation.

Sharia: body of Islamic religious law.

squinch: in architecture, one of several devices that fill the upper corners of a room in order to support a dome. This can be achieved through corbelling, by building arches diagonally, and other methods.

Sufi: Islamic mystic.

tarafdar: governor of provinces. The land management included collecting taxes, both normal and agricultural (lagaan). A tarafdar maintained all the accounts and handled all the monetary/financial transactions for his land.

tepidarium: the warm room in the Roman baths.

ulema: Muslim legal scholars and the arbiters of sharia law.

Wakil al Sultan: one of the highest offices in the administration and an officer of 1,200 horses.

wali: an Arabic word meaning "trusted one" or "friend of God".

zenana: inner area of the household reserved for women.

Deccan: An introduction", *Rivista degli Studi Orientali*, 64: 5–16.

———. 2005. "From Deccan to Hindustan? Gardens in the Deccan and Beyond", *Deccan Studies*, V/2: 42–59.

King, Anthony. 1976. *Colonial Urban Development: Culture, Social Power and Environment*. London.

King, J.S. 1900. *The History of the Bahmani Dynasty Founded on the Burhan-i Maasiri*. London.

Krishnaswami, Mudiraj K. 1929 and 1934. *Pictorial Hyderabad*, 2 volumes. Hyderabad.

Lentz, Thomas W. and Glenn D. Lowry. 1989. *Timur and the Princely Vision: Persian Art and Culture in the Fifteenth Century*. Washington, DC.

Luther, Narendra. 1995. *Hyderabad, Memories of a City*. Hyderabad.

Lynton, Harriet Ronken and Mohini Rajan. 1974. *The Days of the Beloved*. Berkeley and London.

Mackenzie Shah, Alison. 2005. "Constructing a Capital on the Edge of Empire: Urban Patronage and Politics in the Nizams' Hyderabad, 1750–1950", PhD thesis, University of Pennsylvania, Philadelphia.

Mate, M.S. 1967. *Deccan Woodwork*. Poona.

———. 1999. *Islamic Architecture of the Deccan*. Poona.

Merklinger, Elizabeth Schotten. 1981. *Indian Islamic Architecture: The Deccan, 1347–1686*. Warminster.

———. 1986. "Gulbarga", pp. 26–41, in George Michell, ed., *Islamic Heritage of the Deccan*. Bombay.

———. 2005. *Sultanate Architecture of Pre-Mughal India*. Delhi.

Michell, George, ed. 1986. *Islamic Heritage of the Deccan*. Bombay.

———. 1992. *The Vijayanagara Courtly Style, Incorporation and Synthesis in the Royal Architecture of Southern India, 15th–17th centuries*. New Delhi.

Michell, George and Richard Eaton. 1992. *Firuzabad: Palace City of the Deccan*. Oxford.

Michell, George and Mark Zebrowski. 1999. *Architecture and Art of the Deccan Sultanates*. The New Cambridge History of India. Cambridge.

Nayeem, M.A. 2006. *The Heritage of the Qutb Shahis of Golconda and Hyderabad*. Hyderabad.

———. 2007. "Qutb Shahi Gardens in Golconda and Hyderabad during the 16th–17th centuries", *Deccan Studies,* V/2: 5–41.

Nizami, K.A. 1997. *Royalty in Medieval India*. Delhi.

Philon, Helen. 2000. "The murals in the tomb of Ahmad Shah in Bidar", *Apollo*, November 3–10.

———. 2001. "Plaster Decoration on Sultanate-styled Courtly Buildings", pp. 74–88, in George Michell and John M. Fritz, eds., *New Light on Hampi*, Mumbai.

———. 2006. "Early Bahmani mihrabs in Gulbarga, Deccan", pp. 83–95, in Patricia L. Baker and Barbara Brend, eds., *Studies in Honour of Professor Geza Fehervari*. London.

Pieper, Jan. 1985. "The House of Begum Srimati Tahera at Hyderabad", *Environmental Design*: 85–86.

Rötzer, Klaus. 1984. "Bijapur: Alimentation en eau d'une ville musulmane du Dekkan aux XVIe-XVIIe siècles", *Bulletin de l'École Française d'Extrême-Orient*, 73: 125–95.

———. 1989. "Architectures de pierre dans le Dekkan et le Malwa avant l'epoque Moghole", *Techniques et culture*, 14: 51–78.

———. forthcoming. "Water Techniques in Deccani Gardens", in Mumtaz Currim, ed., *Heaven on Earth: Reflections of Paradise in Islamic Art in India*. Mumbai.

Shaikh, Chand Husain. 1940–44. "Literary Personages of Ahmadnagar", *Bulletin of the Deccan College Oriental Research Institute*, 3: 212–18.

Sherwani, H.K. 1974. *History of the Qutb Shahi Dynasty*. New Delhi.

———. 1985. *The Bahmanis of the Deccan*. New Delhi.

Shirazi, Mirza Nizam al-Din Ahmad ibn Abd Allah Saidi. 1961. *Hadiqat al-salatain-i Qutbshahi*. Hyderabad.

Shokoohy, Mehrdad. 1994. "Sasanian Royal Emblems and Their Re-emergence in the Fourteenth-Century Deccan", *Muqarnas*, 11: 65–78.

Shokoohy, Mehrdad and Natalie H. Shokoohy. 1999. "Pragmatic city versus ideal city: Tughlaqabad, Perso-Islamic planning and its impact on Indian towns", *Urban Design Studies*, 5: 57–84.

Siddiqui, I.H. 1984. "Waterworks and Irrigation System in India during Pre-Mughal Times", *Islamic Culture*, LVIII/1: 1–21.

Sohoni, Pushkar. 2007. "Change and memory in Farah Bagh, Ahmadnagar, Metamorphosis of a Deccan palace: From Farah Bakhsh Bagh to a silk factory", *Deccan Studies*, 5/2: 59–77.

Sykes, W.H. 1823. "Notes Respecting the Principal Remains in the Ruined City of Bejapoor, with Traditional Accounts of their Origin, etc.", *Transactions of the Literary Society of Bombay*, 3: 55–63.

Tabatabai, Ali ibn Aziz Allah. 1936. *Burhan-i-Maasir*, Sayyid Hashimi ed., Hyderabad.

Tanindi, Zeren. 1999. "An Illuminated Manuscript of the Wandering Scholar Ibn al-Jazari and the Wandering Illuminators between Tabriz, Shiraz, Heart, Bursa, Edirne, Istanbul in the 15th century", *Proceedings 10th International Congress of Turkish Art*, pp. 647–55. Geneva.

Tavernier, Jean-Baptiste. 1677. *The six voyages of John Baptista Tavernier, Baron of Aubonne; through Turky, into Persia and the East-Indies, for the space of forty years. Giving an account of the present state of those countries, viz. of the religion, government, customs, and commerce of every country; and the figures, weight, and value of the money currant all over Asia. To which is added, a new description of the seraglio.*

Taylor, Philip Meadows. 1866. *Architecture at Beejapoor*. London.

Thévenot, Jean de. 1687. *The travels of Monsieur de Thevenot into the Levant: in three parts. Viz. into: I. Turkey. II. Persia. III. The East-Indies. Newly done out of French.* London. Twist, Johan Van. 1637. Dutch National Archives, VOC 1122: 488v–89.

Varma, D.N. 2005. "Water Management and Gardens in the Qutbshahi Capitals of Golconda and Hyderabad", *Deccan Studies*, Vol. III, 2: 48–63.

Varthema, L. di. 1863. *The Travels of Ludovico Di Varthema in Egypt, Syria, Arabia Deserta and Arabia Felix, Persia, India, and Ethiopia, A.D. 1503 to 1508*, ed. G.P. Badger. New York.

Wagoner, P.B. 1996. "Sultan among Hindu Kings: Dress, Titles and the Islamicization of Hindu Culture at Vijayanagara", *Indo-Islamic Journal of Asian Studies*, 55/4: 851–80.

–––. 1998. "From the Throne of Jamshid to the City of Victory: Islamicate Contributions to the City Plan of Vijayanagara", presented at the Conference on Religion in South India, Raleigh, NC, June 10–13.

–––. 2006. "The Charminar as *Chaubara*: Cosmological Symbolism in the Urban Architecture of the Deccan", pp. 105–13, in Abha Narain Lambah and Alka Patel, eds., *Architecture of the Indian Sultanates*. Mumbai.

Wagoner, Philip B. and John Henry Rice. 2001. "From Delhi to Deccan: Newly discovered Tughluq monuments at Warangal-Sultanpur and the beginnings of Indo-Islamic architecture in Southern India", *Artibus Asiae*, 61: 72–117.

Welch, A. 1996. "Gardens That Babur Did Not Like: Landscape, Water, and Architecture for the Sultans of Delhi", in J.L. Wescoat, Jr., and J. Wolschke-Bulmahn, eds., *Mughal Gardens, Sources, Places, Representations, and Prospects*. Washington, DC.

Worswick, Patrick, ed. 1980. *Princely India: Photography by Raja Deen Dayal 1884–1910*. New York.

Yazdani, Ghulam. 1928. "The Great Mosque of Gulbarga", *Islamic Culture*, 2: 14–21.

–––. 1995. *Bidar, Its History and Monuments*. Delhi (reprint).

Yazdani, Zubaida and Mary Crystal. 1985. *The Seventh Nizam: The Fallen Empire*. Cambridge.

Zebrowski, Mark. 1983. *Deccani Painting*. London.

Zubairi, Muhammad Ibrahim. 1892–93. *Basatin al-Salatin*. Hyderabad.

Index

Page numbers in bold refer to captions

Abbasids 17
Abdur Razzak 25
Achalpur 64
   Hauz Katora 64
Adil Shahis (1490–1686) 10, 15–17, **16**, 21, 66–77
   Ali Adil Shah I 66, 74
   Ali Adil Shah II 73
   Ibrahim Adil Shah I 66
   Ibrahim Adil Shah II 20, 25, 26, 45, 68
   Ismail Adil Shah 66
   Jahan Begum 72, **76**
   Muhammad Adil Shah 71, **76**
   Yusuf Adil Khan Shah 15, 25
Afaqis 15, 51
Agni 51
Ahmadabad *see* Bidar
Ahmadnagar 10, 17, 21, 23, 28, 56–65, **58–65**, 88, 99, 109, 117, **131–33**
   Farah Bakhsh Bagh 10, 23, **58–60**, 61, 63, 65, 117, **131**
   Fort 63
   Hasht Behesht Bagh/Faiz Bakhsh Bagh 23, **23**, 61, **62**, 64, 65, 116, **132**
   Kalawantinicha Mahal 23, 61, 64, **64**, 116, **131**
   Lakkad Mahal **61**, 64, 65
   Manzarsumbah **63**, 132
   Pimpalgaon 64
   Shahi Hammamkhane 64
   Shendi 64
Anatolia 42, 43, 118, 121
Andhra Pradesh 14, 15, 17
Arabs 14
Archaeological Survey of India 11, 71, 94
Asaf Jahis/Nizams (1724–1950) 10, 11, 16, 17, 23, 85, 98–105, **137**
   Asman Jah **100**, 101
   Mir Mahbub Ali Khan, Asaf Jah VI **100**, 101, **105**
   Salar Jang 104
   Viqar ul Omrah 101, 104
Athanasius Nikitin of Twer, Russia 25
Aurangabad 28, 56, 88–97, **94–97**, **107**, 112, 113
   Bibi-ka Maqbara/Rauza 88, 94, **97**, **112**, 113
   Delhi Darwaza 96
   Dr Rafiq Zakaria educational campus 96
   Government School of Art 93, 94
   Himayat Bagh 93
   Ismail Rauza **94**, **95**, 96
   Kham river 93
   Khidki 56, 92, 93
   Naubat Darwaza 93
   Panchakki **107**
   Qila Arg 93, 94
   Shahi Masjid 93
   Soneri Mahal, Begampura 95, **96**
Austria 101

Bahmanis (1347–1528) 10, 14–17, 19, 21, 24–26, 28–30, 34–43, 44–55, **57**, 67, 77, 78–80, 83, **107**, 112–18, 120, 121, **122**, **123**, **125**
   Ahmad Shah 17, 30, 43, 44, 49
   Alauddin Ahmad Shah II 50, 55, **127**
   Alauddin Hasan Bahman Shah 14, 26
   Firuz Shah **16**, 17, 19, 26, 30, 34, 37, 39, 41
   Humayun Shah Bahmani **51**, 52, 55, 127
   Mahmud Gawan 120
   Muhammad Shah 55
   Nizamuddin Ahmad Shah III 55
Baridis (1487–1619) 15, 17, 44–55, 114, 118, 120, **123**, **127**
   Ali Baridi/Barid Shah 48, 53, 54, 113, 118, **123**, **139**
   Qasim Barid Shah II **123**
   Qasim Baridi 15
Beed 64
Berar 15
Bidar/Ahmadabad 4, 10, 14, 15, 17, 20–23, **22**, 25, **27**, 28, 29, 44–55, 79, 83, 88, 108, 109, 112, 114, 116–20, **120**, **121**
   Ahmad Shah Tomb **121**
   Ashtur 4, 17, **51**, 52, 55, 117, **123**, **127**
   Chaubara 20
   Diwan-i Am Palace I **44**, 48–50
   Fort 10, **22**, **27**, 28, 30, 32, **32**, **33**, 37, 38, **44**, 45, **45**, **47–50**, 49, 52, **52–55**, 117
   Gumbad Darwaza 21, 30, **32**, 47, 48, 51, 53–55, 121, **130**
   Kamthana 17
   Karnatik Darwaza 30
   Khazar Kothri **128**
   Manjira river 30, 45, 113
   Nimatabad 17
   Prince's Palace **47**, 48, 52, **52**, 53, 55, **55**, **127**, **129**
   Rangini Mahal 23, 38, 48, 52–54, **53**, 116–18, **118–20**, 121, **129**
   Rani Mahal 82, **136**
   Sharza Darwaza 55
   Solah Khamba Mosque 4, 10, 21, **27**, 47, **47**, 48, 53–55, **54**, **55**, **129**, **130**
   Takht Mahal Palace II 21, 48, 49
   Palace/Zenana III 52
Bijapur 4, 9–11, 15–17, 20, 21, 23–25, 28, 56, 61, 66–77, **66**, **68–75**, 88, **108–11**, 109, 112, 114, **115**, **116**, 117, 118, 121
   Ainapur 17, 72, **76**, 77, **134**, **135**
   Ali Mahal 73
   Anand Mahal 70, **116**, **134**
   Archaeological Museum 71
   Ark Kilah 23, **134**
   Asar Mahal (Palace of the Relic)/Dad Mahal 23, 70–73, **70–72**, 77, 114, 117, 121
   Daulat Mahal (Palace of Felicity) 14, 34–43, 71–73
   Farakh Mahal/Chini Mahal 66–70, **66**, 74
   Gagan Mahal 25, **67–69**, 68, 73, 74, 77, 83, 117, **134**
   Gol Gumbad, tomb of Muhammad Adil Shah 73, **134**
   Haft Mahal **73**, 74, **74**, 76, 77, 115, **134**
   Husseini Mahal 73, 77
   Jahaz Mahal/Ship Palace **70**, 71
   Jalamandir 74, **75**, 76, 77, 118, **134**
   Jami Mosque 121
   Karimuddin's Mosque 68
   Kumatgi 17, 25, 66, 76, 77, **108–11**, 112
   Makka Gate 20
   Mustafa Khan Mosque 70
   Nauras Mahal **21**, 68–70, 72
   Nauraspur 17, 20, 21, **21**, 25, 66, 68, 70, 77, **134**, **135**
   Pani Mahal 4, **72**, 73, 74, 77, 118, **134**
   Pir Mabari Khandayat Tomb 68
   Shah Burj 71
   Shah Nawaz Khan/Mahal **69**, 70
   Zorahpur Gate 20
British 98–101, 103–05
   Victoria, Queen 101
British East India Company 98
British Library, London **15**, **16**
British Museum, London 25, **86**, 87
Bundelkhand 95
Burhan i Maasir 64

Calcutta 98
Central Asia 14, 44, 49, 51, 63, 120
Chalukya 30, **31**
Chaul 58
Chester Beatty Library, Dublin 25
Chinese 66, 104, 117, 120, 121
Chishti 69
Ctesiphon, Iraq/Taq-i Kisra 20, 39
Curzon, Lord 103, 104, **105**

Dakhinis 15
Danda Rajapuri 56
Dattatreya 69
   Narasimha Saraswati 69
Daulatabad/Devagiri 14, 17, 20, 21, 28, **28**, 29, **29**, **31**, 34–43, **35**, **37**, 56–58, **56**, **57**, 61, 64, 65, 80, 88–97, **88–93**, 109, 114, 117, **123**, **124**, **133**, **138**, **139**
   Balakot 88, **88**, **89**, 91, **123**
   Bhandara 63
   Bhingar 63
   Fatehabad 14

Kalakot **29**, **35**, 37, 114, **123**, **124**
Mahakot 29, **29**, **90–93**, 91, **123**, **138**, **139**
Rang Mahal **29**, **32**, **35**, 37, 38, **123**, **124**
Delhi 9, 14, 17, 20, 30, 42, 43
Delhi Durbars 100
Delhi Sultanate 9, 14
Dutch East India Company 72

Egyptian 120
Europe/an 23, 25, 72, 98, 101, 103–05, 114, 121

Ferishta, Muhammad Qasim 24, 50
Firuzabad 17, **18**, **19**, 19, 20, 23, **23**, 28, 34–43, **40–42**, 57, 117, 118, **122**, **124**, **126**
  Bhima river 14, **122**
  Dargah of Khalifat al-Rahman 17, **18**, 19, 23, **23**, 34, 41, 42, **126**
  Jami Mosque 20
French 85, 87, 104
Fuzuni Astarabadi 24

Germany 101
Godavari river 14
Golconda 9, 10, 15–17, 20, 21, 23, 25, **27**, 28, 78–87, **79–81**, 88, 117, 121, **136**, **137**
  Bala Hisar **27**, 79–82, **81**, **136**
  Dad Mahal 87, **136**
  Naya Qila 83, **136**
  Qutb Shahi palace 10, 80, 81, 85, 87
  Rani Mahal 82, **136**
Gulbarga **4**, 10, 14, **14–16**, 17, 19–21, 25, 28–30, **31**, 34–43, **38**, **39**, 44, 68, 70, 76, 88, 117, **122**, **125**, **127**
  Ahsanabad 14
  Bala Hisar **15**, 20, 30, 34, 39, 43, 68, **125**
  Chor Gumbad **4**, 34, **39**, 42, 43
  Firuz Shah Tomb **16**, 43
  Gesu Daraz Dargah **16**, 19, 43, 70, **122**
  Great Mosque **4**, 10, 17, 34, **38**, **39**, **39**, 41–43, **125**
  Haft Gumbad **16**, 19, **122**
  Shah Bazaar/Jami Mosque 19
  Sheikh Mujarrad Dargah **16**, 19
  Sultanpur 10, 17, 19, 20, **20**, 34, **34**, 37, 38, 45, **107**, 117, 124

Habshis 14, 20, 25, 61
  Malik Ambar 56, 61, 92
Hadiqat us-Salatin 87
Hampi 9, 14, 49
Hoysalas 14
Hyderabad/Baghnagar 9, 10, 16, 17, 19, 20, 23, 25, 78–87, **84**, 98–105, **102**, **105**, 121, **137**
  Asman Garh **100**, 101, **137**
  Atapur 87

Badshahi Ashurkhana 87
Bashir Bagh 101, **137**
Bellavista 101, **137**
Bhongir Fort 87
British Residency 104
Chandan Mahal 87
Charkaman 20, **84**, 85, 87
Charminar 9, 20, **29**, **84**, 85, 87
Chowmahallah 23, **99**, 101, 104, **105**
Chowri Thana 87
Diwan Deodhi 104
Falaknuma Palace/Castle 85, 99–101, **102**, 103, **103**, 104, **137**
Hayatabad **85**, 87
Hill Fort 100, 101, **137**
Iram Manzil 100
Khudadad Mahal 87
Koh-i Tur 85
Kotwal Khana 87
Mahbub Mansion 101, **137**
Musi river 20, 78, 84, 85, **137**
Purana Pul 84
Sajan Mahal 87
Salar Jung Museum 25
Sultan Nagar/Dar us-Saltanat 87
Tank Bund 84

Ibn Battuta 42
Imad Shahis 64
Imam Hussein/Husseini Alam 73
India Office Library, London 25
Iran/ian 17, 20, 25, 42, 43, 48, 51, 57, 63, 79, 113, 120, 121
  Shiraz 121
Italian 101, 103
Ithna Ashari *see* Shiism

Jivdhan 56
Jond 56
Junnar 56, 61

Kakatiyas (1083–1323) 14, 17, 28, 30
Karnataka 14, 15
Kaulas Fort 28
Khalji, Qutbuddin Mubarak **29**
Khan Jahan 93, 97
Khuldabad 97
  Aurangzeb Tomb 97
  Hazrat Sayyed Zainuddin Tomb 97
  Lal Bagh 97
Kondhana 56
Krishna river 14, 34
Kulliyat of Quli Qutb Shah 25

Layla and Majnun 87
Lohagarh 56

Maasir i Alamgiri 64
Mackenzie, Colin **15**, **16**, 19, 25
Maharashtra 14, 15, 56
Mahur 28, 30, 33
  Fort 28
  Hathi Darwaza 30
Malik Ambar *see* Habshis

Marathas (1674–1777) 56, 65, 79, 93
Merklinger, Elizabeth Schotten 10
Michell, George 15
Mudgal Fort 28
Mughals (1660–1707) 9, 15, 16, 45, 56, 80, 88–97, 114, 117
  Aurangzeb 9, 10, 64, 88, 91, 93–97
  Azam Shah 88, 97
  Rabia Daurani 88
  Shah Jahan 10, 88, 90, 91, 93
Muhammad, Prophet 69, 71
Muhammad Qasim Ferishta 24
Mukka Malik Qummi 63
Museum and Picture Gallery, Vadodara 96

Narmada river 14
National Library of Russia, St Petersburg 87
National Museum, New Delhi 96
Nauras cult 17
Neimat Khan Semnani 61, 63
Nimatullahi saints 20
Nizam Shahis (1496–1636) 10, 15, 17, 21, 23, 29, **29**, 56–65, 90, 92, 99, 114–17, 121, **133**, **138**
  Ahmad Nizam Shah 15, 56
  Burhan Nizam Shah I 57, 64
  Burhan Nizam Shah II 25
  Murtaza Nizam Shah I 61, 63, 64
  Peshwa Changiz Khan 61
  Salabat Khan II 63, **131**
Nizams *see* Asaf Jahis

Ooty (Udagamandalam) 100, 101
Ottomans (1342–1924) 43, 98, 121

Paigahs **100**, **137**
Pali 56
Pandyas 14
Penukonda 23
  Gagan Mahal 23
Persepolis 42
  Apadana 42
Persian/s 14, 17, 21, 23, 24, 42, 48, 49, 54, 56, 63, 98, 108
Purandhar 56

Qasim Khan 61
Qutb Shahis (1495–1687) 16, 17, 21, 55, 78–87, **86**, 114, 116, 117, 121
  Abdullah Qutb Shah 25, 79, 87
  Abul Hasan 80
  Hayat Bakshi Begum 87
  Ibrahim Qutb Shah 80
  Mian Mishk 87
  Muhammad Quli Qutb Shah 25, 79, 84, 87
  Muhammad Qutb Shah 87
  Sultan Quli Qutb al-Mulk 15, 79, 80

Rafi ud-Din Shirazi 24, 81
Raichur Doab 14, 44
Rötzer, Klaus 10, 11
Russia 25, 87, 101

Safavids (1501–1732) 20, 57
Sagar **4**, 17, 20, 24, 30, 33, 34–43, **37**, 47, 57, 116, **126**, **137**
  Shah Darwaza **4**, 20, 30, 37–41, **37**, 47, 57, 116, **126**
Samarkand 51, 121
  Aq Saray Palace 51
Sasanians 20
Sayyid Ali Tabataba'i 24
Seljuqs 118
Shah Tahir Husseini 57
Shahnama 17
Sherwani, H.K. 81
Shias 17, 73, 74
Shiism/Ithna Ashari 57
  Twelver Shiism 57
Shiva 28
Shivner 56
Sufis 14, 16, 17, 34, 68, 69, 72, **111**
  Gesu Daraz Chishti **16**, 19, 43, 44, 69, 70, 122
  Khalifat al-Rahman 34
  Pir Mabari Khandayat 68
Sunnis 17
Surya 51
Syria 120

Taj Mahal, Agra 63, 88
Talikota 16
Tapti river 14
Tavernier, Jean-Baptiste 87
Thèvenot, Jean de 85, 87
Tikona 56
Tilang 80
Timurids (1370–1506) 25, 63, 121
  Iskender Sultan 121
  Shah Rukh 25
  Ulugh Beg 121
Tughluqs (1320–1414) 17, 29, 34, 42–44, 67, 77, 97, 114
  Muhammad 14, 42
Tung 56
Tungabhadra river 14, 32
Turks 14, 43, 121
Tuscany 101

Udgir 29

Van Twist, Johan 72
Varthema, Ludovico di 25
Vijayanagar 14, 16, 23, 25, 32, 34, 41, 49, 50

Warangal 17, 20, 28–30, 68
  Khush Mahal 20, 68

Yadavas (850–1334) 14, 17, 28–30, **107**, 113, **132**
Yazdani, Ghulam 25, 50, 52, 120
Yusuf and Zulaykha 87

Zebrowski, Mark 10, 25, 69, 72, 121

Contributors

Helen Philon, a freelance Islamic art historian, has founded the Department of Islamic Art at the Benaki Museum, Athens where she was curator for a number of years. In 1981 she published *Early Islamic Ceramics at the Benaki Museum*. Her PhD on the "Religious and Royal Architecture of the Early Bahmanis" (2005) analyses the monuments of this period within their multi-ethnic cultural and religious context. She is interested in intercultural relations.

George Michell was trained as an architect and has been the co-director of the Vijayanagar Research Project. He has edited a number of Marg volumes, including two pioneering works on Hampi, and was the first to bring to the attention of the scholarly community and wider public the Islamic architecture of the Deccan in a volume published by Marg in 1986. In 1999 he co-authored with Mark Zebrowski a book on the *Architecture and Art of the Deccan Sultanates,* in the New Cambridge History of India series.

Klaus Rötzer has spent more than 30 years in India travelling and researching different aspects of its cultural and architectural heritage. He specializes in the study of the water technology and military architecture of medieval India.

Pushkar Sohoni trained as an architect at the University of Pune. He received an MS in Historic Preservation from the University of Pennsylvania, where he is currently a doctoral candidate researching the architecture of the Nizam Shahis of Ahmadnagar.

Mark Brand is currently completing a PhD entitled "The Citadel of Bijapur: The Architecture and Ritual Topography of a Deccan Sultanate Centre" at the Department of Architecture, Cambridge University. He has studied and visited sites of Islamic architecture throughout the world. His major interest is in the architecture of Islamic cults.

Marika Sardar is Research Associate at the Metropolitan Museum of Art in New York. Her dissertation "Golconda through Time, A Mirror of the Evolving Deccan" (2007) from New York University's Institute of Fine Arts is a thorough study of an important royal Deccani centre. She assisted with the organization of a symposium and small exhibition on *The Art of India's Deccan Sultans* at the Metropolitan Museum of Art (2008).

Alison Mackenzie Shah received her PhD from the University of Pennsylvania in 2005, where she trained in South Asian history and history of Islamic architecture. Her dissertation analysed architectural patronage in Hyderabad under the Asaf Jahis, from 1750 to 1950. She is currently an Assistant Professor of History at University of Colorado Denver and a member of the faculty group at the Center of Preservation Research in the university's College of Architecture and Planning.

Clare Arni, the guest photographer, lives and works in India where she specializes as an architectural and travel photographer. She was guest photographer of three previous Marg volumes.

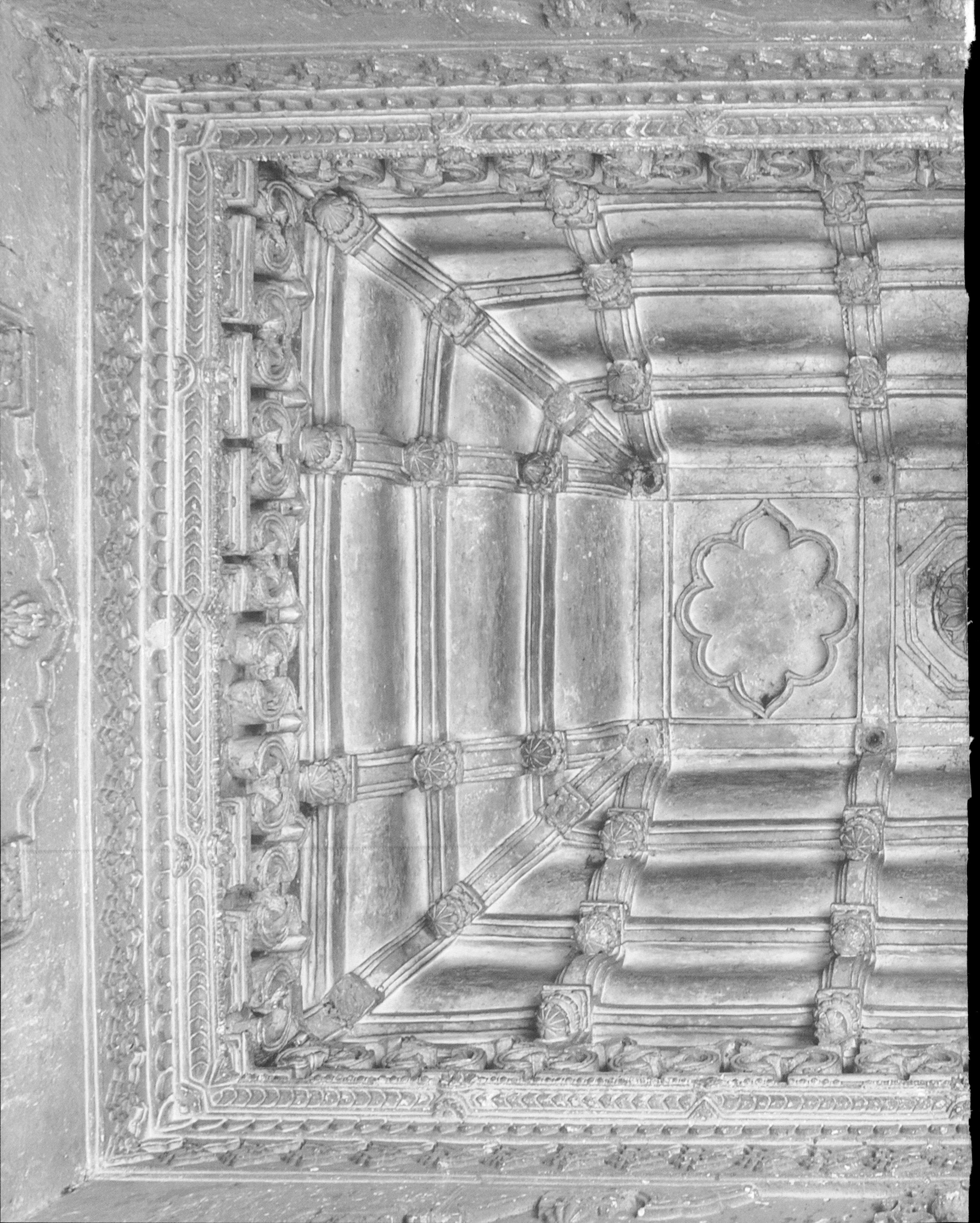